Who Is Muhammad?

Islamic Civilization and Muslim Networks

CARL W. ERNST AND BRUCE B. LAWRENCE, EDITORS

Highlighting themes with historical as well as contemporary significance, Islamic Civilization and Muslim Networks features works that explore Islamic societies and Muslim peoples from a fresh perspective, drawing on new interpretive frameworks or theoretical strategies in a variety of disciplines. Special emphasis is given to systems of exchange that have promoted the creation and development of Islamic identities—cultural, religious, or geopolitical. The series spans all periods and regions of Islamic civilization.

A complete list of books published in Islamic Civilization and Muslim Networks is available at https://uncpress.org/series/islamic-civilization-and-muslim-networks.

WHO IS
Muhammad?

Michael Muhammad Knight

The University of North Carolina Press CHAPEL HILL

Cover art: *Hilyah, Combined with the Relics of the Prophet*, Ottoman Turkey, nineteenth century. Ink, gold, and watercolor on paper, 47 × 29.4 cm. The Nasser D. Khalili Collection of Hajj and the Arts of Pilgrimage, CAL 441. Courtesy Wikimedia Commons.

Library of Congress Cataloging-in-Publication Data
Names: Knight, Michael Muhammad, author.
Title: Who is Muhammad? / Michael Muhammad Knight.
Other titles: Islamic civilization & Muslim networks.
Description: Chapel Hill : University of North Carolina Press, [2023] |
Series: Islamic civilization and Muslim networks | Includes
bibliographical references and index.
Identifiers: LCCN 2023014314 | ISBN 9781469675411 (cloth ; alk. paper) |
ISBN 9781469677262 (paperback ; alk. paper) | ISBN 9781469675428 (ebook)
Subjects: LCSH: Muḥammad, Prophet, –632. | Muḥammad, Prophet, –632—
Biography—History and criticism. | BISAC: RELIGION / Islam /
General | BIOGRAPHY & AUTOBIOGRAPHY / Religious
Classification: LCC BP75.3 .K65 2023 | DDC 297.6/3092—dc23/eng/20230502
LC record available at https://lccn.loc.gov/2023014314

For Jibreel, from Azreal

Contents

Acknowledgments

First, as always, this book materialized through my immeasurable debts to Sadaf; this book becomes possible through a world that I owe to her.

This book was driven by my experiences teaching about Muhammad at three different institutions: the University of North Carolina at Chapel Hill, Kenyon College, and the University of Central Florida, along with other campuses that I have visited through the years. Students and other conversation partners whom I encountered in my academic and community travels helped me to understand why this book was needed.

Writing this book was a dream project, and the dream's fulfillment owes so much to Elaine Maisner at University of North Carolina Press. It was a conversation between us that first sparked the idea, and I am grateful for Elaine's support and guidance through this project as well as *Muhammad's Body*, my first book for UNC Press. I wish Elaine the very best in her well-earned retirement and am grateful for the continued support of her successor, Mark Simpson-Vos. Thank you to Mary Carley Caviness, Alex Martin, Lindsay Starr, and everyone at UNC Press for their work in the execution of this project.

I cannot say enough for the continued significance of Juliane Hammer to my scholarship and the commitments that inform it. I would not still be in this field, writing this kind of book, without having been her student. I am also grateful to Omid Safi, who demonstrates that love for the Prophet can survive the demands of academic rigor, and Carl Ernst, whose scholarly generosity and collaborative spirit guided me to rethink some of my "wrestling promo" writing tendencies. Not everything is a wrestling promo.

My personal possibilities as a Muslim, both on campus and in the masjid, are expanded by the life, work, and struggle of amina wadud.

My life as a writer and reader begins with my mother.

Finally, this book is dedicated to my son Jibreel Husayn, who was named for the Prophet's angelic guide and for his beloved grandson. Jibreel, I made this book using the tools within my reach. I cannot promise that it will answer any questions that you might ask, or even that the questions driving this book are ones that you'll find compelling. But for all its limitations, I hope that you at least see in this work a reflection of your power to ask your own questions and to assemble, disassemble, and reassemble your answers. The world is yours. You are the maker and owner.

Who Is Muhammad?

CHAPTER ONE

My Muhammads

I was sitting in the masjid office with the imam and some community uncles when one of them asked, "Does he have a name?"

"Not yet," another answered. So the man turned to me.

"What's your name right now?"

"Michael."

He taught me to pronounce my name's Arabic equivalent, Mika'il. And then another uncle said, "Muhammad."

"Mika'il Muhammad," said the imam. Now I had a name.

Just moments before, the imam had witnessed as I testified to my belief that there was no god but God and that Muhammad, the man whose name was now my name, was the servant and messenger of God. Repeating the words after the imam in both Arabic and English, I "officially" converted to Islam (insofar as doing something "officially" is possible in a religion without an institution analogous to the Church). I was supposed to think of it not as a "conversion" but as a "reversion" to my natural state. I was sixteen years old. They gave me some books and their phone numbers and I stepped out of the masjid in a new condition, feeling the change on my skin.

As of this writing, I was named after Muhammad nearly thirty years ago. In that time, my relationship to him has gone to all points on the map, even falling off the map into places I could not have imagined. And now I've written this book, *Who Is Muhammad?*, with some sense of the question being answerable. But that sense is delicate, vulnerable. It wouldn't be hard to break.

The idea behind this book is that I can offer a satisfying response to the question as a scholar in the academic study of Islam. This means that I'm not writing as a clerical authority who will speak for some abstracted "real Islam" that exists above the fray of human history. I can't do that. My scholarly training leads me to think not in transcendent essences beyond the clouds but rather on the ground, looking at our traditions as human constructions. But this doesn't mean that I speak from that other transcendence, the imaginary ideal of "objectivity." Everyone who writes a book writes because they have some relationship to the material. They care about it and want to believe, for whatever reason, that their book is worth writing. They come from a position. What's my position? What's the place from which I'll answer, "Who is Muhammad?" Before launching into the project, let's see if I can sort that out.

INTRO TO THE INTRO

Maybe a year before that day in the masjid when I testified to Muhammad's prophethood and then took his name as my own, I was a high school sophomore with feet on two very different paths: I was writing letters to Charles Manson (yes, he wrote back) and reading *The Autobiography of Malcolm X*. Thankfully, I moved away from the former and toward the latter, and Malcolm opened the door for me to consider Islam as a serious possibility. Long before I had done any meaningful readings into the life or words of Muhammad, Malcolm X provided me with a template of what Muslim intellectualism, discipline, conviction, and masculinity were supposed to be. I walked to the local college library and did my best to imitate his obsessive reading regimen, starting with books that he named in his autobiography, such as Will and Ariel Durant's entire eleven-volume *Story of Civilization* series, and philosophers like Friedrich Nietzsche and Arthur Schopenhauer. And of course, I tried to read the Qur'an in translation. Coming from a Christian background, my assumption was that to understand Islam, I just needed to read its "Bible." It's a popular assumption; if you were to survey college and university syllabi across the United States, you'd find more undergraduate courses introducing students to Islam through the Qur'an than those teaching them the life of Muhammad. Like many who approach the Qur'an without a sense of its organization, taking it for granted that one would just start at the first page and read straight to the last page as with any book, I struggled with the lack of linear narrative and the bouncing almost at random from theme to theme. But there was at least a vibe; after reading the Qur'an's first two suras (the short al-Fatiha and the enormous al-Baqara), I felt like I had encountered something sacred.

My early readings of Muslim sources did not immediately produce a developed, fleshed-out idea of Muhammad. Malcolm X's Islam, at least the picture offered by his autobiography, was not centered on Muhammad, not even as Malcolm performed the pilgrimage to Mecca and reinvented himself in a Sunni conversion. In his autobiography, his entire engagement with Muhammad amounts to one remark about the prominence of cigarettes in Saudi Arabia, with Malcolm suggesting that Muhammad would have probably prohibited them if they existed in his time and place.[1] The Qur'an, regarded as God's speech to Muhammad, does not offer much that would help you to understand Muhammad's own life, experiences, and feelings (unless you read the Qur'an with prior knowledge of Muhammad); it's nothing like a Gospel-styled biography. There was some help from the translator, Abdullah Yusuf Ali, whose copious annotations supplemented nearly every verse with his own commentary, but this meant that Yusuf Ali became the first filter through which I'd perceive Muhammad. My earliest sense of Muhammad thus emerged from the context of British-occupied India in the 1930s and from a scholar of English literature who valorized Muhammad as a paragon of self-reflection, reason, and the nation-building, race-uplifting "great man" model of thinking about world history. With an adamant insistence that Islam stood for rational contemplation and opposed all "superstition," Yusuf Ali doesn't take interest in stories of water flowing out of Muhammad's hands or angels cutting open his chest and washing his heart. Other readings, such as the books I received after becoming Mika'il Muhammad, emphasized similar themes: Muhammad was a reformer, revolutionary, social architect, and brilliant statesman. He gave us the perfect template for healthy human families and entire nations on every point from gender roles to taxation policies. They made their arguments for Muhammad's greatness on essentially secular terms.

At some point, Muhammad became something more. I don't know the exact moment when things changed for me. In my senior year of high school, I spent two months at the vast Faisal Mosque complex in Islamabad, which was home to not only the International Islamic University but also a Daw'ah Academy, which offered introductory knowledge of Islam and Arabic to new Muslims. During a trip to Lahore, I had the chance to visit an Islamic bookstore and pick up the most canonically esteemed collection of hadiths, Muhammad's reported sayings and actions, *Sahih al-Bukhari*, compiled in nine big volumes and including both the original Arabic and English translation side by side. I didn't know how I'd get them home, but I ended up carrying them in a duffle bag on my back through airports from Islamabad to Lahore to Dubai to Frankfurt to Rochester, New York. There might have been an easier way, but by that point I had fallen in love with the Prophet, and it felt like an act of sacrifice and devotion to carry that weight on my back. In my seventeen-year-old imagination, it was as if I had carried the Prophet himself.

After high school, I moved to Pittsburgh for college and took up the idea that if I loved Muhammad, I should want to dress like him. So I wore a long white *thobe* and black turban. I began to attend a masjid that I'd later read identified as the local "hotbed of Salafism." As an escape from campus life, I'd sleep there on the weekends. I didn't yet know "Salafism" as a concept, but when I look back at the logics that shaped my world at that time and how I felt about the Prophet, sure, I was a Salafi Muslim.

Salafi Muslims believe in the collective authority of the Salaf, the earliest Muslim generations, arguing that if an idea or practice cannot be supported by its precedent, it cannot be considered legitimately Islamic. All the information needed for understanding Islam, the Salafiyya would claim, rested with those Muslims closest to Muhammad. Beyond them, everything is departure. Because of their proximity to the Prophet, the Salaf constituted the greatest Muslims of all time. This was my understanding; it's not a universal Islamic position but one contained within Sunni views of history. When my readings led me to Shi'i views of history, which call attention to the power struggles and open war that pitted those "greatest Muslims" against each other, I crashed into a deep disillusionment. Reading of the injustices that Muslims inflicted upon the Prophet's own family during what I had been taught to consider our "golden age" broke my heart.

While this collapse of faith in my sources led me to lower my defenses, I was still diving into my nine volumes of *Sahih al-Bukhari* and finding words and actions that couldn't line up with the rational, scientific, modern Muhammad that I encountered in my earliest readings. There came a time when the whole system fell apart in my hands. I couldn't make sense of it anymore. One night I drove to the masjid and left *Sahih al-Bukhari* outside, thinking that I was done with it forever.

Around this time, I also physically mistreated the Qur'an. My shame won't allow me to say more than that, but my previous writings about it are not hard to find. I envisioned the act not as an expression of hatred but rather as proof of my own liberation, a sign that I had freed myself from the pious fears that had once been so powerful (for an example, I had become so obsessed with maintaining ritual purity that I experienced sensory hallucinations of urinating in my clothes). In my own reasoning, there was even something paradoxically Islamic about discarding the Qur'an, a kind of idol-smashing. That night, I went to bed thinking that I was an ex-Muslim; but then I received a dream visit from Muhammad, his cousin and son-in-law 'Ali, and 'Ali's sons, the Prophet's grandsons, Hasan and Husayn. We were at Kauthar, a special fountain in paradise. They embraced me, their arms intersecting to form a protective, nurturing, and healing circle around my body. In my waking life, I wouldn't have known what to do with a moment like that: by everyone's checklist of required faith convictions, I had become an apostate; but somehow my apostasy was blessed by the Prophet himself. I still knew the hadith from *Sahih al-Bukhari* in which Muhammad promises that if you see him in a dream, it's really him. At my lowest points, when I sealed my heart against the sacred sources, that one hadith preserved me.

Over time, I would come to realize that what I initially embraced as Islam was not universal throughout all of Muslim history but in fact a contextually specific—which is to say, *modern*—assemblage that took the particular form that it did through the collisions of all kinds of historical forces. Likewise, Muhammad as I had been taught to understand him (and the proper sources for accessing him) was not the only way of thinking about Muhammad for all times and places. Though my heart had been broken with the loss of the Salafi "golden age" mythology, I would later take some relief from the idea that Muslims never had a perfect golden age; we were always imperfect humans doing what they could, and our collective memory of the sacred past derives from imperfect humans telling their stories. Surrendering the notion that Islam consisted of a singular authentic "orthodoxy," against which everything else could be measured only as heresy and deviation, I could explore the Islamic tradition in new ways and perhaps reconstruct myself as a Muslim.

Through my writing, these explorations connected me to Muslim readers and allowed me new experiences of Muslim community. My novel *The Taqwacores* may or may not have nurtured the flowering of Muslim punk rock. In other works, I documented my travels throughout the United States and abroad, celebrating Muslim multiplicities and heterogeneities wherever I found them. I revisited Pakistan, this time going to the places from which my mentors shielded me the first time: Shi'i and Sufi shrines loaded with concepts and behaviors that my Daw'ah Academy teachers would have condemned as heretical. I also made the pilgrimage to Mecca and visited the Mountain of Light some miles out of the city, home to the cave where Muhammad first experienced revelation and heard what would become the start of the Qur'an (preserved in the ninety-sixth sura). Though not an "official" part of the pilgrimage, and in fact discouraged by the Saudi government, visiting the cave remains a popular practice. I waited in a line extending down the mountain, and when my turn came, I joined two aunties in the cave and made my prayer. Prior to the official days of hajj, I also ventured to Medina, the home of Muhammad's tomb and Jannat al-Baqi, an adjacent cemetery loaded with heroes of early Islam. Between Mecca and Medina, I was struck by the contrast between two visions of the Prophet; Mecca's image of Muhammad as a spiritual seeker alone in a cave outside the city, as opposed to Medina's image of Muhammad as a statesman who signs treaties, collects taxes, and heads an army as the center of power. The way I received it, Mecca's energy was more primordial, the claim to Abraham and even further back; Medina represented the specificities of jurisprudence and later institutional orthodoxies. Shortly after my Medina trip came the hajj itself, during which I walked into a tent of Iranian pilgrims, introduced myself and shared my story, and then asked if they would bear witness to my reconversion as a Shi'i Muslim. They heard me recite the same testimony of faith that I had more than a decade earlier, with an added line bearing witness to 'Ali as the commander of the believers. If Muhammad were the city of knowledge, as a famous hadith went, 'Ali was the gate.

Back home, I married into a South Asian Sunni family, which provoked a rethinking of what "Muslim" really meant in my life. As a convert who became Muslim due to my public affirmation of certain ideas as true, and wondering whether I could call myself a Muslim after experiencing doubts about those ideas, I now entered a context in which being Muslim often had less to do with my stated beliefs than my relationship to a family and extended community. Being Muslim meant many things, but what we believed was only one of them, and not always the most important one. Meanwhile, I continued to search along the margins, accepting initiation in a Moorish Science group led by "anarcho-Sufi" heresiologist Hakim Bey, who gave me the name Mikail El. My disillusionment with Bey ultimately severed the connection. I also developed a relationship with the Five Percenter tradition, which had originated in 1960s Harlem among former members of the Nation of Islam, one of whom made the most unthinkable offense: he renamed himself Allah. This new Allah, formerly known as Clarence 13X, shared that name with his followers, teaching that they were all the gods of their own worlds. I first came to the Five Percenters as an outside researcher, but as so many outside researchers find out, their encounters change their position. I was never "Five Percenter" enough to be a full-fledged member, but I was at least close enough that one of the community's elders gave me a name: in addition to Mika'il Muhammad, I was now also Azreal Wisdom. The idea that we can call ourselves gods was, at first glance, completely opposed to everything I had previously understood as Islam. But while working with the Five Percenters uptown, I also attended a Sufi lodge downtown that drew from the thought of medieval theosopher Ibn al-ʿArabi. Ibn al-ʿArabi didn't exactly call people gods, but his opponents were terrified that this would be the natural consequence of his theology, and supposedly a circle of Sufis in medieval Yemen read his work with that as their ambition. Straddling Five Percenter and Sufi traditions while attending Ibn al-ʿArabi seminars in my graduate program, it all came together for me and felt mostly organic. Moreover, the Five Percenters' claims to Islam while rejecting the notion of transcendent authority from beyond the world—no "mystery god"—sustained me at times when theological abstraction gave out. It almost prepared me for the soul-erasing work of studying religion in grad school.

As my master's program ended and I planned to continue toward a PhD, I feared the impact of more critical training and developing theoretical sophistication on my spiritual life. With their critical guards always up, can academics allow themselves to feel anything? I wasn't sure but could already feel academic rigor starting to wound my trust in the experiences and feelings that made religion meaningful. Anticipating spiritual death in an academic future, I looked to ayahuasca, a psychoactive tea from the Amazon that has grown popular in "New Age" spiritual tourism and wellness networks. Seekers of all religious persuasions engaged in ayahuasca shamanism, but I had not yet seen much of an "ayahuasca and Islam" conversation. Having read reports of men drinking ayahuasca and seeing the divine in feminine form, I went into an ayahuasca ceremony in the deserts of California with an intention to see Fatima, daughter of the Prophet. Before the ceremony, I discreetly ate a piece of a *turba*, a clay token used by Shi'i Muslims in prayer, which had been made from the soil of Karbala, site of the battle in which Muhammad's beloved grandson Husayn was killed by the Umayyad caliphate. It took some time for the medicine to take hold—how much time would be impossible to know—but when it did, I had my Fatima vision, which became the heart of my Islam-and-drugs memoir, *Tripping with Allah*. During the vision, I not only encountered Fatima but even became her for a moment, in order to witness a reconstructed Islamic masculinity in her husband 'Ali. I also witnessed her father undergo a kind of purge and healing in 'Ali's arms, which perhaps really amounted to a purge and healing of my own relationship to Muhammad. The next day, we drove to Los Angeles and I stumbled into a masjid to wash and pray and recite the Qur'an with all of the outer trappings of a publicly "orthodox" Muslim, while my private Islam remained an heretical hallucinatory secret. Appreciating the script of postures and movements that allowed me to function as a Muslim body even while my Muslim brain was in outer space, I started to think about my religion as a set of physical repetitions, not merely a checklist of doctrines that I believed or disbelieved.

I went into the PhD program and spent half a decade thinking about Muhammad's body as it appeared in hadith traditions. I thought about Muhammad's skin and hair; his heart, on which angels had performed surgery; his fingernails; his sweat, saliva, blood, urine, and semen; and his postmortem remains. Reading about Muhammad's Companions seeking linkages to his body through these traces, engaging in practices such as bottling his sweat for the baraka that it contained, I thought about these body parts and by-products while asking what Muhammad's body could *do*, that is, how Muhammad's body could link to other bodies and form a kind of megabody: a baraka-transmitting power grid comprised of these intercorporeal connections. The project led me to further appreciate just how unstable the meanings of Muhammad's body could be, even within a singular sectarian canon such as the Sunni "Six Books" corpus. Among these vast compilations of reports attributed to Muhammad's Companions, we find a multiplicity of ways they thought about his body and what it could do. Companions such as Ibn ʿAbbas and Anas, for example, emphasized the miraculous qualities of Muhammad's body, such as his sweat smelling better than any perfume, or his saliva (and even urine) improving the quality of water in a well; but narrations from Muhammad's widow Aʾisha tend to downplay the marvels of his body, usually presenting a mundane body that's interesting only for answering questions of correct ritual praxis.

And now I'm here, an academic with a weird backstory, attempting to introduce Muhammad in 80,000 words or less. Do you call this an "insider" or "outsider" position? There are lots of insides and outsides. I took *shahadah* as a Shiʾi and then wrote a book called *Why I Am a Salafi*, which I considered a natural complement to my previous book, *Why I Am a Five Percenter*. While studying with the Five Percenters in Harlem, I also spent time at a Sufi lodge downtown. I drank ayahuasca and then wrote a dissertation about hadiths. I'm bad at guarding the borders. Every Islamic tradition that I embrace is disqualified and condemned by another Islamic tradition that I embrace. Some readers would find that orientation helpful or promising, while others would instantly dismiss me as illegitimate. So let's get to it. Who is Muhammad?

This book project might have first materialized because I had confidence in the answers that I could give, having recently completed a doctoral dissertation on Muhammad and then turning that PhD work into a book. The tools that I learned to use in that process, I imagined, were enough. They did not give me a singular answer to the question, but I at least had a grasp of the various terrains on which diverse voices have worked to produce answers of their own. I could historicize the question: here's how Muslims in one time and place viewed him, compared to another; here are different sources that lead to different conclusions; here's how sectarianism colors the sources; here's how the immeasurable disruption that we call "modernity" has changed the question and our expectations for the answer; here's how scholars in the academic study of religion debate whether the "real" Muhammad can be retrieved from the archive, and here's why there's much, much more to the "Who is Muhammad?" question than "But who was he, *really*?"

I came to the question armed with a bag of academic gimmicks. The point is not to answer the question, because there is no answer; rather, we destabilize the question, showing how the question remains so flawed that we have to write a whole book about why it's a terrible question be-fore we can even imagine the possibility of an answer. We start with the problem of facts, or the problems of wanting facts and believing in facts.

What do you *mean*, "Who is Muhammad?"

What do *you* mean, "Who is Muhammad?"

How many ways can we read that question?

I decided to write this book already knowing what my big answer would be. It's the answer that takes up a lot of space in my academic toolbox, and might be the only answer that my particular training equips me to give. Of course, the answer depends on whom you ask, and when, where, and why you ask. We deal in human beings who tell each other stories. The human beings change, the stories change. Somewhere in there might be the Muhammad that you'd recognize as the "real" one, your answer to the question. But the answer can never limit itself to the "facts" of an individual person who lived at a specific moment in time, and the problem of whether or not our sources have reliably recorded that person's behaviors and feelings for us. Muhammad is not a person but an ongoing tradition, always a liquid that matches the shape of his container, forever unstable, forever local and contextual. We each bring our historically specific eyes to Muhammad, and we see in him what our world enables us to see. The real answer to a big question that aspires to stretch across all time and space is to break it down, make the big question into a million smaller questions, and then leave your reader holding the bag. Who is Muhammad? Muhammad is disassembled, de-constructed, Muhammad is what people make him. My academic train-ing has given me all kinds of tools to take things apart but not necessarily put them back together.

I don't disagree with any of this, but sometimes it hurts. When I re-cently performed this kind of deconstruction in my classroom, a Muslim student waited until the end of class to ask me privately, "But doesn't this leave us with nothing? If Islam is whatever Muslims say it is, doesn't that make Islam incoherent and useless? What's the point?" My response—a prepared one, because this happens quite a bit—was a gentler version of saying that it's not my problem. I reminded the student of the differ-ence between prescriptive and descriptive modes of studying religion; rather than attempt to define and prescribe "real Islam," we engage in a descriptive study of what flesh-and-blood Muslims say in their lived worlds. So in the context of the classroom, no, not my problem.

Perhaps because the encounter took place as I was writing this book, thinking in all kinds of ways about how to define Muhammad, it in fact became my problem. For so long, I relied on the deconstructive approach to take myself out of the ring. For years, I did not feel like I needed a position on Muhammad, because any kind of absolute truth claim about him would mean that I was critically unsophisticated. I stepped back from the question as it related to my own life as a Muslim, a member of Muslim communities, now raising a Muslim son with my Muslim partner. If there were no universally "real" Muhammad, I could go on as a Muslim theory nerd with my deconstructed Muhammad and never have to reassemble him.

Writing this book forced me to rethink my own relationship to the question. One challenge (among many) of writing this book during a pandemic was that I lost touch with the social and sensory experiences that could connect me to some sense of Muhammad beyond my cited sources. What I mean is that the experience of stepping into a masjid is not going to change my position on a particular piece of evidence or scholarly argument, but the experience of *being* in a masjid does change my heart, and the experience of being with flesh-and-blood Muslims in brick-and-mortar Muslim ritual spaces does impact my writing voice. When engaging difficult topics such as the Banu Qurayza during our isolation, the writing felt cold, like I was just a machine retrieving and reproducing data without any emotional investment in the work. My voice took on an academic neutrality that could register as cruel, like I had not actually paused to consider the story I was telling. Looking at the statement of "facts" on the page, I wondered how this narrative would have been changed if I'd written it after a congregational prayer or group lamentation for Husayn. My story would be a different story if I wrote it while feeling the energy of other Muslim bodies in the room, seeing and hearing and smelling and touching a Muslim space and walking out of it with my heart softened.

I own a copy of the Qur'an whose cover was made from the green fabric that lines the walls inside the Ka'ba, the interior *kiswa* (as opposed to the more famous black kiswa that hangs over the outside of the Ka'ba), which gets replaced every year. The Qur'an sits inside a special box made from the same material. The box preserves the scent of the perfumes that had been sprayed on the kiswa when it decorated God's house, so opening the box sends all of that kiswa perfume into your face. Sometimes during the writing of this book, I would open that box just to take in the scent. I also have a metal lapel pin bearing the Five Percenters' Universal Flag emblem; it's the pin that Five Percenters would receive after memorizing all of their Lessons and earning a divine name. I actually have a hundred of them in a box near my desk. During the process of writing this book, I would occasionally run my fingers through the pins, or carry one in my hand as I walked outside. It was always the same pin and it took on a talismanic power when I needed that kind of help. And I had ritual technologies like prayer rugs and stringed beads. Sometimes it helped to *touch* my Islam, rather than just read and think about it, but I still felt that the work had been injured by my detachment from Muslim communities. Muhammad is, among so many other things, a mode of connection, but we also find him in our connections to each other.

WHY THIS BOOK?

Muhammad is simultaneously one of the most beloved historical figures in the world and also one of the most contested, challenged, and disparaged. While Muslims defend Muhammad's legacy against Islamophobic polemics, Muslims also challenge each other regarding the proper authorities through which Muhammad's life and message become comprehensible and applicable in our world. Meanwhile, the classical sources themselves are in question, scrutinized from multiple angles both inside and outside the tradition. Many readers—non-Muslims and Muslims alike—either have little to no familiarity with Muhammad or are unsure how to approach discourses (whether polemical or apologetic) that claim superior knowledge of the "real" Muhammad.

I argue that there was never a collective Muslim vision of Muhammad but always a multiplicity of Muslim imaginaries. In the frameworks of the academic study of religion, I treat Muhammad as both a historical figure and a discursive construction. This means that while there was a "real" Muhammad who lived roughly fifteen centuries ago, the Muhammad that we can access remains mediated by constructed textual canons and intellectual traditions that travel through time and space and undergo change. Even the most stable and codified canon remains malleable as its readers change across different historical settings and determine the texts' meanings for themselves. Muhammad is thus always contextual, always contemporary. Exploring various case studies in hadith literature, the collected sayings and actions attributed to

Muhammad, this discussion shows the diversity hiding within a textual body that is often treated as unified and monolithic (indeed, often written as "the Hadith," as though it were a singular self-contained book). This heterogeneity persists as we move from textual canon to historical traditions and the present world.

Monographs focusing on Muhammad tend to either present Muhammad's life as a straightforward "cradle to grave" biography or, as we see in more scholarly work, focus on specific ways Muslims and non-Muslims continue to "create" Muhammad as a discursive construction. Few projects attempt to offer a broad introduction to Muhammad that presents his full complexity—both as a historical figure with a "real life" and as the central personality in Islamic tradition—in concise and accessible fashion. This discussion engages Muhammad in a religious studies framework both as a transformative historical figure of the seventh century CE and as an ongoing construction across diverse traditions. Moreover, as an argument for centering Muhammad, rather than the Qur'an, as an intuitive starting point for introducing Islam, I hope to intervene in the Protestant-informed ways Islam is often defined (that is, presuming the Qur'an to be the "Muslim Bible" and only authoritative text).

Because no Muslim voice speaks for all Muslims, and there's more to a tradition than its most privileged and powerful expressions, I want to give attention to Islamic traditions beyond "classical" and "canonical" sources, engaging not only the "center" but also the "margins" of historical Islam. There is not a singular, timeless Muslim imaginary of the Prophet, defined by a universally accepted body of texts; rather, as Muslims continually encounter Muhammad through their own worlds of knowledge and experience, Muhammad is revealed as malleable for the different contexts in which he is a resource.

THE ARRANGEMENT

Following this introductory chapter, chapter 2 surveys the world in which Muhammad arose, painting a picture of Mediterranean antiquity, beginning with its major superpowers, the Byzantine and Sasanian empires, and the ways religious life was informed by their ongoing power struggles. Attention to the imperial milieu serves multiple purposes: it helps to establish the circulating flows of religious concepts and identities to and from which Muhammad would speak; it demonstrates the linkage of faith confession to imperial identity, which deexoticizes concepts such as the caliphate for unfamiliar readers; and, by examining the weakened state of the Byzantines and Sasanians, it highlights the power vacuum that would be filled by a new empire of faith. This chapter also moves beyond the Byzantine-Sasanian milieu for attention to less-examined aspects of Muhammad's historical setting: first, religion as it existed "on the ground," rather than exclusively the discourses and institutions of rulers; second, the significance of Aksum and Himyar, roughly analogous to modern Ethiopia and Yemen. The purpose of this chapter is to lay out the historical conditions in which Muhammad's movement emerged, while also providing a sense of the "megatext," the surrounding world of references in and to which the revelation of the Qur'an could speak.

Chapter 3 provides something like a "traditional" biography of Muhammad—with critical reminders that we really have no such thing, as there's no universally accepted "Gospel" account of his life—and introduce Muhammad along with key figures in his life and Islamic tradition (such as ʿAli and Aʾisha). This chapter especially draws on my strengths as a writer, as my intention is to tell the story of Muhammad as popularly understood rather than perform critical academic dissection and deconstruction, writing more as a novelist than a professor. This chapter introduces the reader to Muhammad's life as an artifact of cultural memory.

Having introduced hadith texts and questions of the sources, in chapter 4 I delve deeper into the hadith corpus, my area of scholarly specialization. The hadith corpus, like scriptural canons in other religious traditions, invites consideration of the multiplicity and fragmentation that exist under the appearance of universal canon, as well as the power struggles that inform consolidations of scripture and orthodoxy. The hadith corpus challenges notions of Muhammad as reducible to a singular historical individual. Hadith literature does not appear as a monolithic canon or the singular achievement of a lone compiler; rather, it consists of many thousands of distinct textual units, defined by diverse sectarian, geographic, and methodological factors, produced and circulated through multiple networks of transmitters that at times compete, intersect, overlap, and converge, and organized into collections with varying canonical privilege. The messiness of the hadith corpus reflects the diversity of ways Muslims envision Muhammad and understand Islam through his life and words. For a guiding case study as I navigate this messiness, I focus on hadiths attributed to specific Companions such as ʿAbd Allah ibn ʿAbbas, Ibn Masʾud, and Muhammad's widow Aʾisha. Companions and their respective networks, centered in cities such as Medina, Basra, and Kufa, constructed local archives of prophetic memory; between reports traceable to Medina and Iraq, for example, we get different narrations of Muhammad's physical appearance. Different networks also faced different political fortunes that informed their transmissions and place in the developing hadith landscape. Ibn 'Abbas's students were targeted by the Umayyad caliphate, in part for their links to 'Ibadism (one of his most famous students, Sa'id ibn Jubayr, was decapitated after participating in a revolt), but Ibn 'Abbas's descendants became leading figures of the 'Abbasid revolution (so named for their link to the prophetic family through Ibn 'Abbas) that toppled the Umayyads in 750 CE. Both the political positioning of Ibn 'Abbas's students and Ibn 'Abbas's later significance to imperial ideology would be reflected in the content of Islamic discourses. Using Companions' transmission networks and variegated legacies as windows into the complexities of hadith literature, this chapter demonstrates the challenges of navigating sacred sources and the surprising diversity they contain. Within the vastness of the hadith corpus, the possibilities for how Muslims can imagine Muhammad are equally vast. This chapter goes further into hadith sources to highlight the diversity of reporters and networks that produced Muhammad as a discursive construct.

Chapter 5 explores the ways diverse Muslim communities and interpretive traditions have creatively reconstructed Muhammad. Reading Muhammad through the specific lenses of their own knowledge, values, and social contexts, Muslim thinkers have contested each other over the true nature and meaning of Muhammad and, just as important, the question of which Muslims could properly represent Muhammad's legacy in a post-Muhammad world. At numerous points in Muslim histories, most famously the division between Sunni and Shi'i interpretive traditions (and the classical empires and modern nation-states that construct their identities through these traditions), competing claims upon Muhammad and his authority contribute to meaningful political consequences.

Sunni discourses have imagined Muhammad's Companions as collectively authoritative reporters of his words and actions, and depicted Muhammad's authority as resting safely in a tradition of knowledge that had been transmitted from his Companions to later scholars. Shi'i intellectual traditions, meanwhile, envision Muhammad's authority passing through a line of infallible Imams whose claim to supreme truthmaking power came from their descent (both biological and spiritual) from Muhammad's daughter Fatima and 'Ali. Sufi thinkers and orders also define their authority through connection to Muhammad, both through initiatic teaching lineages and direct metaphysical contact with Muhammad in dreams and visions. Mystics have imagined Muhammad as a transcendent light that preexisted the created universe; philosophers imagined him as an ideal representative of their own work, though his understanding came intuitively rather than through philosophical training; astrologers privilege him as a lord of the Saturn-Jupiter conjunction; and in the era of modern nation-states, political thinkers would treat Muhammad as a social engineer who provided the clear instructions for achieving a perfect government, economy, and society. For some Muslims, Muhammad could appear as something like a shaman; others envision him as a model for husbands and fathers. In short, Muslims throughout Islam's history have repeatedly understood Muhammad in ways that could speak to their specific worlds. This chapter surveys the diverse ways Muslims conceptualize Muhammad, including not only the most dominant or "mainstream" templates but also lesser-known representations of Muhammad, such as the vision of Muhammad in some South Asian contexts as an avatar of Vishnu. Muhammad is always contextually specific and remains a contested territory between diverse Muslim projects.

Chapter 6 discusses the varied constructions of Muhammad in contemporary settings. In the modern world, Muslim thinkers have reimagined Muhammad as the founder of a mythic "Islamic state" and a rationalist philosopher whose teachings and practices anticipated scientific breakthroughs many centuries later. Meanwhile, Muslims have also been tasked with reconstructing Muhammad in the face of ongoing polemics from Western voices. This chapter touches upon key issues in modern Muhammad controversies, such as the question of Muhammad images and the popular narrative that an unchanging and united Islam absolutely forbids any visual depictions of Muhammad's face. A closer look at Islamic art history (which offers a considerable archive of visual representations of Muhammad, including his face) enables us to think about the often surprising ways modern transformations of religion can appear to be timeless and "traditional." More broadly, this chapter includes reflection on the immeasurable changes that religion has undergone in modernity.

Chapter 7 pulls together the book's arguments to again assert that Muhammad cannot be reduced simply to his "real life" and the "facts" of his biography; that the earliest Muslims reconstructed Muhammad in diverse ways in their local milieus; and that multiplicity continues to define Muhammad's life and legacy for the immeasurable diversity of Muslims who make claims upon him. Contrary to the rhetoric of Islamophobes, anti-Muslim racists, and various Islamic revivalists and reformers alike, Muhammad's meaning and value cannot be pinned to a singular textual archive or intellectual tradition. In my conclusion to *Who Is Muhammad?*, I present him as both a historical figure and the product of diverse Muslim imaginaries across fifteen centuries of tradition, which continue to transform and multiply. My concluding chapter also reflects on possible futures for Muhammad. As technologies of producing, circulating, and consuming knowledge continue to change, producing new conceptions of community, authenticity, authority, and Muslim selfhood, what happens to Muhammad? What future Muhammads await?

CHAPTER TWO

Muhammad and the World

I don't normally think in terms of the "great man" model of history, in which special individuals are envisioned as the central driving forces that transform the world, but if I did, I could see an argument for Muhammad as the most impactful human being who ever lived. As a teenage convert to Islam, I was struck by a non-Muslim writer making such a case for him, attesting to Muhammad's immeasurable mark on the world stage.[1] But as much as Muhammad remade the world, of course the world also made him, and we can think about the ways his radical breaks and ruptures were also continuities with that world. In other words, Muhammad came from *somewhere*, and this somewhere matters.

Mecca, the city of Muhammad's birth, was 50–60 miles from the Red Sea and about halfway up the Arabian Peninsula's coast, roughly 650 miles from the southern tip of Yemen and 570 miles from the Sinai Peninsula in Egypt. Medina, the city in which he is buried, was nearly twice as far inland and more than 200 miles north. In popular representations of pre-Islamic Arabia, we run into a tension: on the one hand, the Hijaz is portrayed as so isolated and remote that even after a "monotheistic turn" had swept through the Mediterranean world, transforming both northern and southern Arabia, Muhammad's own community remained stuck in its traditional polytheism—deemed *jahiliyya*, "ignorance," in Muslim historical memory—until the advent of Muhammad's prophethood. On the other hand, Mecca is imagined as an economic hub that attracted traders from far and wide, its vibrant market accompanying a pilgrimage site where visitors could find their hometown gods honored with "idols" and shrines. The truth might be somewhere in the middle. Mecca was not so remote that it could remain unimpacted by the world of Mediterranean antiquity and its major powers, but it was still remote enough that the world did not seem to take much notice. Mecca's economic survival relied on the Incense Road, the networks of Red Sea and trans-Arabian trading routes connecting East African, Persian, and Indian markets, but Mecca sat too far inland to become a node on the sea route. In annual overland travel, Meccan merchants made winter trips south to Yemen and summer trips north to Syria. They could sell leather goods, and the nearby town of Ta'if was apparently home to abundant grapes and a small wine industry, but Mecca's local resources did not appear to produce goods that were especially valuable or hard to find anywhere else. Rather, the traveling caravans could pick up merchandise such as perfumes and spices on one end of the Arabian Peninsula and then sell it on the other. Through their cyclical buying and selling adventures, the people of Mecca connected with North Arabian, South Arabian, and East Arabian cultures.[2] The Quraysh, identified as Muhammad's tribe, led the seasonal caravans and navigated their way up and down the Arabian Peninsula through cultivated merchant networks and pacts of nonaggression with local tribes. Peaceful trade was also made possible by religion, through the establishment of prohibitions against fighting in sacred months or at sacred sites, such as the precincts of the Ka'ba in Mecca.

Classical Muslim sources attest to preprophetic Muhammad participating in the caravans to Syria, first as a child with his uncle Abu Talib and later employed by Khadija bint Khuwaylid, a widow he eventually married. In the sources (which I say with all of the necessary caveats for questions of historical accuracy), Muhammad's travels in Syria include encounters with Christian monks who recognize him as a future prophet. From the larger world beyond Mecca, we could say that Muhammad was marginalized but not absolutely disconnected.

The Hijaz sat within a triangle of empires that had defined themselves (and each other) through religious difference. Northwest of the Arabian

Peninsula stood the Byzantine Empire, self-identified as upholder and defender of the Christian faith; to the northeast, the Sasanian Empire, which had developed its own imperial unity around Zoroastrian tradition. Inheriting the Roman-Persian rivalry that had preceded them, these two empires exhausted each other in the centuries prior to Muhammad through ongoing cold and hot wars. To the south and southwest of the Arabian Peninsula, in what is now Ethiopia, stood the kingdom of Aksum, which asserted an imperial presence in South Arabia. As Byzantium and Iran fought much of their conflict through proxies and allies, Aksum's imperial Christianity leaned its allegiances toward Byzantium; we also see South Arabia become a stage of religiously informed strife between Ethiopia's Christians and the Jewish kingdom of Himyar. As a historical materialist, I'm not of the feeling that religions create war (or peace) all by themselves. Ideas and doctrines by themselves do not move the world; instead, they flow through currents of "real life" factors of power relations and economics. But religion did become a potent means through which empires ruling over vast terrains and diverse populations could envision themselves as united, coherent polities, achieve and enforce social and political stability within their domains, authorize and endorse rulers' claims to power, produce negative images of their opponents, and give ideological support to both their alliances and their rivalries.

In the world that made Muhammad, religious ideas flowed between cultures through multiple channels: trade routes, imperial propaganda, wandering "holy men," and war. Reading Muhammad's life through a modern "secular" lens, taking for granted that religion and the state are naturally distinct and separate spheres, might challenge us when we encounter taxation policies and military engagements envisioned as religious issues. But throughout the Christian, Zoroastrian, and Jewish milieus of broader Mediterranean antiquity, faith and empire went hand in hand. It's not useful here to think in terms of "religious" as opposed to "political"; we won't find that modern distinction in the seventh century CE. Muhammad began his movement as an apocalyptic street preacher but died roughly two decades later as the head of a growing territory that entered the world stage alongside other empires of faith that introduced legislation, upheld individual and communal rights, collected taxes, signed treaties, and fought wars as God's representatives on Earth. In this chapter, we'll look at those other empires—Christian, Zoroastrian, and Jewish—that surrounded the Hijaz before finally turning to Muhammad's immediate context.

THE BYZANTINES

Across the fourth and fifth centuries CE, the Roman Empire went from a world of polytheism to a new kingdom defined by Christian confession. Early in the fourth century Constantine (r. 306–37) legalized Christianity; by the end of that century, Theodosius I (r. 379–95) had made Christianity *the* official imperial faith. Emperors unraveled the Roman emperor cult but reauthorized themselves as defenders and enforcers of Christian faith, aggressively stamping out pre-Christian religion through statutes that banned pagan sacrifice. Alongside the persecution of polytheists, imperial statues also targeted Jewish communities, banning Jews from marrying Christians or owning Christian slaves, and punished citizens who left Christianity to become Jews by confiscating their property.[3] But the Christianization of empire did not only come from the top down: networks of Christian monks policed the religious life of Roman society, going after pagans as well as fellow Christians they regarded as "heretical."[4]

In the early fourth century, Constantine, the emperor whose personal conversion changed global religious history forever by linking a formerly persecuted and marginalized religion to Roman imperial power, moved the empire's capital from Rome to Byzantium, leading to Byzantium's renaming as Constantinople, "City of Constantine." In the centuries preceding Muhammad's birth, the Roman Empire had expanded to such a vast domain that one imperial court could not manage its entirety; the territory split into the Eastern and Western Roman Empires, with the latter becoming the Byzantine Empire. But "Byzantine" reflects a later, retroactive term; the people whom we're calling Byzantines here thought of the ruling power in their world as the Roman Empire. When the Qur'an refers to the Romans (as in early verses of the thirtieth sura, popularly titled ar-Rum or "The Romans"), it speaks of the people now known as the Byzantines.

Imperial efforts to achieve a united Christian empire became reinvigorated with the ascent of Justinian I (r. 527–65), who sought to establish his dominion as an empire of faith by persecuting polytheists. He reinstituted antipagan laws that had been neglected, banned polytheists from government jobs, made baptism mandatory, declared sacrifices to the pre-Christian gods to be a capital offense, and condemned to death Christians who reverted to their pagan ways.[5]

In addition to the coercive erasure of non-Christian traditions and communities from the imperial identity, emperors sought unity among

Christians by convening councils of bishops to iron out their differences and establish universal doctrines. Early Christianity was messy, marked by instability over which books to accept as canonical—Christianity existed for a long time without an established "New Testament"—and how Christians might properly understand Christ's nature. How did the Father and Son relate to each other, and how did Christ's status as the Son of God impact his earthly existence: Was Christ entirely divine or entirely human, or both divine and human simultaneously? And if he was both divine and human, how did these two aspects of his being relate to each other? The imperially convened council to establish uniform Christology, identify textual canon, and declare rebellious theologians and theologies to be "heretical" found an early precedent in Constantine's Council of Nicaea (325 CE) and was followed by later councils, such as the Council of Ephesus (convened by Theodosius II in 431 CE), which condemned the Nestorians; the Council of Chalcedon (convened by Marcian in 451 CE), which repudiated the Monophysite theology of Christ's having only a divine nature; and Justinian's Fifth Ecumenical Council in 553 CE, which enforced the Chalcedonian creed against Nestorians and sought reconciliation between Chalcedonian and Monophysite theologies, thus threatening to split the empire in half. Some viewed the emperors' tendency to interfere in religious matters and claim authority over the making of Christian theology as "caesaropapism," a trespassing on the church's domain.

Beyond the imperial frontier, Roman or Byzantine authorities engaged a variety of smaller Arab kingdoms as well as nomadic groups. The most relevant of these for thinking about Muhammad's historical moment would have been the Ghassanids, a Christian Arab kingdom claiming territory in roughly what is now Jordan and Syria. For the Ghassanids and other Arab communities, embracing Christianization could have also promised Romanization, movement from the margins into the imperial center. Living as Christians was often marked by increased use of Greek and Latin (the political and economic lingua francas of the time), particularly in ritual and naming praxis: the Ghassanid ruler al-Harith ibn Jabala, for example, became alternately known as Arethas, Phylarch of the Arabs.

Though Arab adoption of Roman culture and Arab conversion to Christianity would have looked like a singular shift in the centuries immediately prior to Muhammad, they both preceded the Roman Empire's becoming a Christian empire. Of course, Christianity itself had originated on the persecuted margins in Roman-occupied Palestine; the Jesus movement was Arab before it was Roman. Paul writes in Galatians, "I went off to Arabia and again, then, returned to Damascus" (1:15–17). "Arabia" in this context meant the Nabataean kingdom of the northwestern Arabian Peninsula,[6] which would be conquered by the Romans in 106 CE and reconstituted as the Roman province of Arabia.

Sources remain limited on Nabataean religion; the Nabataeans themselves did not leave mythological narratives or accounts of rituals in their own voices, and we lack substantive details about the Nabataeans' major deities.[7] In the Nabataean pantheon, we find the goddess al-Lat, partner (or mother) of the god Dushara. Her name, which literally translates as "The Goddess" (al-ilat), was regarded by Herodotus as the Arabs' name for Aphrodite. Al-Lat worship was especially prominent in Iram and spread throughout Syria and northern Arabia. Another goddess, al-ʿUzza (whose name is the feminine version of al-ʿAziz, "The Mighty"), also identified with Aphrodite and the morning star (Venus), was popular at Sinai and was the supreme goddess worshiped at Petra.[8] Evidence suggests that in northern Arabia, the two were identified as a single goddess, with al-ʿUzza being one of al-Lat's special names.[9] In seventh-century Mecca, according to the glimpse that we have from the Qurʾan and early Muslim sources, Muhammad's contemporaries regarded them as two separate beings, with al-ʿUzza being most popular among Muhammad's tribe of the Quraysh and in a valley to the north of Mecca, and al-Lat enjoying prominence among the Thaqif and Taʾif.[10]

Al-Lat and al-ʿUzza sometimes appear in Nabataean imagery alongside a third goddess, Manat. The Qurʾan condemns them together as a trio believed to be God's daughters and/or angels (53:19–22). Evidence of Manat worship exists far from Mecca at the remains of Hegra, the ancient Nabataean city in what is now northwestern Saudi Arabia, where she was venerated along with a local god named Hubal. Though Hubal did not enjoy a widespread community of devotees or the embrace of Nabataean ruling elites,[11] early Muslim historical sources assert that he was especially prominent several hundred miles to the south in Mecca, where a statue of him with a gold hand had been placed inside the Kaʾba.[12] While al-Lat, al-ʿUzza, and Hubal might have found their ways to Mecca from the north, Manat moved in the opposite direction, apparently originating in the Hijaz and then spreading north into Syria, reflecting an increased Arab tribal presence along the Roman/Byzantine frontier.[13]

A little more than three centuries before the birth of Muhammad, Persian emperor Ardashir (r. 224–42 CE) rose to power and founded the Sasanian dynasty. Mirroring the Roman-Byzantine struggles to create imperial Christian solidarity through councils that established the bounds of "orthodoxy" and "heresy," Ardashir's imperial project pursued a Zoroastrian vision of religious unity. Ardashir came from a Zoroastrian priestly family, further entrenched the priesthood's political power, and established Zoroastrian teachings as the official imperial religion. His imperial Zoroastrianism relied on the systematizing efforts of a priest named Tosar, who assembled textual canon and articulated "orthodox" Zoroastrian teachings. Comparing this process to the development of the Christian Bible, Touraj Daryaee explains, "The canonization of the sacred texts of the Zoroastrians and the Christians was taking place approximately in the same period and would develop in a similar fashion."[14] And as with Christianity in the Roman-Byzantine milieu, Sasanian rulers and connected priestly elites forged a sense of religious unity through the suppression of minority schools: explaining his policy toward "heretics" within Zoroastrianism, the chief priest Kerdir recalled, "Them I punished, and I tormented them until I made them better."[15] Incidentally, Kerdir also received the knowledge of correct beliefs and ritual practice and the nature of heaven and hell through his journey into transcendent unseen worlds, a widespread motif in Mediterranean antiquity that we also find in the life of Muhammad. In the early sixth century CE, imperial Zoroastrian hegemony was challenged not only by complex relations with "foreign" minority religions such as Judaism and Christianity, but also a homegrown Iranian "heresy," the movement of Zoroastrian priest Mazdak, who challenged the established theologies of the priesthood and advocated a radical social egalitarianism, calling for redistribution of property and even a communal sharing of wives. The embrace of Mazdakism by Emperor Kavad I (r. 488–96, 498–531 CE) led to a power struggle pitting the throne against the disenfranchised nobility and priests, during which Kavad was briefly incarcerated at the Prison of Oblivion.[16]

Christianity increasingly represented a threat to the Sasanians' Zoroastrian regime in the fourth century CE after Constantine declared his sovereignty over all Christians, thereby positioning Christians within

Sasanian territory as a potentially subversive element. Sasanian persecution of Christian communities thus intensified during wars between Persia and Rome.[17] Though Christians were marginalized and sometimes persecuted communities within the Persian domain, marked by their links to the rival Byzantines, Sasanian imperial policy engaged Christians and Christianity in surprisingly complex ways. As the Byzantine effort to achieve a united Christian empire led to persecution of Christian "heretics," the Sasanians welcomed Christian refugees such as the Nestorians, who had been condemned by the Council of Ephesus in 431 CE (just as a century later, after Justinian closed the "pagan" School of Athens in 529 CE, Persian emperor Khusru I invited refugee Greek philosophers to Jundishapur near the site of modern Baghdad, where he would establish his own philosophy school in 555 CE).[18] In the fifth century CE, the Persian Christian church received official state recognition; by Muhammad's lifetime, as many as sixty bishops could be found in each of the empire's major provinces.[19] Rather than simply attempt to crush Christianity, Emperor Yazdgird I (r. 399–420 CE) sought to appropriate it, establishing the Church of the East as his own network of loyal churches and bishops, sapping the prestige of Rome's claim to represent all Christians. Persia's Zoroastrian kings thus claimed a kind of Constantinian status.[20] They even made use of Christian symbols such as crosses, and powerful material artifacts, such as relics like the *True Cross*, whose wood "embodied the soteriological purpose of the Roman Empire in the divine economy," and which fell into Persian custody with the conquest of Jerusalem in 614 CE.[21] With control over the most sacred Christian relic, Sasanian rulers could legitimize their dominion in Christian terms, asserting that they had replaced the Byzantines as the Christian God's favored agents on earth.[22]

Though the status of Christians under Sasanian rule improved through the centuries, Jewish communities were more favored for much of Persian history. The positive Persian-Israelite relationship long preceded the Sasanian era, as found in the Bible's treatment of Cyrus, the Persian king who returned the Jews from their Babylonian exile and rebuilt the Temple in Jerusalem, as a liberator and messiah. Yazdgird I also is favorably depicted in the Talmud, treating rabbis kindly, displaying some scriptural knowledge, and marrying a Jewish woman.[23] The argument has been made that Sasanian rulers supported Jewish communities as allies against Byzantine Christian interests in contexts such as Yemen (which the Persians invaded around 570 CE) and Palestine (which the Persians took in 614 CE), though the notion of a consistent Sasanian-Jewish alliance has been challenged.[24] On the eve of Islam, the centers of Jewish scholarship were found in Sasanian Iraq's rabbinical academies. To some readers, early Islamic historical sources and the Qur'an itself would appear to reflect a view of the Arabian milieu as one divided between the competing interests of Roman and Ethiopian Christianity, on the one hand, and a loose partnership of Persians and Jews, on the other.

As Muslim rulers in early Islamic Iran kept many of the Sasanian legal codes and bureaucratic structures that they found in place, much of the Sasanian Empire's engagement of its Jewish and Christian minorities would find echoes in Muslim jurisprudence. Similar to the later Ottoman Empire with its *millet* system, the Sasanians granted considerable autonomy to minority religious communities under a larger legal umbrella of Zoroastrian authority. Jews and Christians in Sasanian Persia could thus regulate their own communities in their own courts, with Iranian state courts intervening when a case involved Zoroastrians.[25] Jews and Christians paid specific poll taxes, like members of a guild, in a taxation system that would persist through early Islamic caliphates.[26] And like later Muslim rulers, the Sasanians regulated relationships between religious communities (and preserved their own religious supremacy) by criminalizing apostasy. The Sasanian policy integrated religious minorities into political spheres without overturning imperial Zoroastrian hegemony (a more urgent concern as Christians entered imperial politics), as well as managed relations between the imperial court and Iran's aristocratic houses.[27]

NORTH ARABIA: THE GHASSANIDS AND LAKHMIDS

As the Romans or Byzantines and Sasanian Persians competed over the course of centuries, the northern and eastern Arabian Peninsula stood between them as a liminal buffer zone.[28] Local powers in this region, facing rivals of their own, aligned with the empires, turning their wars for regional power into proxy battles on behalf of the superpowers. In northern Arabia, covering modern Jordan, Syria, and Iraq, the Ghassanids became allies of the Byzantines; in southern Iraq and the Persian Gulf coast, the Ghassanids' adversaries, the Lakhmids, aligned with the Sasanians. The ruling family of the Ghassan, the Jafnid dynasty, secured patronage from Justinian as phylarchs or "client kings" and served Byzantine interests on the empire's eastern frontier against the Sasanians and the local Sasanian proxies, the Lakhmids. The Ghassanids, however, also sometimes acted as a virtually independent state, fighting their own wars against the Lakhmids rather than battling only as Byzantine proxies against Iranian proxies. "Encapsulated by Rome," writes Greg Fisher, "the Ghassanid confederation was neither wholly part of the empire nor fully separate from it."[29]

Though the Ghassanids aligned with the Byzantines in a righteous Christian war against the unbelievers of Iran, they also found themselves at odds with the Byzantines' official theology. The Byzantines supported the Chalcedonian creed (Christ having both divine and human natures) while the Ghassanids upheld and promoted Monophysite theology (Christ having only a singular divine nature) in the face of imperial disapproval. Relations between the empire and client state soured in the late sixth century CE, due either to this Christological controversy or perhaps to a more pragmatic Byzantine concern with the Ghassanids' growing autonomy. The Ghassanid confederation would meet its end with the Persian invasion of 614 CE, during the same period that, 1,000 miles to the south, Muhammad struggled in the early years of his mission.

Countering the Roman-Ghassanid alliance, the Sasanian Persians forged a clientage relationship with the Ghassanids' enemies, the Lakhmids. The militarily powerful Lakhmids buttressed the Sasanians' western edge and experienced a resurgence in the decades prior to Muhammad's birth; with the Persian conquest of Yemen, Emperor Khosru I handed the region over to Lakhmid king Monder III (r. 503–54 CE). Around the start of the seventh century CE, however, Khosru II ordered the assassination of the Christian king No'man III (r. 580–602 CE), which marked the end of Lakhmid autonomy and absorption of the territories into Sasanian direct rule. The loss of the Lakhmid support on the Arabian frontier greatly increased Sasanian vulnerability and exhaustion.[30]

Unlike the Ghassanids, the Lakhmids did not share in their imperial patron's religious confession: rather than embrace Zoroastrianism, the Lakhmids apparently maintained their indigenous traditions. The Lakhmids' capital of Hira became a site of extraordinary cosmopolitanism where, Isabel Toral-Niehoff explains, "the cultural spheres of Rome, Iran, Arabia and the Syrian world interacted and overlapped."[31] Trade routes connected Hira to the Hijaz, and later Muslim sources even record the Persian emperor Kavad I's attempt to impose Mazdakism in Mecca. The account serves to glorify Muhammad's great-great-grandfather 'Abd

Manaf, who remained steadfast and refused to desert the religion of Abraham and Ishmael; "The tradition may be spurious," M. J. Kister suggests, "but it points to the contacts which seem to have existed between al-Hira and Mecca."[32]

Hira's diversity included Christians of various cultural backgrounds and competing theological orientations. The city attracted missionary activity from both Monophysites and adherents of the Nestorian doctrine, which advocated faith in Christ's having two natures, divine and human, that remained radically separate. Monophysites reached Hira in part due to Syrian monks fleeing Justin I's anti-Monophysite persecutions of 518–23 CE, seeking refuge and new converts among the Bedouin; in 540 CE, decades after Byzantine emperor Zeno closed the Nisibis school due to its Nestorian alignment, Nestorian scholars reestablished the school in Hira.[33] As Hira became a refuge for exiled monks and scholars, Lakhmid Christians were regarded as highly literate, and it was believed that early forms of the Arabic script had originated in Hira and made their way to the Hijaz in the century of Muhammad's birth.[34]

The Nestorians of Hira benefited from greater compatibility with the official doctrines of the Persian church. By Muhammad's lifetime, Hira had become a Nestorian stronghold. In the 590s, when Muhammad would have been in his twenties, the last of the Lakhmid kings, the ill-fated No'man III, converted to Nestorian Christianity. Though the Sasanians might have been concerned with their Arab proxy's becoming Christian, the entanglement of Byzantine politics with competing visions of "orthodoxy" and "heresy" made it possible to position some brands of Christianity as anti-Byzantine. Though Justinian had sought to differentiate his Chalcedonian orthodoxy from the Nestorian heresy, Monophysites regarded the theologies of Chalcedon and Nestorius as indistinguishable from one another. Conversely, while Chalcedonians and Monophysites condemned each other as illegitimate, Nestorians regarded them as equally guilty of the same heresy. The Nestorian Christianity that flourished under Lakhmid rule and in the Persian churches, therefore, remained a mark of opposition against both the Chalcedonian Byzantines and their Monophysite Ghassanid clients.[35]

Hira's Christians became known as a community of *ibad*, "servants" or "devotees" of God and the Messiah.[36] Scholarship has speculated that, as a transtribal community defined by religious faith, the ibad of Hira produced a new model of society that could have been relevant for the concept of *umma* that emerges later in Islam.[37]

To the extent that the Ghassanid-Lakhmid wars were informed by religious difference, especially at the level of their imperial patrons, the Ghassanids understood their wars through a Christian lens; they maintained a concept of warfare that could be fought in service of Christ. This seems to be important for our consideration of Muhammad's world. Islamophobes like to argue that Muhammad was influenced by the diverse cultures and communities that he could have accessed, which included not only his local milieu of "pagan" religion but also Jewish and Christian groups, both within his immediate surroundings and the flows of trade routes that connected him to the larger world. The question of "influence," in their eyes, would expose Muhammad's program as an earthly one, a result of historical accidents and borrowing of ideas, rather than a divine revelation from outside the world. But despite this fixation on "influence," modern critics of Muhammad who look at Islam as simply a derivative plagiarism from other traditions still tend to assume that jihad, or Muslim just-war theory (often considered the "lesser jihad" in contrast to a "greater jihad" of inward spiritual struggle), represents something uniquely and exclusively Islamic. The Islamophobic narrative would claim that while Muhammad freely appropriated monotheism and biblical stories from his Jewish and Christian sources, his ideas about fighting and conquering for God were entirely his own.

When talking about jihad, we're usually talking less about Muhammad and more about a later juristic conversation, as Muslim clerical scholars in the generations and centuries after Muhammad theorized about the justifiable causes of military action and the codes of conduct for Muslims who take part in it. I don't want to project later just-war theories and legal discourses backward onto Muhammad's life, but multiple Islamophobic narratives fall apart with a closer look at Christian warriors in Muhammad's setting. Besides the matter of God's commanding war in the Bible and entitling the victorious Israelites to plunder, enslave, or outright exterminate conquered populations (Deuteronomy 20, Joshua 10), we can think of Muhammad's military campaigns as a mirror to the ways a regional Christian power had linked faith to war.

Recent scholarship has called for focused attention on the Ghassanids as an Arab kingdom that connected with the Byzantine sphere through both Christianization and Romanization, joining with Byzantine forces against their "pagan" enemies with faith that God supported their expeditions and raids.[38] When the Ghassanids raided Hira in 575 CE (when Muhammad would have been five years old), they destroyed polytheists' sites but left Christian churches standing (even those of the heretical Nestorians).[39] Michael Lecker has even argued for a direct Ghassanid presence during Muhammad's prophetic career, pointing to genealogical links between the Ghassanids and various groups in Medina and suggesting that the Ghassanids (and their Byzantine patrons) had directed the city's leadership to encourage Muhammad's migration there.[40] In other words, Christian jihad preceded Muhammad. Imperial Christian networks with their own concepts of sacred war were already active forces in Muhammad's landscape.

AKSUM AND SOUTH ARABIA

Let's now head southward into what is now Yemen and cross the Red Sea into Ethiopia, site of the third major power in this triangle of faith-driven empires. In Muhammad's time, the Ethiopian empire of Aksum was one of the world's foremost, one of only four kingdoms in that period to issue its own gold coins.[41] Early in the fourth century CE, contemporary to Constantine, King Ezana I converted to Christianity and spent much of his four-decade rule (ca. 320–60 CE) working to Christianize his territory. Scholarship on early Islam has increasingly come to recognize Aksum as extraordinarily significant for the historical setting that gave rise to Muhammad. After all, of Rome, Persia, and Ethiopia, only Ethiopia appears to have made any serious attempt to conquer the Hijaz region, in a wave of invasions that Islamic historical memory depicts as having approached Mecca itself in the year of Muhammad's birth.

Much of Ethiopia's significance in Muhammad's historical setting relates to its power moves in South Arabia and the Christian-Jewish conflicts between the kingdoms of Aksum and Himyar, in what is now roughly Yemen. In the fourth century CE, Himyar's ruling elites began to embrace Judaism; by the early fifth century CE, references to indigenous gods had seemingly disappeared from royal inscriptions without a trace, and a new Jewish kingdom was in power. Of course, the problem with royal monuments is that they speak with a royal voice, representing the values and aspirations of ruling elites. The religion expressed in monuments of power may or may not correspond to popular lived religion, but it also appears that the temples of local gods had been in rapid decline.[42] Prior to the royals' Jewish conversion, different indigenous gods were worshiped in different regions of the kingdom; consolidation of the kingdom did not mean a singular united religion but recognition of the varied local gods in the capital.[43] The state promotion of monotheism could have reflected an effort to express an imperial unity on different religious terms. Christian Robin additionally considers that as both the Persians and Byzantines sought Himyar's allegiance in their contest over Arabia, the Byzantines offered impressive gifts with hope that the Himyarite king would accept baptism; but the historical Byzantine-Ethiopian alliance, and the Ethiopians' developing Christian conversion (Aksum's king Ezana announced his Christian faith around 360 CE), could have diminished Christianity's appeal for the rulers of Himyar.[44]

How Jewish communities came to southwestern Arabia is unclear, but we know of a Yemeni synagogue datable to the third century CE. In 70 CE, centuries before the rise of Jewish Himyar, Vespasian's siege of Jerusalem and destruction of the Temple apparently caused a flight of Jewish refugees seeking sanctuary in Arabia, a possible origin of the Jewish communities of Yathrib (Medina) that Muhammad would encounter.[45] South Arabian monotheists called upon God as Rahmanan (which would appear in the Qur'an as "Rahman," typically translated into English as "The Merciful"), in contrast to North Arabia, where the God of Abraham was called Allah. The Qur'an references a possible confusion among Muhammad's audience, who might have suspected that Rahmanan or Rahman and Allah were two different gods. The name "Allah" was apparently better known in Muhammad's locale, with some possibly regarding Rahman as an entirely different god worshiped in the south, but the Qur'an would embrace both names: "Call upon Allah, or call upon Rahman; by whatever name you call him, to him belong the most beautiful names" (17:110). Robin suggests that a similar distinction between Rahmanan or Rahman and the God of Abraham could have existed in South Arabia. Rabbinical literature condemns Jews who believe in "two powers in heaven"; Robin points to an inscription in which Rahmanan appears to be a distinct character from the "Lord of the Jews" (identified as YHWH, God of Abraham), possibly the "God of converts" (in distinction from Judean-origin Jews).[46]

Around 518 CE, roughly fifty years before Muhammad's birth, the Ethiopians invaded Himyar and installed a Christian king of their choice, Ma'dikarib Ya'fur, but this regime did not last long. The "fanatically Jewish" Dhu Nuwas, also known as Yusuf, took power in Himyar ca. 522 and embarked on a program of killing Ethiopians, burning churches, and attacking settlements on the coast.[47] In Najran, near the modern Saudi-Yemen border, he engaged in an act of religious genocide so heinous that it became a "global" event: he slaughtered the city's Christians, which included not only Ethiopians but also Byzantines and Persians,[48] burning them alive in their church. The atrocities at Najran became so notorious, and their historical ramifications so far-reaching, that more than 500 miles north and a century later, an early sura of the Qur'an made reference to the massacre: "Condemned are the companions of the trench, the fire filled with fuel, when they sat around it, watching what they were doing to the believers whom they resented for no reason but their belief in God, the Almighty, the Praiseworthy" (85:4–8). Najran also appears in the long prelude of Ibn Ishaq's biography of Muhammad, as part of the "universal" sacred history in which Ibn Ishaq situates the Prophet's life.[49]

In an official statement read by a messenger, Dhu Nuwas unapologetically boasted of his brutality to a diplomatic conference in Ramla, providing horrifying details to the Byzantine and Persian officials in attendance. Speculating as to why Dhu Nuwas would have been so forthcoming to the international community about his violent persecution of Christians, G. W. Bowersock suggests that Dhu Nuwas might have been seeking support from the Persians, who had historically supported the Jewish rulers of Himyar, against the Ethiopians, who would have been aligned with the Byzantines.[50] Dhu Nuwas's hope for Persian backing apparently went unfulfilled, but his concerns about a Byzantine-Ethiopian Christian alliance were well founded: When the Byzantine emperor Justin learned of the Najran massacre, he called upon Aksum to seek justice and offered the support of his own soldiers. Ethiopian forces moved into Arabia in 525 CE, killing Yusuf and putting an end to South Arabia's Jewish kingdom. Churches were restored or built anew and Himyar again became Christian in its imperial faith.

After the successful invasion, many Ethiopian troops remained in Himyar. One of them, a Christian general named Abraha, rose to power in the 530s and established Himyar as an Ethiopian-ruled kingdom independent of Aksum. He held a conference in 547 CE, where he presented himself in front of representatives of the Byzantine, Persian, and Ethiopian kingdoms as Arabia's new power player. In 552 CE he sent two armies on northward expeditions, one heading northeast against Ma'add, the other moving northwest to advance up the coast.[51]

Classical Muslim historical sources link Abraha's northward advance to a short passage in the Qur'an. In its 104th sura, the Qur'an describes the "Companions of the Elephant" (ashab al-fil), who were attacked by birds that pelted them with stones. The Qur'an gives no more information about who these Companions of the Elephant might have been, or when and where this event took place; but interpretive tradition holds that Abraha's forces had actually entered Mecca and attempted to destroy the Ka'ba, possibly with an ambition to create a new site for Arab pilgrimage in Himyar. As the story goes, the army's elephants refused to advance upon the Ka'ba, God sent birds from the sea to bomb them with stones, and Abraha himself met a gruesome end with his fingers falling off and his heart bursting out of his body.[52]

Popular Muslim tradition also dates the event to 570 CE, regarded as the year of Muhammad's birth, connecting the Prophet's arrival to another miraculous intervention from God. Of course, naming precise birth years for someone in Muhammad's setting would be difficult, and if we accept that Muhammad was born in or around 570 CE, he's roughly two decades removed from Abraha's expedition into Arabia. The years around Muhammad's birth also saw the Persian king Chosroes I, in response to the appeals of a South Arabian Jewish leader named Sayf ibn dhi Yazan, send troops into Himyar and completely annihilate the Ethiopian regime. With the end of Ethiopian imperial power, South Arabia became Persian territory.[53]

THE HIJAZ

After circling through the major empires surrounding the Arabian Peninsula and the various interactions of smaller kingdoms and tribal confederations with great powers, we zero in on the Hijaz, the region on the Red Sea coast in which Muhammad was born. The Arabian Peninsula's deserts and mountains were too forbidding to invite a complete Byzantine, Sasanian, or Ethiopian conquest. Again, while the Hijaz was too isolated to become a major trading hub or absorbed within a larger power's territory, it was not so removed that it could remain completely untouched by the major historical forces in its milieu—or transformative moments like the monotheistic turn that swept through the ancient Mediterranean world. Mecca existed near the Red Sea segment of a land caravan trade route, the Incense Road. At one time the land and sea routes in this area, connecting South Arabia and East Africa to the Mediterranean, were protected by the Ethiopians. The Qur'an refers to the Meccans' summer and winter caravans (to Syria and Yemen, respectively) in its 106th sura.[54]

The same sura calls upon them to worship "the lord of this house" (106:4) in gratitude for their success and security. "This house" was the Ka'ba, a structure that matched other sacred places in the post-Christian shrine culture of the area.[55] Robert Hoyland writes of sacred spaces as "legion in Arabia" and usually designated with a term signifying protection and prohibition: in the case of the Ka'ba's precincts, the area came to be known as its haram.[56] Such spaces were often established around areas that provided vegetation and water, which would have been prized in the desert and therefore likely causes of violence: marking the area as sacred would have deterred fighting.[57] The Ka'ba was constructed at the site of a sacred well, Zamzam. As with other holy places, the Ka'ba attracted seasonal pilgrimage, the success of which depended on correct ritual praxis. As Hoyland explains, pilgrims to these sites were required to abstain not only from violence but also sexual intercourse and wore special pilgrims' garb that signaled them as "temporarily exempt from the usual rules of tribal behavior."[58]

Pilgrimage to the Ka'ba, which would have been not only a spiritual event but an economic one as well, attracted pilgrims from a diversity of traditions, both "pagan" and biblical. In Muhammad's time, the Ka'ba was reportedly dedicated to Hubal (according to some traditions, the only god with a statue *inside* the Ka'ba), but 360 "idols" would have been found in the shrine's surrounding precincts. Sources also indicate that images of Mary, baby Jesus, and Abraham (possibly conflated with Hubal) were placed in and around the Ka'ba;[59] though officially a "pagan" shrine, the Ka'ba could also have been, at least to some of its visitors, a Christian one.[60] It seems to have been believed by at least some participants in the Ka'ba's ritual life that Abraham and Ishmael were not only their biological forefathers but also the builders of the original Ka'ba (it was also believed that the Zamzam well first appeared as a miracle to save young Ishmael and his mother Hajar), endowing the Ka'ba with another layer of meaning as a site of ancestor veneration.

Drawing from his study of Safaitic inscriptions in Syria and Jordan from centuries before Muhammad, Ahmad al-Jallad speculates on North Arabia's pre-Islamic worldview as one defined by the forces of an impersonal *Mny* ("Fate") and the various gods and goddesses that could help human beings who made proper appeals to them.[61] Among these gods was Allah, whose name literally signified "the God" (*al-ilah*) and his feminine equivalent, al-Lat. Arabic-speaking Christians in North Arabia also used the name Allah for the God of Abraham. In the Qur'an, al-Lat appears with al-'Uzza and Manat as three goddesses and/or angels and/ or daughters of God (53:19–22).

Reading the Qur'an for a glimpse at its original audience, it also appears that Muhammad's contemporaries called upon jinns (root of the English "genie"), beings created from smokeless fire, for help (6:95–100, 37:158, 72:6). When the Qur'an emphasizes that God created both humans and jinns, provides refuge from the evil of both humans and jinns, and will ultimately judge both species as their lord (sura 114), a modern reader might miss the polemical thrust of these verses.

Islamic historical memory presents the Mecca of Muhammad's time as dominated by local indigenous polytheism (termed "jahiliyya," meaning "ignorance"), while acknowledging the presence of Jewish and Christian communities. Efforts to contextualize the Qur'an by linking verses to specific times and places, along with biographical material on Muhammad, encourage a view that while the Meccans were primarily polytheists, Yathrib (Medina) was dominated more by monotheists: in the earlier, Meccan revelations, the Qur'an tends to argue for belief in one God over indigenous deities such as al-Lat, while the Medinan revelations focus more on engaging Jews and Christians. Yathrib or Medina was home to both Jewish and polytheist tribes. A number of theories have been suggested for the Medinan Jews' origins, with scholars arguing that they could have been a remnant of a first-century CE Israelite sect, descendants from the Qumran community, or linked to Samaritans.[62] A curious claim in the Qur'an—"The Jews say that 'Uzayr is the son of God" (9:30)—provokes some speculation as to the specific Jewish communities that Muhammad encountered. 'Uzayr is usually identified as the scribe Ezra, last high priest of the First Temple, but there is no evidence of a Jewish tradition that imagined Ezra as the son of God. Since Muhammad was arguing with people to their faces, it's not enough to simply pronounce him "ignorant" of true Jewish beliefs; Crone suggests a connection to trends of angel worship that existed between monotheists and polytheists alike.[63] We could at least speculate that the Qur'an refers to a now-lost local tradition or sectarian group in Medina.[64] The specific Jewish communities mentioned in this charge, whatever they might have believed, no longer exist to give their side.

The classical narrative of Muhammad as a courageous voice for Abraham's God against a polytheism-dominated social order reads in tension with the available material evidence. Robin's study of several hundred South Arabian inscriptions points to 380 CE (two centuries before Muhammad's birth) as the moment at which references to the regional pantheon of gods vanish in favor of exclusively monotheist inscriptions.[65] In North Arabia, al-Jallad writes, references to "pagan gods" were gone from inscriptions by 500 CE (seventy years before Muhammad's birth).[66] Examining pre-Islamic "Paleo-Arabic" inscriptions, al-Jallad and Hythem Sidky observe monotheistic inscriptions, some specifically Christian, that "together imply the widespread penetration of monotheism across Arabia . . . even in areas previously believed to have been late bastions of paganism," such as a route between Mecca and al-Lat's alleged stronghold of Ta'if.[67] If Muhammad's movement represented a fight against polytheism, how much polytheism was there left to fight?

While acknowledging the region's Jewish tribes, Christians, a local kind of unaffiliated monotheist (*hanif*), and significant numbers of enslaved Ethiopians with origins either in Christian Aksum or Christian and Jewish South Arabia, Islamic historical sources present the Hijaz as polytheism's last holdout. But as one might guess from their designation of pre-Islamic Arabia as "jahiliyya," these sources remain ideologically loaded, relying on polytheism as a device to establish a severe distinction between pre-Islamic and Islamic eras. Similar to individual "born again" conversion narratives such as the lives of Saint Paul and Malcolm X, the sources present Arabia at its lowest possible low before the Truth arrives. As historical sources, they're not especially helpful. As al-Jallad observes, these narratives work as theological warnings and entertainment for their audiences but do not present a grasp of pre-Islamic religion that resonates with other forms of evidence, such as archaeological evidence and inscriptions. "What is noticeably absent from such works," al-Jallad explains, "is any sense of a mythological framework—the gods are isolated idols, stones, statues, and carvings, each one revered by a different social group with no narrative connection between them or any description of their role in cosmos."[68] Additionally, "None of the information contained therein comes directly from practitioners of these traditions."[69]

One could argue that the text of the Qur'an, which is reliably datable to the time of Muhammad (or, at its most conservative and critical estimate, the generation of people who had known Muhammad), gives us a picture of pre-Islamic religion. The Qur'an condemns Muhammad's contemporaries for their worship of "idols" that they had fashioned with their own hands and false deities that cannot help them, especially the three figures that they regarded as God's daughters: al-Lat, al-ʿUzza, and Manat. Though we can speak of pre-Islamic goddesses across Arabia more generally, there remains the problem of knowing precisely what these figures meant for Muhammad's own community: what we can say about the religion of al-Lat and al-ʿUzza at the Nabataean capital of Petra does not give us a perfect window into the goddesses' significance in another setting removed by several centuries and hundreds of miles. The Qurʾan does not deeply probe and engage polytheists or give us much information about a polytheistic religion beyond the names of key deities; polytheism appears in the Qurʾan almost more as an abstraction than as a real worldview held by flesh-and-blood human beings. Through a close read of the Qurʾan's arguments against polytheists, G. R. Hawting has argued that the Qurʾan actually targets people who already understand themselves to be monotheists.[70] As Patricia Crone provocatively writes, "The Messenger and his pagan opponents worshipped the same God."[71] Crone draws this conclusion from the Qurʾan's own arguments against them: if asked who created the heavens and earth, the "pagans" would affirm that it was God (29:61, 31:25, 43:9); these same "pagans" insisted that they venerated lesser gods in order to get closer to God (46:28) and mediate between God and themselves (39:43).[72] The Qurʾan does not charge Mecca's "polytheists" with wrongly identifying the creator of the universe as another being besides God; when the Qurʾan brings up God's creative power, it seems to reference a fact that both Muhammad and his opponents take for granted. The Qurʾan even recognizes that in their most vulnerable situations (such as traveling by sea), the "polytheists" pray to God alone (10:12, 16:54, 29:65). Crone additionally points out that the Qurʾan's mentions of "idol worship" appear in its references to Bible stories, rather than living contemporaries in Muhammad's own community, and that the Qurʾan's mentions of "sacrificial stones," appearing in the context of ritual slaughter, refer to altars, not idols. Contrasting the Qurʾan's direct engagement of Muhammad's community against the way his community is depicted in later sources such as hadiths and prophetic biographies, we get two very different pictures. Assessing the picture that the Qurʾan paints of pre-Islamic Meccan religion, Crone writes, "One would not guess from this that the Kaʾba is supposed to have housed a deity called Hubal, that three hundred and sixty idols are supposed to have surrounded it, that every house in Mecca reputedly had its own idol, that one of the Prophet's opponents was an idol-maker, and that no Meccan would go away without stroking his idol before leaving and doing so again on his return."[73] The Qur'an makes no mention of Hubal, or shrines other than the Ka'ba in a landscape that was supposedly littered with them. Perhaps most important, Crone observes, the Qur'an never calls for or threatens the destruction of any such artifacts or structures, nor do the verses following Muhammad's conquest of Mecca make a single reference to his destroying or removing anything from the Ka'ba.[74] The *mushrikun* or "polytheists" of the Qur'an, Crone argues, were monotheists who worshiped the God of Abraham and recognized this God as the singular creator of heavens and earth but believed in a variety of unseen beings ("and perhaps also in some cases the sun and moon") who could mediate between God and themselves.[75] They engaged these beings as routes *to* God, not *instead of* God.

Crone focuses her analysis on the Qur'an as the most reliable representation of pre-Islamic Mecca; in contrast, the reported sayings and actions of Muhammad, the hadith traditions, come with added problems of vetting the sources. But if we casually survey the most canonical hadith sources, looking for concrete fact-claims on the details of "idolatry" in pre-Islamic Mecca (excluding legends about the far distant past, the use of "mushrikun" as a vague social category, or hypothetical prescriptions about law and practice), we run into a similar phenomenon. The notion that 360 idols surrounded the Ka'ba comes from a singular source: a narration from the traditionist Sufyan ibn 'Uyayna (725–814 CE), who was born roughly a century after Muhammad's death. Sufyan tracks his transmission through a chain of three sources and then to the Companion Ibn Mas'ud, who receives more attention in a chapter 4. With one exception that refers to the idols as *sanam*, all versions of Sufyan's account depict Ibn Mas'ud using the word *ansab*, which, as Crone explains in her work on the Qur'an, signifies the stone altars *on* which sacrifices were performed, not idols *to* which worshipers offered sacrifices. Ibn Mas'ud narrates in canonical collections that Muhammad jabbed at the stone altars with a stick, reciting verses of the Qur'an proclaiming truth's arrival and falsehood's powerlessness (17:81, 34:49).[76] Muhammad's younger cousin Ibn 'Abbas, another Companion on whom we will focus more later, becomes our only source in canonical hadith traditions for claims that the pre-Islamic Ka'ba contained images of Abraham and Ishmael; the attribution to Ibn 'Abbas comes from 'Ikrima, a notoriously troubled source.[77] And nowhere in these hadith traditions do we encounter a claim that the Ka'ba housed a statue of Hubal. Al-Lat and al-'Uzza are mentioned sparingly, and the only mention of the goddess Manat in canonical hadith literature comes from Muhammad's widow A'isha, who narrates to her nephew 'Urwa, who in turn reports to his son Hisham. The account depicts the Ansar, the Muslim converts in Medina, as having formerly entered into a pilgrim's ritual purity (ihram) to worship Manat. Out of reverence for Manat, the goddess's devotees abstained from walking between Safa and Marwa, the hills adjacent to the Ka'ba; citing the Qur'anic verse revealed to address this situation (2:158). A'isha commands the now-Muslim Ansar to forget their pre-Islamic taboo and walk between the hills, which had become part of the required Islamic pilgrimage rites.[78] Al-Nasa'i's canonical hadith collection depicts Muhammad's cousin 'Ali as smashing idols of al-Zutt, an Indian community that had migrated to the Persian Gulf in Sasanian times.[79] Ibn Hanbal's *Musnad* provides the hadith of Muhammad helping 'Ali reach the top of the Ka'ba to knock idols off its roof, but later canonical sources did not include it.[80] Hadith sources generally treat idolatry more as an abstraction—clarifying that you cannot sell idols or swear oaths by idols, comparing drunkenness to idolatry, addressing the afterlife fates of idolaters' children who die before reaching maturity, and so on—than a historical reality contemporary to the narrators. If we want a more detailed picture of pre-Islamic polytheism than the Qur'an provides, the hadith corpus—even before we approach the question of hadiths as trustworthy historical sources—offers little help, instead further challenging our assumptions about Meccan "idolatry."

This issue will come up again as we zoom in from Muhammad's broader historical context to his own biography. Whether or not the venerators of God's daughters were "real" monotheists could say more about our own personal religious feelings than about an "objective" historical reality, since monotheism is a bit of an unstable concept, and monotheists regularly charge each other with not being "real" monotheists. Muslims commonly argue that the Christian doctrine of God's begetting a son violates true monotheism, and that the theology of the Trinity amounts to a worship of three gods; Protestants accuse Catholics of idolatry in their veneration of Mary and the saints. Both insiders and outsiders often presume a pure and absolute monotheism (*tawhid*) to represent the truest essence of Islam, but Islam is also characterized by an abundance of disagreement over what exactly that means. Muslims of diverse intellectual and sectarian positions regularly accuse each other of violating tawhid and falling into the offense of *shirk*, assigning "partners" to God. If the Qur'an calls for a purification or revival of Abraham's religion, it also portrays Muhammad's contemporaries as already believing and practicing what looks *to them* like monotheism. Muhammad's claim to prophethood seems to have encountered severe opposition from the people of Mecca, but I don't know that his testimony to divine unity, *la ilaha illa Allah* ("There is no god but God") was necessarily the reason.

While classical Muslim historical memory presents Muhammad's movement as a radical and absolute break from what had been thinkable in his world, there's space for thinking about Muhammad's revelation and revolution as reflecting a continuity, a natural flow from the historical forces that made him possible. Whether as a rupture or a flow, his life marks the point of departure between old empires of late antiquity and a new world.

CHAPTER THREE

The Life of Muhammad

For me, this chapter is simultaneously the most basic and the most frustrating part of the book. I want to provide an introductory biography of Muhammad, a story told so often that the chapter should write itself. I could tell a version of his life off the top of my head. But at every step of the way, I find a reason to slow down and rethink the narrative.

It might seem weird that this basic introduction to Muhammad's life is the chapter that causes me the most trouble. It feels completely incompatible with my academic training in the study of religion. But if a scholar in Islamic studies cannot speak with confidence on Muhammad's life, what's the point of becoming a scholar in Islamic studies? I am confronted with two choices, each burdened by specific challenges. I could simply present the "traditional" and "canonical" biography of Muhammad. Or I could subject that story to critical scrutiny, scrutinize the sources, expose fictions and forgeries and mythmaking embellishments, radically deconstruct Muhammad's life, and try to recover a kernel of the "real Muhammad" that would satisfy even the most rigorous academic skepticism. I'm torn by these competing impulses. When introducing a figure like Muhammad, do you start with a foundation of what we can reliably claim as "real" history and then move into myth? Or do you prioritize Muhammad as he exists in popular cultural memory?

The "real" history remains a source of scholarly debate. I am not an extreme skeptic who believes either that Muhammad was entirely a fictional character or that the mass corpus of reports on his character, behavior, and discourses was entirely fabricated, forever burying Muhammad under so much mythmaking and fiction that we cannot confidently say anything about him. Beyond the question of what we can reasonably know about the historical Muhammad, there's the question of whether this "real" Muhammad is more important than the vast and diverse traditions that have imagined and reimagined Muhammad in countless ways. If you're looking to Muhammad as the portal into a better understanding of Islam, I can't claim that "real history" is necessarily what matters most here. Muhammad's significance in Islam includes all kinds of concepts and expressions that may or may not reflect the ideas, words, or life of the historical person. You may or may not believe that Muhammad flew from Mecca to Jerusalem on a winged animal called the Buraq and then ascended through the vertical tiers of the heavens, interacting with angels and long-dead prophets, but these stories, whether or not they reflect historical reality, remain historically impactful. Meanwhile, giving you the "mythical" Muhammad doesn't mean I can abandon all interest in evidence and sources. Even if someone writes from a nonbeliever perspective and does not believe that claims of heavenly ascension can ever have serious evidence, they would still consider the question of which versions of these stories might reliably trace back to Muhammad's own claims about himself. On both sides, we have choices. Whether or not we resolve the historical authenticity problem, we face some issues that won't go away.

If you want the "traditional" or "canonical" biography of Muhammad, I'm sad to confess that technically, there's no such thing. Though Muslims do consider some texts to be canonical sources for learning about Muhammad (and disagree over which sources are best), they have not produced an "official" cradle-to-grave biography of Muhammad with the kind of transcendent authority that Christians give to the Gospel accounts of Jesus's life. The Qur'an is not, as many might assume, the "Muslim Bible," and it does not say much as a source for detailed history or biography; because the Qur'an presents itself as God's communications *to* Muhammad, it provides virtually no concrete details *about* him. Nor did Muhammad's Companions or their students work together to construct an account of his life. And the most respected scholars of Muhammad's life in Islam's first centuries simply weren't interested in telling his life story, even though they were intensely interested in things that he said and did. For reasons I'll get into here, their particular investment in Muhammad's life did not lead them to think about that life in terms of a chronologically ordered biography.

This doesn't mean that Muslims never wrote biographies of Muhammad; in fact, they wrote many, *many* biographies, each reflecting the values and priorities within a specific historical context and ideological concern, and again, none taking on full "Gospel" authority. Some of these have become extremely important and influential, even enough to claim a kind of "canonical" status. But there's a tension in Muhammad's biography over questions of who collects the material, how do they get it, how do they organize it, and for what purpose. Scholars in the oral traditions of hadiths, Muhammad's reported sayings and actions, became privileged relatively early in Islam as the foremost custodians of his memory. They were principally interested in issues of practice, collecting reports of Muhammad's life for the purpose of knowing how to live in accordance with his example. This means that they engaged his life not as a cradle-to-grave narrative with a moral lesson at the end but as thousands of distinct incidents in which his actions, words, or silence provided an example to imitate, instruction to follow, or at least adequate material through which someone could surmise what he *would* have done in a particular situation. The scholarly authorities that would have been most trusted as biographers of the Prophet, therefore, were not really interested in giving his life a biography treatment. They were collectors of evidence for theological, legal, and ritual arguments.

Early hadith scholars even expressed suspicion toward biography as a project, largely for the methods that it required. To write a biography of anyone, you'd need to gather evidence from a wide range of sources to develop the most comprehensive account possible; and then you'd have to combine these materials into a singular, coherent narrative, which would inevitably require cutting and pasting and altering the material. The practice of combining reports existed early in Muslim historical writing, and the hadith scholars reviled it for its lack of scholarly rigor. To write Muhammad's biography, you would have to reconcile or synthesize contradictory reports and force them into a singular narrative, force multiple narrators to surrender their own personal subjectivities and speak as a Companion "hive mind"; and as you skillfully manipulated these diverse voices into the image of a united voice, you would inescapably inject your own personal feelings and priorities into the work. The united voice, then, is your own. Compiling hadiths into one massive story would have been hopelessly subjective and methodologically sloppy, and even the most piously intentioned biography of the Prophet risks inflicting a particular harm on his story. In this way, early hadith scholars and contemporary postmodern theorists would raise almost the same challenge to Muhammad's biography. Muhammad is not "a life," that is, a narrative that some author assembles and arranges from outside to convey some ultimate and universal life lesson; rather, Muhammad is a catalog of thousands of events, best accessed in a topic-based arrangement.

These hadith scholars were well aware that forgers and fabricators would make up reports about Muhammad for any number of reasons, whether for financial gain; to puff up the honor of a particular tribe, region, or king; or to give evidence for a sectarian claim. They also grew intensely hostile toward marketplace storytellers who enthralled crowds with epic sagas, with or without formally citing their sources. Hadith scholars developed a sophisticated method of vetting reports about Muhammad to assess their likely authenticity; but did these methods do what they promised? If you'd hope to mine hadith literature to produce a critically satisfying "academic" biography of Muhammad with the strongest evidence, this would be exceedingly short and would still have to acknowledge gaps in our knowledge or confidence in the sources. Scholarship is not yet settled on the question of whether, or to what extent, premodern hadith scholars have preserved a reliable picture of the "historical" Muhammad. The strongest arguments for deriving "authentic" reports on Muhammad from classical hadith sources have often prioritized the narrations of A'isha, as opposed to narrations attributed to other Companions.[1] While these projects cannot recreate documentary evidence for "facts" of Muhammad's life, they can plausibly date some traditions to the first century of Islam.[2] If we only used A'isha's narrations, however, we would access Muhammad's life as filtered through A'isha's account of her own experience, an ideologically loaded source, given A'isha's polarizing position between Sunni and Shi'i visions of Islamic history. The source-critical approach would additionally leave out some important material: If you want to learn more about Muhammad due to his immeasurable significance for Muslims, what do you need to know—the verifiably "real" details of his life, or the stories that express his significance?

That the source considered the earliest extant biography of Muhammad is the *Maghazi* of Ibn Ishaq (d. 767 CE), and that this work survives in the recension of later scholars such as Ibn Hisham (d. 833 CE), would raise some red flags: we rely in part not only on a scholar who lived a century after Muhammad but in fact on his mediation through a scholar in the following generation, editing the work several decades later in accordance with his own values and sensitivities. This brings us to the early ninth century CE, two centuries after Muhammad. That could be a problem. Ibn Ishaq was not a highly regarded hadith expert; he comes from an era before the boundary intensified between professional, jurisprudence-minded hadith scholars and more popular, entertainment-centered storytellers. But even in that time, hadith transmission circles didn't care for him; the imam Malik ibn Anas reportedly called Ibn Ishaq a *dajjal* (antichrist), leading to Ibn Ishaq's exile from Medina. Nonetheless, the *Maghazi* became the most popular and widely read biography of Muhammad; while Muslims could critique specific details or some of his weak citations, it provides a telling of Muhammad's life that would broadly work for most readers.

My general approach to these sacred narratives leans on the deconstructive side, but we can't take a thing apart before it's put together. I have to assemble something and call it "The Life of Muhammad" before we can subject it to our critical disassembling. In this chapter, I would like to put together Muhammad's story, with the idea that we'll complicate it later; but I'm afraid that it's always going to be complicated. Almost everything here is up for grabs.

BIRTH, EARLY YEARS, AND THE QUESTION OF MUHAMMAD'S PREPROPHETHOOD RELIGION

Muslim historical memory has identified Muhammad's tribe as the Quraysh, though contemporary scholarship has questioned the process by which the term *Quraysh* (which appears in the Qur'an but is not explicitly named a "tribe") came to be understood as a tribal unit.[3] Within this designation, Muhammad came from the Banu Hashim clan, whose social power was ritualized in its prominent role during pre-Islamic rituals around the Ka'ba. Muhammad's grandfather, 'Abd al-Muttalib, provided food and water to the pilgrims, a role that he had inherited from his uncle and in turn passed on to his son ʿAbbas.

Before he received God's guidance and became the Prophet, what exactly was Muhammad's religion? This might be more complicated than we think, especially when we surrender a binary opposition that has been retroactively imposed on the scene, namely that of pre-Islamic polytheism defined against Islam and other monotheistic traditions. The distinction between polytheism and monotheism is never so absolute; after all, monotheists throughout history can't agree with each other over what "monotheism" really means, and they regularly accuse each other of violating its terms. Rarely are two traditions absolutely walled off from each other, with no possibility of contact or exchange; instead, encounter and mixture historically are the rules of the day, and the borders between identities often are more open than anyone expects. Accounts of Muhammad's family background exhibit some of that messiness. On the one hand, we have no account that presents Muhammad as having been born into a Jewish or Christian family; all sources point to his family having practiced pre-Islamic Arab polytheism, which Islamic narratives derisively brand as jahiliyya ("ignorance"). But on the other hand, the Quraysh apparently claimed descent from Abraham through his son Ishmael; it was also believed that Abraham and Ishmael had built the Kaʾba, and that the adjacent well of Zamzam (rediscovered by Muhammad's grandfather ʿAbd al-Muttalib, who was instructed to dig up the well in a miraculous dream) had originally appeared as a divine intervention to save Ishmael and his mother, Hajar. When ʿAbd al-Muttalib and the Meccans recovered the lost well, they proclaimed, "Allahu akbar!" ("God is the greatest") and spoke of divine judgment in ways that seem to read as essentially "Abrahamic."[4] Muhammad's own parents are presented as having names with ostensibly monotheistic implications, ʿAbd Allah ("Servant of God") and Amina ("Faithful" or "Believing"). According to Ibn Ishaq, Amina was told during her pregnancy that a voice from the unseen realm informed her, "I put him in the care of the One," and instructed her to name her baby Muhammad, meaning "deserving of praise."[5] Before Muhammad's conception, a blazing light appeared in the forehead of his father, which caused a woman to pursue him because she knew (having heard from her knowledgeable Christian brother) that he could conceive the apostle of God. After ʿAbd Allah married Amina and conceived Muhammad, the light disappeared from him: it was now transferred to her womb, from which a light shone that could show her the castles in Syria.[6]

In other stories of biblical monotheists recognizing Muhammad's destiny in advance, we see members of Muhammad's "pagan" family, such as his uncle Abu Talib and wife Khadija, taking the assessments of learned Christians seriously. Echoing the Gospel of Luke, in which Zoroastrian priestly astrologers (the Magi, rendered today as generic "wise men") recognize the star signaling Jesus's birth and journey from Persia to honor him, Ibn Ishaq provides an account of a Jewish man making a declaration of astrological knowledge: "Tonight has risen a star under which Ahmad is to be born."[7]

For a reportedly "pagan" family in a world dominated by "pagan" religion, that's a lot of Abraham. We can read these connections in two ways. First, maybe the linkages to Abraham and biblical monotheism were layered onto the story later, retroactively "Abrahamizing" Muhammad's background. Second, we can consider that Muhammad came from a family that already understood itself as monotheistic in some sense, and already valued its connection to Abraham's religion. The Qur'an's anti-idolatry polemics, as some scholarship has suggested, would therefore reflect not an effort to convince polytheists to embrace monotheism but rather a critique that self-identified monotheists were not sufficiently monotheistic in practice.[8] The two options are not mutually exclusive by any stretch.

Reading narratives of Muhammad's life as they developed in the generations after his death, we can see a growing anxiety about the possible connections to polytheism and so-called jahiliyya. This anxiety related to the evolving notion of 'isma, a prophet's protection from error, and intensifying interests in Muhammad's transcendent authority. Even though Muhammad was regarded as "unlettered" in biblical traditions and did not receive divine revelations until he was forty years old, Muslim historians nonetheless cleaned Muhammad's biography to keep him distanced from polytheism. A tradition in which Muhammad appears to have eaten the meat of an animal that had been slaughtered on a goddess's altar, for example, circulates in different versions that further remove him from participation in jahiliyya religion.[9]

As God's speech to Muhammad, the Qur'an does not give us much in the way of biographical material; it doesn't narrate Muhammad's life back to him. But the Qur'an does make references to his past and present experiences: in 93:6, the revealed verse asks, "Did he [God] not find you as an orphan and then gave you shelter?" The biographical tradition would affirm that 'Abd Allah died before Muhammad was born, and that Amina died when he was only six years old. He then went to the home of 'Abd al-Muttalib, who in turn passed and left Muhammad in the care of Abu Talib, who loved Muhammad like his son. In addition to asserting that God gave Muhammad shelter when he was an orphan, the Qur'an consistently presents orphans' welfare as a central concern—whether as a means to highlight the wickedness and greed of those who would exploit orphans for their inheritances or turn them away, or to praise those believers who care for orphans and guard their property.[10] Someone who reads the Qur'an as a nonbeliever, regarding the text as a product of Muhammad's own mind, could see the Qur'an's preoccupation with orphans' security as a hint of his formative experiences, or at the very least (since we have no evidence that Abu Talib or anyone else mistreated young Muhammad) as supporting the tradition's accounts that he had lost both parents early in life.

Similar to popular tellings of the lives of Jesus, Buddha, and other world teachers, accounts of Muhammad's childhood abound with tales alert us to his special destiny: besides the miracles of his birth and his periodic recognition by Jews and Christians as a future prophet, his childhood was also marked by an episode in which two angels abducted him and cut open his chest, removed his heart, and washed it before restoring him. In some versions, the angels extract a black portion, identified as "Satan's share," before restoring Muhammad's torso. The incident appears to treat Muhammad's body as requiring a supernatural modification before it can perform the later functions of prophethood; in some variants of this "chest-opening" tradition the incident occurs not as a prerequisite for prophethood but rather before Muhammad's heavenly ascension.[11]

Muhammad's birth, childhood, and early years are perhaps the most "literary" or "mythical" portions of his biography, by which I only mean that these reports fit him into a particular narrative mold: the character of the history-making "great man" whose special future reveals itself in miraculous signs and promises early in his life. There's nothing close to documentary evidence for these events, and the Companions who became the most important reporters of Muhammad's life, such as his cousin Ibn 'Abbas and wife A'isha, were too young to have witnessed his preprophetic years firsthand. While I'm oscillating a bit between interest in the "traditional" story and the effort to spot "real history," his early life leaves us dealing almost entirely in the former.

THE PROPHET

While we're limited in what we can say of Muhammad's preprophetic religious life, since the sources want to keep him simultaneously distant from jahiliyya polytheism and "unlettered" in Jewish and Christian book knowledge, he at least emerges in these accounts as a young man of exceptional character. Muhammad's reputation for honesty and honor led a wealthy widow, Khadija bint Khuwaylid, to hire him to sell her goods. According to Ibn Ishaq, in a narrative for which we don't otherwise have evidence, Muhammad transported Khadija's merchandise as far as Syria. Ibn Ishaq also reports that Muhammad traveled on these trading journeys with Khadija's slave Maysara, who upon returning to Mecca informed Khadija of the marvels that he had seen: a monk identifying Muhammad as a prophet, and even angels shading Muhammad from the sun. Khadija, already impressed by Muhammad's trustworthiness and ethics, proposed marriage, which Muhammad accepted.[12]

In his off time, Muhammad took to spiritual hermitage on a small mountain outside Mecca. In the month of Ramadan in the year 610 CE, at the age of forty (with a caveat that precise years in the premodern world might be a problem), he was visited by the angel Gabriel, who commanded, "Iqra!" (Read!). In this context, in a setting of oral tradition and poetry prior to the Arabic script's full development, "read" more precisely meant "recite." Muhammad answered that he was not a reader (or reciter); he was not one of those poets and seers in Mecca who claimed that their words came through them from unseen beings such as jinns. Gabriel again ordered, "Iqra!" and this time physically squeezed Muhammad. Then the words came: "Recite [or read] in the name of your lord who created! Created humanity from a clot. Recite, and your lord is the most generous, who taught by the pen, taught humanity what it did not know" (96:1–5). This was the start of the twenty-three-year process that would become the Qur'an.

Though the Qur'an contrasted itself to the recitations of poets—its words came not from mere jinns but from the Creator of all the worlds—it did so in part through besting the poets on their own terms, by surpassing their eloquence and aesthetic power. The Qur'an invited any doubters of its divine origin to produce superior verses. The Qur'an's original audience did not experience it as a "book" but as an ongoing flow of unpredictable revelations: the Qurʾan's first listeners engaged not a "text" to study and interpret but an expression of divine presence that marked itself as such through the sensory power of its words. The Qurʾan showed and proved itself as divine through the experience of listening to its recitation. This power would remain a mark throughout Islamic tradition, as scholars theorized about the Qurʾan's divine inimitability (*iʾjaz*), seeking to understand the truth of the Qurʾan's claims about its own aesthetic merits. Classical literature on the Qurʾan's transcendent properties includes catalogs of devout Muslims who were so physically impacted by listening to recitations that the Qurʾan literally *killed* them, granting a kind of martyrdom.[13]

Muhammad did not come down from the mountain in a state of mystical bliss or calm contentment that his spiritual yearnings had finally been answered: instead, his first experience of revelation was violent and traumatic. He believed that he was insane and momentarily considered ending his own life. When he returned home and told Khadija what had happened, she reassured him in monotheistic terms ("I take refuge in God," she said, in "him in whose hand is Khadija's soul")[14] and suggested that Muhammad was the prophet for his people. She then went to her cousin Waraqa, a Christian knowledgeable in the Torah and Gospel. According to Khadija, Waraqa instantly affirmed that her husband was guided by the same angel who guided Moses.[15]

These expressions of continuity with biblical tradition, whether historical or not, are worth noting. While the first revelation could be considered the start of something called "Islam," evidence does not suggest that Muhammad saw himself as the "founder" of a new religion. The Qurʾan certainly does not frame him as such, instead emphasizing that God's religion is one for all of the prophets, and that Muhammad only represents a continuation of what God had revealed to past messengers.

THE QURʾAN, EARLY PREACHING, AND PERSECUTION

The revelations that would become the Qurʾan started with a handful of verses on that night in the cave. The rest of the Qurʾan did not come immediately but rather in bits and pieces over the next twenty-three years, sometimes slowing or stopping, and often directly engaging issues facing Muhammad and his community. It's important to remember that the Qurʾan did not really function in Muhammad's lifetime as a "book," and it certainly could not have been the "Muslim Bible," for a number of reasons. Besides all of the ways our human experience of religious scripture has changed in recent centuries (paper technology and modern printing making books cheaper, standardized education making books more accessible, the Protestant ethos of religion as inherently scripture-centered circulating across the world through Christian missionary work and European colonialism, and the new hegemon of digital media), we have to note that until the end of Muhammad's life, the Qur'an remained a fluid, growing, changing artifact.

Classical Muslim scholarly tradition and contemporary academic engagements of the Qur'an have sought to identify the historical contexts for specific verses, enabling readers to more effectively relate them to Muhammad's life and mission and perhaps date the order in which these verses were revealed. The Qur'an is not organized chronologically: suras generally regarded as the earliest, such as the command that Muhammad recite in the cave (96:1), appear near the end of the Qur'an (in the 96th of the Qur'an's 114 suras), while the verse commonly regarded as the Qur'an's conclusion appears near the front of the book, in the fifth sura. Considerations of the Qur'an's chronology and Muhammad's life lead us to note some stylistic and substantive differences between early and late revelations. Verses dealing with things like marriage and divorce or inheritance laws come from later in Muhammad's mission; in contrast, the early revelations do not give detailed plans for building a pious society or address finer points of ritual practice and moral codes. Nor do the first revelations launch into obscure theological arguments. At the start of Muhammad's prophetic career, the Qur'an spoke in both its content and structure like loud knocks on a door—short, abrupt, and commanding, jarring witnesses into action. Early suras condemned the Meccans for their greed and arrogance, compared them to ancient nations that were destroyed for ignoring the messengers that God sent them, and called them to remember that this world was not permanent, on either the personal level (since we are all bound to die) or a macrocosmic scale (since the Qur'an seems to warn of an imminent apocalypse in which the mountains will be ripped apart, the oceans overflow, and the earth shake before vomiting up its contents).

Some years ago, as I prepared for my pilgrimage to Mecca, a loved one gave me some advice. He said that if I ever found myself challenged by severely overcrowded environments, which would inevitably invite some mistreatment and rude behavior from other pilgrims, who were themselves frustrated and stressed, I should remember this: no one has been treated worse by the people of Mecca than the Prophet. That lesson jumps out at me as I reflect on the early reception of his message. Muhammad's message of monotheistic revival and piety, and in part his appeal to the powerless and vulnerable of Mecca, could have been a shock to the system. For the first three years of his mission, Muhammad only preached privately. When he slowly began to gather a following and his movement grew public, Mecca's social elites came to view him as a threat to their way of life. Muhammad's apocalyptically tinged social critiques and condemnations of his society's religion and ancestral traditions encountered increasing antagonism from Mecca's powerful clansmen, who not only found their pride hurt by his attack on Mecca's traditional religion but also held an economic stake in Mecca as a local pilgrimage center. It was pilgrimage that turned Mecca into a minor trading hub; if Muhammad destroyed the old ways, what would happen to the economy that had grown around the shrine? Ibn Ishaq tells of twenty Ethiopian Christians (possibly coming from Najran, he notes) who visited Muhammad at the Ka'ba, reportedly having been sent to learn about the new movement, and embraced Muhammad as a genuine prophet after hearing him recite the Qur'an.[16]

Muhammad attracted followers from varying social and economic ranks, including enslavers and the enslaved alike. Muhammad's more privileged opponents would mock him for teaching Mecca's lower classes, scoffing at the idea that the poor could have access to a prophet before them.[17] They doubly stung Muhammad with a class-based critique, claiming that he not only was a fraud but had been taught by a young enslaved Christian named Jabr. The Qur'an would answer their charge by asserting that "the language of the one to whom they refer is foreign, and this language is clear Arabic" (16:103).[18] Ibn Ishaq reports that the Meccans persecuted Muhammad's followers with strategic regard for their class status. One of Muhammad's most famous adversaries, known in Muslim memory as Abu Jahl ("Father of Ignorance"), would verbally insult Muhammad's followers who had high status or familial protection, threaten Muslim merchants with boycotts, and even beat and torture Muslims who were most socially vulnerable, such as the enslaved.[19]

Muhammad received some protection thanks to his uncle Abu Talib, who mediated between Muhammad and the leading Meccans and advocated for his nephew. Because this protection did not extend to the rest of

Muhammad's growing community, Muhammad sent more than eighty of his followers to seek refuge in Ethiopia, confident that it was a hospitable country ruled by a just king, the Negus. While the term "hijra" in popular Islamic vocabulary most often refers to the later migration from Mecca to Medina (which provides the basis for the Islamic calendar), this earlier flight to Ethiopia is recognized in Muslim memory as the first hijra.[20]

The Meccans sent a delegation to Ethiopia after the Muslims, hoping to convince the Negus to deport the Muslims back to Mecca. The most threatening weapon in the Meccan argument was that the Muslims followed neither their ancestral ways nor the Negus's Christianity but their own made-up religion. Muhammad's cousin Ja'far ibn Abu Talib pleaded that prior to Muhammad's prophethood the people of Mecca were "an uncivilized people, worshiping idols, eating corpses, committing abominations, breaking natural ties, treating guests badly, and our strong devoured our weak."[21] When the Meccans asserted that Muhammad taught his followers to regard Jesus as a mere created being, not the son of God, Ja'far countered with affirmation of Jesus as the servant of God, "his apostle, and his spirit, and his word, which he cast into Mary the blessed virgin."[22] The Negus gestured to a stick on the ground, declared that Jesus "does not exceed what you have said but the length of this stick," and declared that the Muslims would remain safe in his kingdom.[23]

While remaining in Mecca with most of his followers and enduring harassment and even violence from the Meccans, Muhammad experienced a devasting pair of losses during a period (usually dated 619 CE) termed his "Year of Sadness." Khadija, his wife of nearly twenty years and the first to believe in his message, died, followed by Abu Talib, his uncle who had protected him first as a young orphan and later as a persecuted prophet. Whether Abu Talib ever formally converted to Muhammad's religion is a complicated question, and an ideologically loaded one, due to the spiritual and political significance of Abu Talib's son 'Ali. Sunni sources, with some exceptions, crystallized around a narrative that Abu Talib refused to bear witness to his nephew's prophethood and was condemned to hellfire; some traditions place Abu Talib in the least severe level of hell, in which a fire at his feet causes his brain to boil. In contrast, Shi'i traditions tend to regard Abu Talib as a sincere Muslim who kept his faith secret so he could keep Muhammad safe from the Meccan elites (which he could not have done if he lost his own elite status).[24] Whatever his fate might have been in the next world, Abu Talib's death had massive consequences for Muhammad's safety and security in this world. Losing his wife and uncle in the same year left Muhammad not only emotionally devastated and alone but also more vulnerable to Meccan violence with the loss of Abu Talib's protection.

THE ASCENSION

The Year of Sadness represents the low point of Muhammad's prophetic mission and the loneliest time in his life. While he struggled with the loss of his wife and uncle, the Meccans' persecution intensified. His surviving family supported him as they could; his daughters would clean him after the Meccans dumped animal intestines upon his head as he prayed. Seeking the security that some of his followers had found in Ethiopia, Muhammad journeyed to the town of Ta'if with hopes of refuge; but upon his arrival, the inhabitants threw stones and garbage at him. Muhammad was isolated, persecuted, and facing threats to his life and the well-being of his new community.

During this time Muhammad experienced something miraculous. The Qur'an describes it in vague terms: "Glory to the one who caused his servant to journey by night from the sacred masjid to the furthest masjid, whose surroundings we have blessed, to show him some of our signs. Indeed he is the hearing, the seeing" (17:1).[25] What does this mean? The "sacred masjid" (*masjid al-haram*) would refer to the precincts of the Ka'ba in Mecca; what was the "furthest masjid" (*masjid al-aqsa*)? What were the signs that Muhammad saw? The Qur'an doesn't identify the two masjids, but the hadith corpus and biographical literature report a celestial adventure in which Muhammad, accompanied by the angel Gabriel and riding a supernatural steed known as the Buraq, flew from Mecca's "sacred masjid" to Jerusalem's "furthest masjid." He then ascended from Jerusalem into successive tiers of heaven, interacting with prophets and a variety of beings from the unseen, such as angels and—depending on what you read, and how you read it—God.

This is one of those points at which I must pause and repeat that there's no singular "canonical" version of Muhammad's journey through the heavens. Even within a specific community's notion of "canonical sources," such as the "Six Books" of hadiths that Sunni Muslims hold in high esteem, we can find multiple versions with meaningful differences. It would also be important to remember that the "canonical sources" aren't the only things that drive a tradition; through the centuries, Islamic art has produced its own "canonical" imagery of Muhammad's night journey that can depart from textual sources. The animal that Muhammad rides into the heavens, the Buraq, is described merely as an animal "larger than a donkey and smaller than a mule" in Sunni tradition's Six Books; but Islamic art, in conversation with less canonical textual sources, embellishes the Buraq into a supernatural hybrid with a Pegasus body, human face, and peacock tail. This depiction of the Buraq remains powerfully "canonical" in its own way, proliferating throughout the world and becoming the Buraq's most famous image.

Zooming our lens back out to consider religion in the ancient Mediterranean world, we can see Muhammad's Night Journey within a popular truthmaking genre. Spectacular accounts of holy men traveling in the skies appeared throughout religious imaginations; the account that we have from Muhammad (and/or later Muslims who assembled and elaborated the event into a coherent story) fits into a preexisting template. In biblical traditions, we see sky travelers such as Enoch (1 and 2 Enoch), who is popularly identified as the prophet Idris named in the Qur'an, John (Rev. 4:1–2), Paul (2 Cor. 12:1), and most obviously Jesus, who physically enters the heavens (Luke 24:50, Acts 1). The world of the transcendent was "up there," physically beyond human reach; Muhammad's account of his celestial travels meets Mediterranean antiquity exactly where it was.

The Night Journey would reflect not only the religious narratives of Muhammad's world but also the *physical* science of his time: his ascension through the heavens as a series of seven vertically ordered tiers was not simply a spiritual event. While we might think of the seven heavens today in purely metaphysical symbolic terms, people regarded this as the actual shape of the universe: the earth was in the lowest celestial sphere, the "sublunar" realm, and advancing toward God meant journeying upward through these successive spheres. However, early sources also present a view that Muhammad's journey was not physical. Though Ibn Ishaq includes the account of Abu Bakr earning the honorific title *as-Siddiq* (the Trustworthy) for believing in Muhammad's journey when others did not, Ibn Ishaq also presents Abu Bakr's daughter A'isha as stating that God had only transported Muhammad's spirit and that his body remained in place through the night.[26]

Ibn Ishaq's version of the journey, which overlaps with more formally canonical tellings, emphasizes that Muhammad was a prophet in the biblical tradition. The Buraq first takes Muhammad to Jerusalem, where he sees Abraham, Moses, Jesus, and other prophets, and joins them in prayer. Muhammad then undergoes a test in which he is asked to choose between vessels containing water, wine, and milk. Muhammad passes the test by choosing the milk, meaning that his people will be rightly guided. In his later accounts of the prophets, Muhammad would describe their physical appearances: Moses was tall, curly haired, and had a hooked nose; Jesus was of medium height with straight hair. As for Abraham, Muhammad asserted, "I have never seen a man more like myself."[27] If we think of Judaism, Christianity, and Islam as cousin religions within a larger "Abrahamic" tradition, and position Moses, Jesus, and Muhammad as the embodied stand-ins for these religions, these physical descriptions of the prophets take on an added significance: their bodies mark their relationships. Muhammad and Abraham match each other perfectly.

It was after this Night Journey (isra') to Jerusalem that Muhammad experienced his ascension through the heavens (mi'raj). Today, Muslims generally treat these two events as a singular journey taking place on the same night, and the terms "Night Journey" and "ascension" have essentially become interchangeable. In his work on these varied and evolving narratives, Frederick S. Colby observes that "early sources differ on whether the terrestrial and celestial journey are in fact one and the same, or whether they refer to distinct events happening at different times"; but he also notes that Muslims clearly regarded these two journeys as a singular combined event by no later than the ninth century CE (two centuries after Muhammad).[28]

Muhammad's account of his ascension includes another polemical swipe against the followers of Moses. It was during this journey that Muhammad received the assignment of five daily prayers; the command was originally for fifty prayers each day, but Moses, pessimistic that Muhammad's followers could uphold such a duty, convinced Muhammad to ask God for a lighter burden.[29]

According to Ibn Ishaq's material on the ascension, Muhammad "reached the seventh heaven and his Lord."[30] What kind of access to God, exactly, did Muhammad experience? In a particularly controversial point for Islamic theology, Muslim traditions differ as to whether Muhammad's amazing visions include a direct vision of God. Hadith literature presents a difference of opinion among Muhammad's close companions: Muhammad's cousin Ibn 'Abbas, who would have been a small child when the journey took place, appears to report that Muhammad saw

God; Muhammad's wife A'isha would later insist that Muhammad only saw Gabriel in his true form, not God.[31]

It was also during this time of anguish, loss, defeat, and despair that Muhammad, according to a tradition that was once widely believed but gradually fell out of the textual canon, accepted a theological compromise with his opponents and recited verses that affirmed the beings al-Lat, al-ʿUzza, and Manat as worthy intercessors with God. When the Meccans heard these verses, they celebrated as though the conflict between their traditions and Muhammad's new movement had ended. After all, both sides worshiped the same God, and they had now come to terms on the legitimacy of seeking help from the three angels or goddesses as mediators between God and themselves. Muhammad, his followers, and those he condemned as *mushrikun* performed prostration (*sujda*) together. But God then corrected Muhammad's error, revealing that Satan had corrupted Muhammad's recitation with his own "Satanic Verses," and replacing these "Satanic Verses" with the true Qur'anic recitation.

Did this "really" happen? I hope that by now, I've made it clear that I don't have video recordings from Muhammad's lifetime fifteen centuries ago, and my confidence regarding "real" history isn't the strongest. But perhaps the more interesting question would ask how Muslims approached the story. It's possible to track historical change in Muslim responses to the Satanic Verses incident, as the late Shahab Ahmed had labored for many years to do, as a way of tracking the development of Islamic "orthodoxy" over time. Muhammad's early biographer Ibn Ishaq, for example, narrates the incident as a historical fact. His treatment places emphasis on Muhammad's compassion for his people and the pain of his alienation from them, a human weakness that could render even God's Messenger vulnerable to Satan's manipulation.[32] In his extraordinary but sadly unfinished project on the Satanic Verses in a dynamic and changing Islamic tradition, Ahmed establishes that the event was accepted by early Muslims as historical. Ahmed's posthumously published survey of the Satanic Verses as it appears in the earliest sources contrasts this widespread acceptance with later "orthodoxy," which would treat it as unthinkable to suggest that Muhammad succumbed to a compromise with Mecca's pre-Islamic religion. As Muslim ideas about Muhammad's divine protection from error intensified through the centuries, it became heretical beyond repair to imagine Muhammad lapsing in this way, even momentarily.[33]

The turning tide of momentum in Muhammad's prophetic mission was not only expressed with a mystical ascension; in "real life," on the ground, things were changing. Though he failed to win over the Meccans and was turned away violently at Ta'if, his message had spread to other communities. The first glimpse of a better future came in 620 CE, during the pilgrimage season in which devotees from throughout the region, apparently polytheists and monotheists alike, came to Mecca to perform rites at the Ka'ba. A handful of men from the Khazraj, a polytheist tribe, met with Muhammad outside Mecca. As Muhammad recited the Qur'an to them, they marveled that Muhammad must be the prophet they had been anticipating. Though not monotheists themselves (again, with all of our critical disclaimers about categories of "monotheism" and "polytheism" in this time and place), the Khazraj came from the city of Yathrib, an assemblage of tribal forts a little more than 200 miles north of Mecca, where they lived in close contact with Jewish tribes and were apparently familiar with biblical traditions. During the next year's pilgrimage, Muhammad received pledges of allegiance from pilgrims of both the Khazraj and their rivals the 'Aws. During the pilgrimage of 622 CE, even more pilgrims came to meet with Muhammad; this time, they not only repeated their earlier pledge but invited him to come to Yathrib and act as a judge between the two tribes. If we want to project modern terms onto the situation, we could say that Muhammad was about to become a statesman.

The gradual relocation of Muhammad's movement to Yathrib concluded with Muhammad himself, whose exit from Mecca reads in the sources as a daring escape with Abu Bakr from a conspiracy to assassinate him, during which he is assisted both by the bravery of 'Ali (who takes Muhammad's place in Muhammad's bed, so his opponents do not notice that Muhammad had left) and supernatural intervention. When Muhammad and Abu Bakr hid in a cave, a spider spun a web that covered the entire cave's entrance; seeing the unbroken web, the Meccans hunting Muhammad assumed that the cave must have been empty, and passed over it in their search for him.

As Muhammad's followers left everything behind for new life in his Yathrib (Medina) community, the hijra proved traumatic for many. The hadith corpus provides a trace of this trauma in the account of a migrant who cut his hands with arrow heads until he bled to death. His friend Tufayl later saw him in a dream with his hands bandaged but otherwise in peace; the man told Tufayl that God had brought him into paradise. When Tufayl reported the dream to Muhammad, Muhammad affirmed that it was true and prayed that God heal the man's hands.[34]

From what we can gather, Muhammad's Medina years reflect a complex and increasingly antagonistic engagement with the city's Jewish communities that eventually ended in Muhammad's pushing them out. Muhammad's invitation to Yathrib (Medina) had come from members of the city's major polytheist tribes, the 'Aws and Khazraj, not the Jewish communities. Muhammad's Medina treaty (often erroneously termed his "Medina Constitution"), drafted between his followers and various tribes and clans of Medina, includes some Jewish communities—promising them safety, security, and "aid and equal rights"—but notably makes no mention of the three major Jewish tribes, the Qaynuqa, Nadir, and Qurayza.[35] This could explain the Qur'an's apparently inconsistent treatment of Jews, which reads as positive in some verses and negative in others. Muhammad did not interact with a singular Jewish community in Medina but several. Juan Cole has suggested that when the Qur'an speaks of *the* Jews, it often means *those* Jews, "appearing to speak globally but actually referring to a particular group."[36] Muslim hadith traditions present virtually a whole subgenre of reports in which Medina's Jews attempt to expose Muhammad as an imposter by challenging him with questions of theology and law. These sources even depict a Jewish sorcerer enacting a magical attack upon Muhammad that requires angelic intervention to undo.[37]

It has often been noted that the prophet most frequently mentioned by name in the Qur'an is not Muhammad (by a long shot) but rather Moses, with the suggestion that the Qur'an treats Moses as a stand-in for Muhammad, depicting a rhyme or symmetry between their respective struggles. This calls us to further consideration of Muhammad's decade in Medina, where he faced different audiences, both friendly and adversarial, than in Mecca. We see changes in Muhammad's movement that point both to Judaism's relevance as an adjacent tradition and danger as a "proximate other" requiring a clearer line of demarcation. It was in Medina, for example, that the prohibition against eating pork was revealed. But it was also in Medina, less than two years into the posthijra era, that God changed Muhammad's qibla, the direction he faced in prayer, from Jerusalem to Mecca, seemingly signifying a break from the Israelite tradition. The Qur'an also expresses this growing sense of Muhammad's movement as something distinct from both Jews and Christians but not exactly "new," since it only amounted to a restoration of the single, timeless religion of all prophets from Adam onward. Intervening in disputes among the biblical monotheists, the Qur'an would declare that their shared father Abraham was "not a Jew and not a Christian but a *hanifan musliman*," that is, a "true submitter" (3:67). This resonates with Muhammad's experience during his heavenly journey, in which he led the pre-Islamic prophets in prayer, observed the perfect physical resemblance between Abraham and himself, and engaged in an exchange with Moses, who doubted the ability of Muhammad's followers to keep up with rigorous prayer requirements (with the implication that Moses spoke from disappointment with his own followers). While Muslim history dates Muhammad's celestial ascension prior to the hijra, it's possible that these anti-Jewish polemics speak from a posthijra context; even if we faithfully accept the hadith reports as coming from the exact sources that they claim, these sources tend to be Companions of Muhammad who were too young to hear his ascension narrative in "real time." Narrators of Muhammad's ascension, such as Anas ibn Malik and most famously his cousin Ibn 'Abbas (who was reportedly born in the same year that the ascension took place!) would have necessarily learned about the ascension years after it happened.

In contrast to Muhammad's decade in Mecca, during which he was a marginalized street preacher calling "idolaters" to piety and speaking of an imminent end-of-times scenario, Muhammad's Medina decade exhibits the project of building a new society. His community's distinct practices crystallized: the five daily prayers were instituted just before the migration, reportedly during his ascension; in Medina, Friday afternoon became the time for congregational prayer. *Zakat*, a charitable tax the Prophet collected to distribute among those in need, was instituted, along with the prescribed fast in the month of Ramadan. While Muslim scholars would later debate the exact parameters of the Qur'an's prohibition against drinking wine (asking, for example, whether this prohibition applied to *all* intoxicating beverages, whether a beverage such as coffee could be considered an "intoxicant," or whether nonliquid drugs also fell under the prohibition), the ban on wine also came during this time.[38] It was also in Medina, as Muhammad assumed the role of a theocratic statesman, acting as judge, tax collector, and signer of treaties, that he now headed a military force and could directly engage the Meccans who had tortured his followers. And while he had endured persecution in Mecca with patience and nonviolent resistance, in Medina he could directly confront his opposition. Speaking to these changed circumstances, new verses of the Qur'an announced, "Permission for those who are being fought [to fight back], because they are wronged" (22:39) and commanded the believers, "Fight the polytheists together as they fight you together" (9:36).

CAMPAIGNS, BATTLES, SIEGES

Situated north of Mecca, Medina provided a base from which Muhammad's followers could launch raids on the Meccans' summer caravans on the latter's way to and from Syria. In his first twenty months in Medina, Muhammad and his followers launched several raids on Meccan caravans. During the winter months, when the caravans went south, the Qur'an's ongoing revelation allowed a surprise tactic of fighting in "sacred months" that had been forbidden: "They ask you about fighting in the sacred month. Say, 'Fighting in it is great [sin] but obstructing people in the way of God, and disbelief in him, and in the masjid al-haram, to drive his people out of it, is greater [sin] than fighting'" (2:217). These raids were not "holy wars" in the distinctly modern sense of the term, though participation came with a special gravitas as service to God and the Prophet. With the raids on trading caravans, exiled refugee believers struggled to sustain themselves economically against the wealthy elites who had boycotted them, driven them from their homes and livelihoods, and sought to deprive them of tribal protection.

This series of expeditions culminated in an event that would permanently upend the balance of power: the battle of Badr. When Muhammad learned of an especially lucrative Meccan caravan heading home from Syria, he ordered an expedition against it. The Meccans, however, heard that Muhammad had been planning to intercept their caravan, and sent word back to Mecca for reinforcements. In the resulting confrontation, Muhammad's outnumbered fighters achieved miraculous victory over a Meccan army several times its size. Muhammad ransomed his prisoners rather than kill them, and released those who accepted him as Prophet—including his own uncle 'Abbas, who confessed that he had been a believer in Muhammad since long before that day.

Muhammad's underdog triumph at Badr, and conversely the Meccans' humiliating defeat, marked the first glimpse of a new order in the Hijaz. It was perhaps at this moment that both Muhammad and his opponents, including not only the Meccan polytheists but also other monotheists in Medina, realized that Muhammad could become the singular ruler of Arabia. In particular, tensions increased between Muhammad and Medina's Jewish tribes, which finally manifested as violence with Muhammad's raid on the Banu Qaynuqa. The conflict's causes are a bit murky in the sources; we read of a collective Jewish rejection of their agreements with Muhammad after he emerged from Badr as the new power; we also see the battle sparked by an assault on a Muslim woman in the Qaynuqa's market.[39] The conclusion of the siege, however, was clear: the Qaynuqa surrendered and Muhammad exiled them from Medina.[40] Verses of the Qur'an were then revealed in which God told Muhammad not to take Jews or Christians as his friends (5:51). Muhammad targeted another of the city's three Jewish tribes, the Banu Nadir, after becoming aware of a plot to assassinate him. The Nadir surrendered and accepted exile from Medina, settling primarily in Syria and nearby Khaybar.[41] The Qur'an is believed to refer to the Banu Nadir's defeat and exile in its fifty-ninth sura.

The battle that would shift the balance of power permanently in Muhammad's favor took place in 627 CE, when a Meccan-led coalition, supported by Bedouin horsemen, besieged Medina. On the advice of his Persian follower Salman, Muhammad ordered a ditch to be dug around Medina, and the event came to be known as al-Khandaq ("The Ditch" or "The Trench"). The ditch blocked the soldiers on horses from advancing into the city, and as the stalemate dragged on, the alliance of forces surrounding Medina gradually broke apart. The victory marked a true turning point in Muhammad's career, perhaps even more than the miraculous triumph at Badr. Momentum was now firmly on the side of the Prophet and his movement. But it's also after Khandaq that we turn to one of the more difficult points in Muhammad's biography: the fate of the Banu Qurayza, the last of Medina's Jewish tribes.

Muslim historical tradition recalls that during the Battle of Khandaq, the Qurayza had violated the terms of their treaty with Muhammad, which required that each party would help the other against outsiders. As Muhammad's community, trapped in Medina, waited out the long siege, the Banu Qurayza apparently did business with and supplied the anti-Muslim coalition. With the Battle of Khandaq concluded, Muhammad turned his attention to the Qurayza, ordering a siege of their forts. The Qurayza finally surrendered on agreement that their community's fate would be decided by Sa'd ibn Mu'adh, who was on good terms with both sides. Sa'd gave the verdict that all of the Qurayza's men would be killed, while their women and children would be sold into slavery. According to some accounts of the surrender, Muhammad affirmed that Sa'd's judgment came from the heavens. Muhammad's soldiers cut the neck of every Banu Qurayza male over the age of puberty—an estimated 400 to 900 executions. The Qur'an does not explicitly mention the event, though Muslim interpretive tradition links the massacre to a pair of verses in the thirty-third sura: "And those of the People of the Book who backed them, God took them from their forts and cast terror into their hearts. You killed a group and took a group prisoner. And he caused you to inherit their land, homes, properties, and a land that you had not trod. God has power over all things" (33:26–27).

Some scholarly consideration has been given to the story's sources. A degree of variation exists between the different Companions who narrate their knowledge of the event, highlighting their own subjectivities as reporters. In some versions, for example, Sa'd appears more willing to pronounce his judgment than in others, and Sa'd is sometimes depicted as announcing his verdict while suffering from mortal wounds.[42] The version attributed to Ibn Maslama, a member of the Khazraj tribe, depicts the Khazraj more favorably than their rivals, the 'Aws; and the only version in which Sa'd does not speak as the official judge of the affair, but rather as an informal advisor to Muhammad, is attributed to Sa'd's own grandson.[43] But these versions agree on the basic outline of events. The extent to which we can trust the earliest textual account on the Banu Qurayza, found in Muhammad's biography by Ibn Ishaq (who died nearly 150 years after the event), has also been the subject of debate.[44] Investigation of the sources is not going to prove whether the story is "true," but it has at least established that the story is "old"— namely, that it circulated very early in Muslim history, and that reports traced back to the authoritative scholar 'Urwa ibn al-Zubayr can be reliably treated as at least the "gist" of what he actually heard from his aunt, the Prophet's widow A'isha.[45] Scholars have argued that the most strongly evidenced narrations of A'isha speaking to 'Urwa allow us to confidently assemble a limited outline of Muhammad's life.[46] Of course, not all 'Urwa-from-A'isha narrations are equally authoritative, as later transmitters (including 'Urwa's own son Hisham) could have forged A'isha narrations while naming 'Urwa as their source.

Settling questions of "What really happened?"—to the extent that such projects are possible—cannot themselves provide the key to a true "essence" of Muhammad's character, mission, and legacy. Even when two Muslims can agree on the bare "facts" of Muhammad's life, they still must determine what the events *mean*; that is, what we're supposed to do with them in our world.

HUDAYBIYYA AND THE *FATH*

Muhammad's change of his qibla, the direction that he faced in ritual prayer, from Jerusalem to Mecca has been described as a shift in the "center of exilic nostalgia," an intensified longing for the homeland from which he had been driven.[47] Inspired by a dream, Muhammad decided in 628 CE that he would make a physical return to Mecca and perform the customary pilgrimage. He set out accompanied by as many as 1,400 men. Reaching Dhu-l-Hulayfa, he entered ihram, a pilgrim's state of ritual purity. Knowing that the Quraysh, aware of his intention, were sending a force to intercept him, Muhammad went another route, which would pass through the village of al-Hudaybiyya just a few miles from Mecca. Muhammad camped at al-Hudaybiyya with plans to reach Mecca the next day, but the Quraysh met him there in an attempt to negotiate. Muhammad agreed that he would not perform the pilgrimage that year, but with an understanding that he could return the following year and make the pilgrimage with his followers. Muhammad and the Meccans also agreed to a ten-year peace between them, acceptance of all tribes' rights to make their own agreements with Muhammad or the Quraysh, and Muhammad's promise that he would turn over any of his followers who attempted to flee Mecca in the future. In a special humiliation, Muhammad acquiesced to the Quraysh demand that the treaty open not with Muhammad's *bismillahir Rahmanir rahim* ("in the name of God, ar-Rahman, the merciful") but instead the more traditional *bismikalla-humma* ("in the name of God") and that Muhammad himself was named in the agreement not as the Messenger of God, but simply Muhammad ibn 'Abd Allah.

Though some of Muhammad's followers were dejected by what had looked like a surrender (especially as Muhammad, abiding by the terms of the agreement, sent a refugee back into Meccan custody), the Qur'an's next revelations called the Hudaybiyya treaty a "clear victory" (48:1). Muhammad's followers could not see it immediately, but the Qur'an was right, as the concession at Hudaybiyya served a long game. Mecca, which stood south of Medina, had entered an alliance with the Jewish colony of Khaybar to Medina's north, with an agreement that each would side with the other against Muhammad. But when Muhammad reached a peace agreement with his enemy to the south, it canceled the threat of a two-front war, enabling him to head north and conquer Khaybar less than a month after the treaty. From the plunder, which included captured women, Muhammad freed a young woman named Safiya, whose husband and father had both been killed in battles against his followers, and married her. Though Muhammad had been monogamous in his marriage with Khadija, Safiya joined a growing household of co-wives.

It has been argued that our understanding of the Hudaybiyya treaty would be enhanced by zooming back out at the international context. The Mecca-Khaybar alliance reportedly reflected not only a shared antagonism toward Muhammad but a shared affinity for the Persians, while Muhammad was more sympathetic to the Byzantines. A month prior to the Hudaybiyya treaty, the Byzantines defeated the Persians; according to some sources, Muhammad and his followers learned this news, at which they rejoiced, on the very day of the treaty.[48]

Muhammad continued to consolidate his power and launch raids for resources in the north. According to later Muslim sources, the northward campaigns advanced far enough to encounter Byzantine forces in an inconclusive skirmish. If it seems counterintuitive to imagine Muhammad, who by all appearances favored the Christian emperor Heraclius against the Zoroastrian Khosru, moving against Byzantine territory, we have reason to question the narrative: during these years, the lands bordering northern Arabia were controlled by the Persians, leaving essentially no opportunity for Muhammad's forces to advance upon the Byzantines.[49]

He performed the pilgrimage to Mecca in 629 CE, as per the terms of the Hudaybiyya pact. But just two years into their ten-year treaty, Muhammad judged the Meccans to have violated the agreement, and in 630 CE moved upon Mecca with 10,000 troops. Muhammad's conquest of Mecca, though nearly bloodless, could be read as in tension with the repeated efforts that we see in the Qur'an's Meccan suras to persuade its audience. The necessity of conquest means that the Qur'an's arguments and warnings did not work. Mecca became Islamic territory through military action, not a convincing discourse. As Walid A. Saleh writes, "There is no escaping the conclusion that Muhammad's mission in Mecca was a failure. His arguments, style, and preaching all proved in vain."[50] Whatever "idols" might have once surrounded the Ka'ba were destroyed, but not because the "idolaters" were moved by the message, came to their own conclusions, and decided that Muhammad was a true prophet. After fleeing Mecca as persecuted refugees, Muhammad and his followers formed new connections that increased their power, and it was their return to Mecca with these outside forces that enabled a take-over of the city. Muhammad's opponents among Mecca's ruling elites, such as Abu Sufyan and his wife Hind, saw the writing on the wall and accepted the new regime. Though Muhammad's new position of power would have entitled him to take revenge on his former adversaries, he forgave them, accepted their conversions, and absorbed their political, social, and economic clout into his project of rebuilding Meccan society. Muhammad did not permanently resettle in Mecca but headed back to Medina. Along the way, he stopped at Ghadir Khumm and addressed his traveling party with cousin and son-in-law 'Ali at his side. He declared, "For whoever I was his *mawla*, 'Ali is his *mawla*." This moment has been preserved in sources of both Sunni and Shi'i traditions, though these tra-ditions differ as to what exactly Muhammad meant by "mawla," which can be translated as "master" or as "protecting friend."

After the conquest or "opening" (*fath*) of Mecca, Muhammad subdued the final traces of opposition to him in the region, the tribes of Hawazin and Thaqif, based respectively in the cities of Hunayn and Ta'if. Later sources depict him as pursuing a rematch with the Byzantines (though, as stated above, it's historically implausible that he had ever fought the Byzantines) at Tabuk, more than 300 miles north of Medina, but returned home after waiting twenty days for a Byzantine army that never arrived. The adventure brought him into contact with Christian tribes from the Gulf of Aqaba region, where the Red Sea meets the Sinai Peninsula and northwestern Arabia. Muhammad and the tribes agreed that they would not become his followers but rather enter into a *dhimma*, a covenant of protection. As the more powerful party in the covenant, Muhammad guaranteed the safety of the tribes, who would keep their own religion under his domain. In exchange, the tribes compensated Muhammad with taxes (termed "jizya," as opposed to "zakat," the alms tax that Mu-hammad collected from Muslims). Once a marginalized and persecuted preacher who was pelted with stones and garbage, Muhammad now boasted a force that could collect taxes hundreds of miles from his own base. As empires around him crumbled, Muhammad's *umma* emerged as the regional superpower.

The new imperial thrust is reflected in later suras of the Qur'an, in which divinely revealed legislation resonates resoundingly with Roman law under Justinian (r. 527–65 CE). The sura al-Ma'ida ("The Table"), though only the fifth sura in the Qur'an's arrangement, comes from later in Muhammad's life, and includes a prescription for punishing "those who spread disorder in the land" with crucifixion or amputation (5:33) that perfectly matches Novel 134.13 of Justinian's legal code. For Cole, this correspondence between legal codes is "so exact as to rule out co-incidence,"[51] but the match is not reducible to the Qur'an's "borrowing" or plagiarism from Roman law. Rather, the Qur'an's appropriation of Justinian "underlines a Qur'anic political claim on parallel power" and could even reflect the pro-Christian, pro-Byzantine Muhammad's effort to join a Roman alliance against Zoroastrian Iran.[52] And it's in this same sura that the Qur'an privileges Christians as "the nearest in love" to Muhammad's followers, over the Jews and polytheists, who are grouped together as his most hateful adversaries (5:82).[53]

THE DEATH OF MUHAMMAD

The Qur'an's fifth sura, traditionally dated within the last two years of Muhammad's life, also includes a verse that Muslims widely regard as the closure of the revelation, with God's statement, "Today, I have completed your *din* for you, and have completed my blessing upon you, and chosen surrender as a *din* for you" (5:3). The Arabic word "din," related to meanings of duty and judgment, appears in English translation today as "religion," though the concept of religion (like our concepts of race and gender) undergoes so much change between different historical contexts that translation might be doomed to fail. The Arabic word translated here as "surrender," *islam*, does not appear in the Qur'an as a self-evident, properly capitalized name for a religion: speaking again to the ways "religion" changes over time, we might note that the Qur'an refers to *communities* of Christians and Jews but has no words for "Christianity" or "Judaism" as *religions*. One could choose to read the excerpt of 5:3 as "chosen Islam as a religion for you" or "chosen surrender as a duty for you."

Muhammad lived only two years after taking Mecca. According to some narrations, he was assassinated by a Jewish woman who poisoned his food after the victory over Khaybar. But the battle of Khaybar had taken place years earlier: Why did the poison take so long to affect him? Even more curiously, some versions depict the woman as confessing that her motive was to test Muhammad: if he was not a genuine prophet, her poison would kill him. But it is still asserted that the poison *did* kill him. Since all of our sources for the story are Muslim traditionists, this seems odd: Why would people who obviously believed that Muhammad was a genuine prophet circulate a story in which he failed the test? We also have stories, however, in which the poisoned meat warns Muhammad before he eats it (or eats too much), apparently saving his life (at least in the short term). The depiction of Muhammad ingesting poison that only takes hold years later could represent an amalgamation of stories with competing interests, allowing two contradictory narratives—one in which Muhammad miraculously survived an assassination attempt, another in which he receives the blessing of martyrdom—to simultaneously be true. Etan Kohlberg has argued that the story of miraculous intervention and survival came first, later developing into an account of martyrdom.[54] As with other aspects of Muhammad's life that we've seen here, traditions concerning Muhammad's death have changed over time.

Sources present some of Muhammad's Companions, most famously 'Umar, as refusing to accept that Muhammad had died. Given the apocalyptic tenor of Muhammad's early preaching, in which the Qur'an seemed to promise an imminent end of the world, it might have been inconceivable that Muhammad would not live to see the conclusion of earthly time. It also appears that some of Muhammad's Companions feared that if he died, their prayers and good deeds would go unrecorded.[55] Muhammad's father-in-law Abu Bakr brought peace to the community by reminding them while Muhammad was dead, God does not die.

As much as these sources could tell us about Muhammad's final days, they also point to the worldviews of later narrators. Looking at accounts of Muhammad's death over time, for example, we see changes in the ways Muslims thought about Muhammad's physical postmortem condition. Early sources depict the uncertainty over Muhammad's death as having been resolved by the fact of his body's normal decomposition: rather than Abu Bakr's poignant theological reminder, Muhammad's uncle 'Abbas corrects 'Umar's denial of his death by stating that "his flesh decays like any other person's."[56] According to early sources, Companions even recognize normal signs of decomposition in Muhammad's body, such as a bloating stomach and changes in his fingers.[57] But these accounts would fall out of later canonical narratives as Muslim scholars favored traditions in which Muhammad would remain not only conscious in his grave (so that he could bear witness to the deeds of his community) but physically intact and performing prayers.[58] Muhammad had reportedly said that the earth was forbidden from consuming the flesh of prophets, and that he had personally seen Moses praying in his grave.[59]

Reports of Muhammad's final illness and death often seem to reflect an interest in the crisis that would immediately follow: the disputed matter of how one might best connect to Muhammad in a post-Muhammad world, or rather, which people best offered that connection. When we think about the Sunni-Shi'i divide, there's a tendency to imagine the crisis of Muhammad's death strictly in political terms: since Muhammad died as a head of state without having established a clear system for the transition of power, who could succeed him? And we often imagine "Sunnism" and "Shi'ism" existing as fully formed sectarian identities, immediately and obviously distinct from each other, and doomed to eternal conflict from that day forward. Certainly, there were high political tensions following Muhammad's death, not only because there were two prime candidates (Abu Bakr and 'Ali) but also because support for these candidates was related to preexisting tribal beefs and factionalisms within the community. Tensions had already been brewing between the Muhajirun (Emigrants), Muhammad's followers who left Mecca with him to build a new society in Medina, and the Ansar (Helpers), his followers in Medina who welcomed the Muhajirun into their city.

As the archive of Muslim communal memory developed in subsequent generations, Muslims would circulate narratives that privileged one candidate or the other: so we read of Abu Bakr leading communal prayer during Muhammad's final illness, suggesting that Abu Bakr was the right man to embody Muhammad's position in his absence; but we also read of Muhammad declaring that for whomever Muhammad was their mawla, 'Ali was also their mawla; and the stories of Muhammad's death include reports that he died in the arms of his wife (Abu Bakr's daughter) A'isha as well as competing accounts that he died in the arms of 'Ali. Even the question of Muhammad's bodily powers can be related to earthly power struggles. Since 'Ali was a biological cousin of Muhammad, and his children with Fatima were direct descendants of the Prophet, we see an abundance of narrations from 'Ali, his supporters, and descendants attesting to special qualities of Muhammad's body. In contrast, A'isha's accounts often downplay the prophetic body.[60]

No, the death of Muhammad did not instantly produce two rival sectarian groups that would remain in place until the end of time. But it did result in a power struggle that would, over the course of multiple generations, contribute to the crystallizing of Sunni and Shi'i traditions. But it's important to note that no one who lived early enough in Muslim history to have been a contemporary of Muhammad's great-grandchildren would have recognized the easy binary opposition of "Sunni versus Shi'i" as it would look in our modern terms.

The sources tell us that while 'Ali washed Muhammad's body for his funeral, an election was held that resulted in Abu Bakr's becoming the first caliph (although *khalifa* or "caliph" is a bit of a retroactive term, and it doesn't appear that any of the earliest caliphs actually referred to themselves by this title).[61] Almost immediately, the community was fractured by a number of tribes that broke away, declaring that because their agreement had been with Muhammad, Muhammad's death ended their obligations to the new community. Abu Bakr charged that the rebel tribes had committed *ridda*, which literally translates to "reverting" and would come to signify apostasy out of Islam—a bit of an irony, since "revert" has become a popular term for new Muslim converts in English-speaking Muslim communities. Abu Bakr declared war on the apostate tribes to bring them back into Islam, in this case meaning "submission" and "surrender" in the most literal sense; notions of religious apostasy were entangled in political secession and tax evasion. Upon victory in the Ridda Wars, Abu Bakr was able to consolidate his power and preserve the community. The tensions and rivalries that troubled Muhammad's followers at the time of his death, however, would not go away but resurfaced decades later, when Muhammad's widow (and Abu Bakr's daughter) A'isha led a military challenge to the caliphate of 'Ali.

CONCLUSIONS

As a Muslim teenager in the 1990s, I was regularly advised by masjid brothers and uncles to see Muhammad's life as an example for imitation and a source of limitless guidance, but there wasn't a specific biography to which everyone pointed me. Ibn Ishaq's *Sira* was well circulated, but my more conservative, hadith-centered mentors found fault in his scholarship. The source we most respected for its scholarly prestige and presumed authenticity, *Sahih al-Bukhari*, was not designed for a cover-to-cover reading to provide a grand narrative of Muhammad's life; rather, it was conceived as an encyclopedia of mostly decontextualized anecdotes about Muhammad.

There was a charisma to the hadith books, a power. I remember the feeling of coming home from Pakistan with Bukhari's volumes on my back. It seemed like an act of love for the Prophet to let the books weigh me down, like I was performing some ascetic feat in his service. But looking back on the meaning of those heavy books for me, I can say that their real value was in the promise of a technology that could make someone more Muhammad-like, rather than as a resource for knowing the ins and outs of Muhammad's journey.

The biography of Muhammad, as it would come to exist in my young Muslim consciousness, took form as a composite of materials. Ibn Ishaq's biography remained a major resource even for those who would qualify his work with critical notes, often through the filter of modern perennialist Muslim scholar Martin Lings. The most important biography of Muhammad for me at the time was produced by a non-Muslim author, Karen Armstrong, whose *Muhammad* (1993) offered a humanizing portrait of the Prophet; like many Muslims, I once placed great stock in the power of non-Muslims writing sympathetically of Muhammad. Beyond these books, I accessed Muhammad through other media, such as a very cautious film depiction of his life, *The Message* (1976), starring Anthony Quinn as Muhammad's uncle Hamza (no actor portrayed Muhammad himself; the camera often shot from a "Muhammad's eye view" and characters would speak to him by addressing the camera, which ostensibly turns the viewer into Muhammad). The life of Muhammad as I understood it took shape through these various colliding artifacts.

With this chapter, I set out to provide a short and generally acceptable biography of the Prophet, to the extent that such a thing is possible. But I still had to make choices. Every act of storytelling faces natural obstructions, starting with the limits of space: this is a story that cannot rightly fit within one chapter of a book. To this end, every historical narrative is a work of fiction, even if the facts are "right." Scholarship has argued for recognition of this reality even when it comes to the earliest presentations of Muhammad's life, those of his Companions such as

A'isha, who narrated as eyewitnesses but still had to make choices when telling their stories.[62] Working in this restricted space, I make choices about the budgeting of my pages and words. Even if we somehow all agree on the bare skeletal outline of "facts" that require mentions, I still decide for myself the "facts" that matter most. I decide when to step in and give further context or explain how a particular episode appears in multiple versions. The decision to *not* step in or give any additional context or comment would reflect not only the "objective" or academically detached approach but another set of feelings and attachments.

CHAPTER FOUR

Prophetic Networks

Most readers of hadith literature, Muslim and non-Muslim alike, tend to read the hadiths as if they form a homogenous block and speak with one voice. This could feel intuitive, since we access hadiths through big archives, whether as books or online databases, that give the impression of unity. The most prestigious and popular Sunni hadith collection, *Sahih al-Bukhari*, is named for its compiler, Muhammad ibn Isma'il al-Bukhari, and typically conflated with the man himself: someone could assert a hadith's validity by stating, "It's *in* Bukhari." It's as though the thousands of hadiths become identifiable with Bukhari's body. This goes for all of the collections in the broader Sunni hadith canon, the "Six Books," which are all popularly referred to by their compilers' names. The fact that these canonical collections have been arranged by topic can also encourage a view of the hadith corpus as one mass, undifferentiated database, rather than as a multiplicity of voices.

To think about the hadith corpus as one united voice also comes from—and in turn enforces—a Sunni view of Muhammad's Companions, the Sahabas, as collectively authoritative, meaning that someone could not accuse a Companion of lying about the Prophet and still be considered a Sunni Muslim. The doctrine of the Companions' universal reliability as reporters of Muhammad's sayings and actions is uniquely a Sunni concept, not shared by all Muslims. It is also a concept that developed over time, as early hadith scholarship crystallized into both a professional field of knowledge and something of a sectarian identity. And it is a concept that would have been unrecognizable to the Companions themselves, who fought each other on battlefields and accused each other of lying. After all, even the concept of "Companions" as a coherent category or class was not one that the Companions themselves knew, at least not in its later recognizable terms.

This all means that if we approach the hadith literature as though it speaks with one voice, through one textual canon, produced by one united community, reflecting the knowledge of the Prophet's Companions who mutually affirmed each other's authority as the Prophet's Companions, we're denying something fundamental about these sources and the *thousands* of voices that they represent. Careful engagement of hadith literature requires disassembling the monolith and looking at the ways its different pieces relate to each other. We do not simply need to determine whether Muhammad "really" said something that was attributed to him; we must also consider the different subjectivities that we find mediating between Muhammad's world and our own.

To think about the multiplicities that make up hadith traditions, I turned away from the most canonically privileged sources to examine the precanonical *Musnad* collection of Ahmad ibn Hanbal (d. 855). The advantage of Ibn Hanbal's *Musnad*, besides Ibn Hanbal's immense gravitas as a classical hadith master, lies in his collection's arrangement. The *Musnad*'s 30,000 (give or take) hadith reports are organized not by topic but by the Companions to whom they are attributed. This makes the *Musnad* much harder to use if you have a question about a specific issue but more convenient if you are interested in one specific Companion's reports, or if you wish to read two Companions against each other to see the points at which their stories conflict or converge. In this chapter, I'll extract one Companion, the Prophet's cousin 'Abd Allah ibn 'Abbas (more popularly known as Ibn 'Abbas), pick apart the hundreds of reports attributed to him, and then bring his corpus into conversation with that of another Companion, 'Abd Allah ibn Mas'ud.

First, let's introduce Ibn 'Abbas. He was the son of Muhammad's uncle 'Abbas ibn 'Abd al-Muttalib (d. 653), making him a patrilineal cousin to the Prophet. This would become especially meaningful several decades after his death, when the 'Abbasid caliphate—so named for its rulers' alleged descent from him—established its right to power in part through a kinship argument. Ibn 'Abbas's father 'Abbas opposed Muhammad's movement, even fighting against Muslims and briefly becoming a prisoner of war. 'Abbas ultimately became Muslim, but as Andreas Gorke writes, 'Abbas's later significance for the 'Abbasid caliphate makes it difficult to sort historical fact from imperial propaganda in these details.[1] Ibn 'Abbas was too young to take any action in these struggles: when his father was captured at Badr, he could not have been more than five years old. In a tradition that appears with different versions, Ibn 'Abbas gives his age at the time of Muhammad's death as either ten or fifteen years old.[2]

Let's pause on these accounts of Ibn 'Abbas telling us his age, since the numbers might not be mere biodata. Ibn 'Abbas's effort to establish his age addresses a tension in his sizeable body of reports: How could someone who was only a boy at Muhammad's death possess his depth of knowledge in matters such as the meanings of the Qur'an, the correct performance of rituals, and jurisprudence? Ibn 'Abbas's section in the *Musnad* amounts to nearly 2,000 reports, ranking him among the five most prolific narrators among Muhammad's Companions. In his later years, authorized by the strength of his childhood memories and close relationship to the Prophet, he taught a younger generation that could not have known Muhammad. Had he seen enough of Muhammad, and was he old enough to have processed what he saw? Ibn 'Abbas's clarifications of his age could establish credibility, if only barely: to have been ten years old would mean that he had been circumcised (and a version that doesn't provide a number states that he had just been circumcised at the time), meaning that he had entered puberty, and the age of fifteen would have meant that he was technically an adult.

An adolescent or teenager during the initial power struggles after Muhammad's death, Ibn 'Abbas only became politically active in later years. In the 650s, when his cousin 'Ali ascended to the caliphate and faced opposition from an alliance led by their uncle Zubayr, the Prophet's widow A'isha, and early convert Talha ibn 'Ubayd Allah, Ibn 'Abbas led troops as a general in 'Ali's army. He also fought for 'Ali against

Mu'awiyya, founder of the Umayyad caliphate, appeared on 'Ali's side during arbitration with Mu'awiyya, and met with members of the Kharijiyya, a sect formed by 'Ali's disillusioned followers who abandoned 'Ali after he agreed to arbitration.[3] 'Ali appointed him governor of the military garrison city of Basra, but he reportedly left over a question of misappropriated funds.[4] Ibn 'Abbas eventually returned to Mecca but was forced out of that city and then imprisoned for some time in 684 during the anticaliphate of his cousin 'Abd Allah ibn al-Zubayr. He was said to have died in Ta'if sometime between 684 and 690, his age ranging from his late sixties to mid-seventies.[5]

Over time, due in no small part to his political importance as the 'Abbasid dynasty's ancestor, Ibn 'Abbas's significance as an especially knowledgeable scholar of the law, interpreter of the Qur'an, and close Companion to the Prophet swelled to mythic proportions. In addition to narrations attesting to Ibn 'Abbas's superior knowledge, supernaturally tinged and miraculous legends developed around him; hadiths depict him as seeing the angel Gabriel, for example.[6] He has been famously linked to the Prophet's ascension through the heavens as an important source for the event, though this manifests more in *tafsir* (Qur'an commentary) than hadith literature. It should also be noted that in canonical hadith, he appears as an advocate of the idea that Muhammad saw God (in conflict with A'isha, the most emphatic denier of the vision); but in tafsir literature, he appears as a source for the "Satanic Verses" episode. We'll see in the following discussions that our sense of Ibn 'Abbas and his teachings depends on which students and genre of Muslim literature we engage.

MAKING IBN 'ABBAS

Examining Ibn 'Abbas's presentation of his prophetic cousin can shine a light on the ways our views of Muhammad are so dramatically informed by these filters. We don't access Muhammad directly but rather through the subjective memories and interpretations of figures such as Ibn 'Abbas, who essentially become "founders" of Islam in their own right. But to make things more complicated, our mediator also passes through mediation, since we depend on a network of people—Ibn 'Abbas's students, and their students, and *their* students—to give us Ibn 'Abbas. With or without a verdict on the historical authenticity of their narrations, these hadith transmitters "made" Ibn 'Abbas—not in the sense of Ibn

'Abbas being a fictional character but as the filters that produce Ibn 'Abbas in social memory. And it doesn't even stop there, because these students themselves became popular "brands" and citable names that could be dropped to bolster an argument. Ibn 'Abbas, like his cousin the Prophet, manifests in the literature not simply as a historic individual but more as an assemblage of voices.

So who were they?

Thankfully, premodern scholars obsessively cataloged information on hadith transmitters. In the *Tuhfat al-Ashraf* by Yusuf al-Mizzi (1256–1341 CE), an important encyclopedia of transmitters whose reports appear in canonical hadith collections, we see roughly 200 people named as "direct" reporters of Ibn 'Abbas material, meaning that they report on Ibn 'Abbas without naming another source on whom they depend. This does not mean that they all sat at Ibn 'Abbas's feet and heard his narrations directly from his lips. Nor are these reporters all substantive sources for his words: most of them appear as the source for only one or two reports, and even Ibn 'Abbas's sons and grandsons are only minor sources. Some early scholars, however, did seek out Ibn 'Abbas, spend a great deal of time with him, and become highly productive transmitters of his teachings. Sa'id ibn Jubayr reportedly traveled from his home in the garrison town of Kufa to study under Ibn 'Abbas, motivated first by disagreement among the Kufans over the meaning of a specific Qur'an verse (4:93, which promises hell for anyone who intentionally kills a believer).[7] As we see throughout hadith literature, a small number of people did the vast majority of work when it came to preserving a specific sage's knowledge. Going through the *Tuhfat's* listed sources for more than 2,000 narrations traced to A'isha, for example, we find that half of these narrations (49.95 percent) come from her nephew 'Urwa ibn al-Zubayr, and nearly a third of 'Urwa's narrations from A'isha come from 'Urwa's son Hisham. 'Urwa's cousin, al-Qasim ibn Muhammad ibn Abi Bakr, also provides roughly 7 percent of A'isha's narrations, meaning that two of A'isha's nephews provide more than half of her corpus.[8] In the *Musnad*, Ibn 'Abbas's top ten transmitters provide 73 percent of his hadiths.

Iraqi hadith critic Yahya al-Qattan (d. 813 CE) narrated that Ibn 'Abbas's "companions" were six: Mujahid ibn Jabr, Tawus ibn Kaysan, 'Ata ibn Abi Rabah, Sa'id ibn Jubayr, 'Ikrima, and Jabir ibn Zayd.[9] Of Ibn 'Abbas's hadiths in the *Musnad*, these six men count for 775 combined reports, 63 percent of the total; the giant among them is 'Ikrima

(303 reports, 25 percent of the *Musnad*'s Ibn ʿAbbas material), followed by Saʾid (225 reports, 18.3 percent), with ʿAta at a distant third (98 reports, 8 percent). These three alone are responsible for 51 percent of the *Musnad*'s Ibn ʿAbbas collection.

Yahya had not known Ibn ʿAbbas's six companions personally: they all died roughly a century before him, in a range from 713 to 733 CE, which was in turn three to nearly five decades after Ibn ʿAbbas himself. Like Ibn ʿAbbas and his contemporaries in the first generation of Muslims, who acted as custodians of sacred memory for those who had never seen Muhammad, these six students represented the traces of an absent elder from the past; in turn, they became critical links in a sacred chain. It seems that by Yahya's time in the late eighth and early ninth century CE, scholars had recognized their names as linked to a larger Ibn ʿAbbas brand. Whether this brand reflects historical reality remains somewhat unsettled, as skeptical scholars would charge that Ibn ʿAbbas's significance as an authority, particularly on Qurʾan interpretation, is less historical than mythic. "If there is a 'school of Ibn ʿAbbas' in the sense that certain methodologies or specific interpretations were shared by hadiths ascribed to Ibn ʿAbbas and to his 'students' such as Mujahid, Ibn Jubayr and ʿIkrima," Herbert Berg writes, "that school was not formed by the aforementioned exegetes learning at the feet of Ibn ʿAbbas."[10] Important figures such as Ibn ʿAbbas and their students are not just "real" individuals occupying a certain time and place but complex assemblages that continue to grow and develop long after the individuals have died.

What can we say about them? First, they came from the margins of the Arab empire. They were overwhelmingly mawali, that is, they were non-Arabs and/or freed slaves who had entered honorary membership or "clientage" with Arab tribes. When the caliph ʿUmar officially banned the enslavement of Arabs, his policy intensified the flow of non-Arabs into Islamic society as enslaved peoples.[11] Ibn ʿAbbas's three most prominent reporters were all Africans: ʿIkrima was a North African Berber; Saʾid ibn Jubayr was of Ethiopian heritage; and ʿAta ibn Abi Rabah was a Nubian born in Yemen, described in biographical literature as "flat-nosed" and *shadid al-aswad* (intensely black). Mujahid ibn Jabr was described as *al-aswad* (black). Tawus ibn Kaysan was born in Yemen, but of Persian ancestry, and Jabir ibn Zayd had come from Oman. How might their maula status have informed their work?

Contrary to the imaginary of a color-blind utopia in early Islam, they would have encountered racism (or what we might more carefully call "proto-racism," recognizing that scientific categories of "race" did not yet exist in their modern forms). Ibn ʿAbbas reportedly tried to deflect anti-mawla prejudice for his student Saʾid. The story holds that Ibn ʿAbbas asked Saʾid to identify his people, and Saʾid answered that he had come from the Banu Asad; Ibn ʿAbbas then asked Saʾid, "From their Arabs or their mawali?" When Saʾid replied that he was from the mawali, Ibn ʿAbbas advised that Saʾid should only answer, "I am from those Banu Asad upon whom God had bestowed favor."[12] Nonetheless, while ʿAta served as the official mufti of Mecca, Saʾid's appointment as judge in Kufa was opposed by that city's Arabs, who protested that only Arabs could be judges, and Saʾid lost his office.[13] When Mujahid tells us that Ibn ʿAbbas told him that the Prophet had declared, "I have been sent for the reds and the blacks"[14]—with "red" signifying a complexion and proto-racial concept that would more commonly be called "white" today, meaning that Muhammad came for all human families of the planet—we can't forget the lived contexts of our sources. Muhammad's legacy of antiracism comes to us in part through the lived experiences of those who endured premodern racism.

Besides being non-Arabs, Saʾid, ʿAta, and Mujahid were also former slaves; ʿIkrima was Ibn ʿAbbas's own freed slave, gifted to him in Basra. Beyond the six companions, other formerly enslaved people appear among Ibn ʿAbbas's reporters. Perhaps it's not a coincidence that in his discussion of commentary on the Qurʾan's verse 24:33, which refers to the freeing of slaves, Ramon Harvey observes, "The exegetical activity around Q. 24:33 associated with Mecca in the first/seventh to early second/eighth centuries is dominated by the circle of Ibn ʿAbbas."[15] When Ibn ʿAbbas speaks in the *Musnad* on slavery, his reports come through the mediation of formerly enslaved people, most prominently ʿIkrima.

In addition to the factors of their ethnic, tribal, and freed/slave contexts, Ibn ʿAbbas's six companions experienced varying relations to ruling elites, revolts against the state, and sectarian identities. In the aftermath of Ibn al-Zubayr's failed rebellion against the Umayyads, ʿAta's hand was chopped off.[16] At the turn of the eighth century CE, the Umayyad caliphate struggled to maintain control over Iraq, where the caliphate's ruthless governor, Hajjaj ibn Yusuf, enflamed tensions as he brutally suppressed resistance from various corners. Tensions culminated when Ibn al-Ashʾath, an Umayyad general, led an Iraqi rebellion against Syrian Umayyad oppression. Saʾid was commissioned by an Umayyad chief of bureau administration to compose a commentary on the Qurʾan; but he also fought in Ibn al-Ashʾathʾs army at the Battle of Jamajim. After Ibn al-Ashʾathʾs defeat, Saʾid fled but was ultimately captured and imprisoned along with ʿAta, Mujahid, and ʿAmr ibn Dinar, another traditionist who appears frequently in the Ibn ʿAbbas archive. Though the others were released, Saʾid was executed.[17]

Since we're looking at these six companions of Ibn ʿAbbas for their contributions to the Sunni hadith corpus, it might seem natural to think of them as uniformly card-carrying Sunni partisans. But the Sunni-Shiʾi divide didn't really work that way at the turn of the eighth century CE; those categories did not yet exist in a binary opposition. Using these terms retroactively, we can say that Shiʾism (or "proto-Shiʾism," to be more precise) was a major presence in the Ibn ʿAbbas network. Saʾid's tribe, the Banu Asad, was known for its proto-Shiʾism; ʿIkrima, Mujahid, and Jabir were all associated with the Khawarij, the proto-Shiʾi partisans of ʿAli who abandoned him after he agreed to arbitration with Muʾawiyya; Jabir in particular became a leader of Basra's Ibadi community, which is regarded as espousing a moderate Kharijism. He is considered a foundational figure in Ibadism at large. Writing that "the circle of Ibn ʿAbbas was targeted" by the government, Harvey suggests that the circle's persecution was likely due to the alleged "proto-Ibadism" of some members; Harvey also observes that captured Berbers (such as ʿIkrima) and other prisoners of war who experienced slavery were especially drawn to the social egalitarianism they found in Kharijism and Ibadism.[18] Ibn ʿAbbas's material in Sunni sources, in other words, comes to us mostly from people who don't appear all that "Sunni" in retrospect. Though the Sunni hadith corpus has operated in many settings as a machine for making "orthodoxy," many of its producers, now remembered as foundational figures of Sunni tradition, were affiliated with stigmatized and marginalized communities in their own lifetimes.

They successfully became custodians of Ibn ʿAbbas's knowledge and legacy in no small part through the recognition and acknowledgment they received from their colleagues and later scholars. Their Basran contemporary Qatada ibn Diʾama, who narrated a large number of Ibn ʿAbbas traditions but does not appear to have met him, reportedly hailed ʿAta as the most learned of the *tabiʾun* (the generation after Muhammad's Companions) in asceticism, Saʾid the most learned in Qurʾan commentary (tafsir), and ʿIkrima as the most learned in the Prophet's biography (*sira*).[19] Sufyan al-Thawri named Mujahid, Saʾid, and ʿIkrima as three of the four authorities from whom one could take Qurʾan commentary (the fourth, Kufan scholar Dhahhak ibn Muzahim, was a student of Sa'id, 'Ata, and Tawus, and also appears as an important source of Ibn 'Abbas material, though he had not personally met Ibn 'Abbas),[20] and in another account named 'Ata, Tawus, and Mujahid as the most desirous of knowledge.[21]

The literature abounds with reports of their exceptional piety and devotion. Mujahid went through the entire Qur'an with Ibn 'Abbas three times, stopping at every verse to ask him about its context, and allegedly died while prostrating in prayer.[22] 'Ata was considered the world's leading expert on hajj, and even as a weakened elderly man he would recite 100 verses from the Qur'an's longest sura, al-Baqara, during the standing portion of prayer.[23] Sa'id recited the entire Qur'an between the early evening (Maghrib) and night (Isha) prayers on the first night of Ramadan, as well as during a short prayer inside the Ka'ba, and regularly completed a Qur'an recitation within two nights.[24]

Some accounts of their holiness take the form of hagiography, saintly biographies leaning into the miraculous and magical. After his execution by the Umayyad governor of Iraq, Sa'id's severed head recited the first testimony of faith, la ilaha illa Allah (There is no god but God) three times.[25] Their authority was affirmed in dreams: Mujahid had a dream in which he saw Tawus praying inside the Ka'ba with the Prophet;[26] a woman witnessed the Prophet in a dream declaring 'Ata to be the "Master of the Muslims."[27]

Praise of them was not uniform, as scholars disagreed over the relative merits of these figures. Even affirmation of one figure's authority—naming Sa'id as the greatest expert in Qur'an interpretation, for example—could read as a subtle jab at those who go unnamed; but scholars also explicitly compared and criticized the early authorities. 'Ikrima in particular receives a mixed review in Sunni hadith criticism. Two heroes of early proto-Sunnism, Sa'id ibn al-Musayyib (who had met Ibn 'Abbas and narrated hadiths from him) and Ibn 'Umar, were depicted as telling their freed slaves, "Don't lie on me like 'Ikrima lied on Ibn 'Abbas."[28] Even 'Ata, Mujahid, and Tawus charged 'Ikrima with lying.[29]

The tradition includes reports of comparisons between Ibn 'Abbas's students: 'Ali ibn al-Madini said, "There was no companion of Ibn 'Abbas like Sa'id ibn Jubayr," which led someone to ask, "And not Tawus?" 'Ali ibn al-Madini replied, "And not Tawus, and not one."[30] Moreover, Yahya al-Qattan's roster of Ibn 'Abbas's six most important students was not the only list; an alternative Basra-exclusive assessment names Jabir along with Hasan al-Basri and Muhammad ibn Sirin as the three great students of Ibn ʿAbbas.[31] Yahya's list excludes transmitters who provided more Ibn ʿAbbas material than Jabir's meager seventeen reports (1.4 percent of Ibn ʿAbbas's *Musnad* corpus), including mawlas such as Kurayb and Miqsam, as well as ʿUbayd Allah ibn ʿAbd Allah ibn ʿUtba, each of whom provided twice as many reports as Jabir. Kurayb was said to have possessed a camel load's worth of written material from Ibn ʿAbbas, and Ibn ʿAbbas's own son ʿAli regularly looked to Kurayb as an archivist of his father's knowledge.[32]

Beyond the six companions of Ibn ʿAbbas named by Yahya al-Qattan, the Ibn ʿAbbas transmission network includes a wealth of historical snapshots. Abu al-ʿAliya al-Basri (d. 708–14) was a former slave who studied the Qurʾan with Ibn ʿAbbas (who reportedly gave him preferred seating over the Quraysh during Ibn ʿAbbas's reign as governor of Basra) and became "one of the most important Qurʾan scholars of the first century."[33] Ibn ʿAbbas's reporters also include ʿUbayd Allah ibn ʿAbd Allah ibn ʿUtba ibn Masʾud (d. ca. 717), who served as mufti of Medina and was one of the city's renowned "seven jurists," as well as one of the "four seas of knowledge." He was also a major teacher of Umayyad court scholar al-Zuhri. In a noteworthy detail due to al-Zuhri's relationship to the Umayyad ruling elite, ʿUbayd Allah serves as al-Zuhri's source for stories in which Muhammad sends letters to kings. We also encounter the Medinan or Kufan and retroactively labeled Shiʾi scholar ʿAbd Allah ibn Shaddad (d. ca. 701), whose mother was the widow of the Prophet's uncle Hamza. Ibn Shaddad left Kufa to join Ibn al-Ashʾath's rebellion against al-Hajjaj, during which he was killed. Ibn Shaddad appears in the *Musnad* as source for only two Ibn ʿAbbas reports, both of which relate to concern over one's private distractions during prayer. In contrast to Ibn Shaddad's political position, Maymun ibn Mihran (d. 735), a former slave, did his best to stay unproblematic at a time of political and theological turmoil, and refused conversation about four topics: ʿAli, ʿUthman, predestination (*qadar*), and the stars. He fled his hometown of Kufa during the Iraqi-Umayyad War's Battle of al-Jamajim and made his way to al-Jazira (modern Qatar), eventually becoming a leading jurist, state-appointed tax collector, treasurer, judge, and teacher.[34]

It was common, particularly in Iraq, for hadith scholars to claim exceedingly exaggerated ages, which served to shorten the distance that separated them from the Prophet and the original Muslim community—and thereby enhance their own authority and prestige. Among these

Basran *mu'ammarun* appearing in Ibn 'Abbas's corpus, we find that Abu Raja al-Utaridi had supposedly converted after the Prophet's conquest of Mecca and was said to have been between 120 and 135 years old when he died.[35] Abu Raja also seems to have been the originator of an Ibn 'Abbas hadith in which Muhammad claims that the majority of people in hellfire will be women.[36]

Did Ibn 'Abbas's six companions (and/or the larger body of Ibn 'Abbas transmitters) constitute a collective "Ibn 'Abbas school?" To what extent might these transmitters of Ibn 'Abbas's knowledge comprise a coherent, self-contained network? The six companions and other transmitters reported what they had heard from each other—Mujahid appears in transmission chains as a significant reporter from Tawus, for example—and often shared students in common. Some transmitters of Ibn 'Abbas material appear to be primarily or even exclusively connected to one or two of the six companions: Ibn Jurayj is a minor reporter from Tawus but far and away the prime transmitter of 'Ata's reports. 'Ata, Sa'id, and Tawus all narrate reports to their own sons (as did Ibn 'Abbas himself), but among them, only Tawus's son becomes a substantial source. But sometimes we get the impression of a self-contained circle, as many in the Ibn 'Abbas network provided narrations from numerous other key figures in the network: the Basran scholar Abu Bishr, a major transmitter for Sa'id, also transmitted from Mujahid, Tawus, 'Ata, and 'Ikrima, among others. The scholar 'Amr ibn Dinar, a Yemeni of possibly Persian or Ethiopian heritage who became mufti of Mecca, would have been a small child when Ibn 'Abbas died, but he studied under numerous students of Ibn 'Abbas, including five of the six companions: Mujahid, Tawus, 'Ata, 'Ikrima, and 'Amr's primary mentor in jurisprudence, Jabir.[37] 'Abd al-Karim ibn Malik al-Jazari also transmitted from five of the six, missing only Jabir.

It's important to remember that the Ibn 'Abbas network was not a bubble existing in pure isolation from other Companion networks; Ibn 'Abbas had obviously interacted with other Companions of Muhammad, and most of his students would have also been plugged into other Companion networks, whether indirectly (through students of those Companions) or directly (hearing directly from the Companions themselves). The *Musnad*'s collection of reports from Ibn 'Umar, son of the caliph 'Umar and a prolific hadith narrator, includes accounts of Sa'id ibn Jubayr hearing Ibn 'Umar narrate a statement of the Prophet forbidding *nabidh*, an alcoholic drink made in earthenware jars, and Tawus narrating that according to Ibn ʿUmar, the Prophet had banned earthenware jars alto-gether.[38] According to Yaʾla ibn Hakim, the transmitter to whom Saʾid re-lated his account, Saʾid then went to Ibn ʿAbbas for corroboration.[39] ʿAta narrated from other Companions, though Motzki observes an important difference in the ways ʿAta cites his sources: ʿAta usually (but not always) clarifies that he had heard something directly from Ibn ʿAbbas, but he does not use this same language when reporting statements or actions of other Companions.[40] Muhammad ibn Sirin, recognized as an important student of Ibn ʿAbbas, claimed direct contact with many of the Prophet's Companions and apparently became a significant channel through which hadiths of the most prolific Companion reporter, Abu Hurayra, passed from Medina to Basra.[41] Reading a specific Companion's hadith corpus, we can spot specific tendencies, as well as distinct networks of students and transmitters, but Companion "schools" could also blend into each other both in their producers and their content.

Now that we've looked at the Ibn ʿAbbas hadith corpus with an eye for how it was made, we can ask, What does it *say*? What are the teachings of the Ibn ʿAbbas school? Reading his material in the Musnad, the first thing that jumped out at me was the sizeable share of his narrations that directly concern the Mecca-centered pilgrimages, hajj and *ʿumra*, addressing details of correct practice and clarifying what someone could do while in ihram, the pilgrim's state of ritual purity (major topics in this regard being fasting, cupping, and marriage). Ibn ʿAbbas frequently cites his aunt Maymuna's marriage to the Prophet as evidence that the Prophet did marry while in pilgrim status; he also relies on a night that he and Muhammad spent at Maymuna's home for evidence regarding Muhammad's nighttime prayers. There's a disjointedness to reading Ibn ʿAbbas's reports together, since these come together not as a singular large work of which we can call Ibn ʿAbbas the "author" but rather a mass of hundreds of short quotes and anecdotes, with some topics surfacing more often than others.

Below I examine some key themes in Ibn ʿAbbas's narrations that illustrate the challenges of navigating hadith literature.

NARRATING THE FITNA

In the "First Fitna," the civil war that afflicted the original Muslim com-munity after Muhammad's death, Ibn ʿAbbas's position was unambigu-ous. He led troops in his cousin ʿAli's army against Aʾisha at Basra and again to oppose Mu'awiyya, future founder of the Umayyad caliphate, at Siffin. Retroactively speaking—again, with the disclaimer that "Sunni" and "Shi'i" did not exist as clearly or consistently drawn sides among the earliest Muslims—Ibn 'Abbas's alignment would seem to place him on the Shi'i side of history, though his relationship to 'Ali became complicated later. Ibn 'Abbas broke with 'Ali over 'Ali's violent response to the Kharijiyya (and Ibn 'Abbas's own circle included links to Kharijism); the hadith corpus depicts Ibn 'Abbas objecting to 'Ali's burning of apostates.[42]

At several points in his *Musnad* material, Ibn 'Abbas narrates hadiths that reflect the Shi'i (or proto-Shi'i) sentiments that we've seen with him and his students. Sa'id ibn Jubayr reports that Ibn 'Abbas witnessed Muhammad praying for the protection of his grandsons Hasan and Husayn from threats such as devils, poisonous animals, and the evil eye.[43] In a more overtly political report from 'Amar ibn Abi 'Amar, Ibn 'Abbas narrates that on the exact day of the battle of Karbala, he saw Muhammad in a dream, tired and disheveled, collecting Husayn's blood in a bottle; only after the dream, 'Amar ibn Abi 'Amar recalled, did they learn that Husayn had been killed that day.[44] Ibn 'Abbas also provides a version of the famous "hadith of the cloak," in which Muhammad embraces 'Ali, Fatima, Hasan, and Husayn within his garment and prays for them. The same sequence of reporters transmitting this account—Abu 'Awana narrating from Abu Balj, who narrated from 'Amr ibn Maymun, who reported from Ibn 'Abbas—also provides a report in which Ibn 'Abbas affirms that other than Muhammad's wife Khadija, 'Ali was the first to become Muslim and pray with Muhammad.[45]

Despite Ibn 'Abbas's military service to 'Ali's cause and the apparently proto-Shi'i lean of his immediate network, hadith transmitters sometimes cite Ibn 'Abbas as a source for more ambiguous narrations and even anti-Shi'i reports. Ibn Abi Mulayka (d. 735), a Meccan judge who transmitted directly from A'isha, provides a narration (sometimes presented as his report from A'isha's slave Dhakwan Abu 'Amr) in which Ibn 'Abbas visits A'isha on her deathbed and honors her.[46] Though it's not impossible that the event actually took place, it matters that our sources for the episode are Ibn Abi Mulayka and Dhakwan, rather than figures regarded primarily as intimate members of Ibn 'Abbas's circle, such as Sa'id. While possibly privileging A'isha over Ibn 'Abbas, this narrative could also reflect later efforts to smooth over the differences and conflicts among Muhammad's original followers and imagine the "Companions" as a united community. Additionally, the Ibn ʿAbbas archive even includes narrations from Aʾisha's father and the first "rightly guided" caliph, Abu Bakr. According to an ʿIkrima report, Ibn ʿAbbas witnessed Muhammad announcing that if he had a close friend, it would have been Abu Bakr.[47] ʿUbayd Allah ibn ʿAbd Allah reports Abu Bakr kissing the Prophet after his death, and names both Aʾisha and Ibn ʿAbbas as his sources.[48] Kufan traditionist ʿArqam ibn Shurahbil relates that Ibn ʿAbbas told him about Abu Bakr leading congregational prayers during Muhammad's fatal illness, but one of the three versions of his account includes the detail of Muhammad asking first for ʿAli, and Aʾisha encouraging him to call for Abu Bakr instead. ʿArqam also tells us that according to Ibn ʿAbbas, Muhammad left no will or final instructions; in one ʿArqam report from Ibn ʿAbbas, the "illness prayers" and "last will" tropes are combined into one narrative.[49]

It must also be recognized that decades after Ibn ʿAbbas and all of his students had passed away, the Islamic political context—and Ibn ʿAbbas's historical significance—radically transformed. In 750 CE, the Umayyad caliphate fell to the ʿAbbasid revolution, which claimed a kinship relation to the Prophet through Ibn ʿAbbas himself; as descendants of Ibn ʿAbbas's son ʿAli ibn ʿAbd Allah ibn ʿAbbas, they traced their lineage to the Prophet's patrilineal uncle ʿAbbas, whom they regarded as the rightful heir to Muhammad's authority. That authority, naturally, passed to the ʿAbbasid caliphate.

Though this relation to Muhammad's family enabled the assembly of a broad Muslim coalition against the Umayyads—again, defying the later binary of "Sunni versus Shiʾi" that we so often impose on early Islam—the claim to power through Muhammad's uncle ʿAbbas put the ʿAbbasids at odds with the proto-Shiʾi ʿAlids, who believed in the rightful authority of Muhammad's cousin ʿAli. As Nabil Husayn observes, the ʿAbbasids thus recognized the supporters of ʿAli and descendants of ʿAli's sons Hasan and Husayn, endowed with their own claim to inherited authority, as their most threatening competition. Hadiths disparaging ʿAli's father Abu Talib as a polytheist who never accepted Islam, and who was known to his nephew Muhammad to have been condemned to hellfire (even if Abu Talib receives a lesser punishment, out of God's mercy to the Prophet), served to discredit the Hasanids and Husaynids.[50] In his only Ibn ʿAbbas hadiths in the *Musnad*, Abu ʿUthman al-Nahdi (d. ca. 715)—a famed muʾammar who allegedly lived to be 130 years old—presents Ibn ʿAbbas as a source for Muhammad describing Abu Talib's brains boiling in the hellfire.[51] 'Abd Allah ibn Ka'b ibn Malik (d. 716), allegedly a Companion of the Prophet, shares an Ibn 'Abbas report that during Muhammad's final illness, Ibn 'Abbas's father 'Abbas wanted to ask the Prophet about the matter of succession; 'Ali refused for fear that the news wouldn't favor Muhammad's family. As with Abu 'Uthman, this is 'Abd Allah ibn Ka'b's only Ibn 'Abbas tradition included in the *Musnad*.[52]

While an isolated tradition in Ibn 'Abbas's corpus places 'Ali's father in hellfire, the image of Ibn 'Abbas's father 'Abbas, who had fiercely opposed Muhammad's movement and appeared to have become a Muslim only in Muhammad's later years, is rehabilitated. The *Musnad* presents Ibn 'Abbas reporting that 'Abbas was captured by an angel at the battle of Badr, and that in custody 'Abbas declared that he had become Muslim even before his capture; 'Abbas even gives Muhammad sage guidance while still a prisoner in chains.[53] The Ibn 'Abbas corpus also presents Muhammad protecting his uncle 'Abbas from retaliation after 'Abbas had slapped a man, proclaiming, "'Abbas is of me and I am of him." The hadith's chain traces its attribution to the trusted Sa'id ibn Jubayr but is considered weak due to the man who presents it as Sa'id's report, 'Abd al-A'la.[54] In a similarly discounted transmission (traced to a disreputable reporter, Husayn ibn 'Abd Allah, who claims 'Ikrima as his source), 'Abbas prays to God for the right man to bury his prophetic nephew; the story ends with clear political consequences, as 'Abbas's prayer leads to Abu Talha, who dug graves for the Ansar, becoming favored over Abu 'Ubayd who dug graves for the Mujahirun.[55]

Neither Ibn 'Abbas nor his students lived to see the caliphate founded by his great-grandson; Ibn 'Abbas's later years were defined by the rise of the Umayyad dynasty, founded by 'Ali's rival Mu'awiyya. Ibn 'Abbas's posthumous importance as eponymic ancestor of the revolutionaries who overthrew the Umayyads, however, means that reports of Ibn 'Abbas's interactions with Mu'awiyya and the early Umayyad caliphate could have been filtered through—or even created by—the 'Abbasid propaganda machine. Ibn 'Abbas's hadith corpus includes a number of narrations in which he criticizes Mu'awiyya's practices, demonstrating that his knowledge is superior to the caliph's and exposing Mu'awiyya's departure from authentic precedent. 'Urwa ibn al-Zubayr, A'isha's nephew and a scholar entrenched in the Umayyad court, sometimes bears the brunt of Ibn 'Abbas's (and/or the network's) polemic. These episodes could read at first glance as mere disagreements over religious rituals, but they carry special weight as both Ibn 'Abbas and Mu'awiyya become stand-ins for entire dynasties. Mu'awiyya and his junior scholars embody the Umayyads' lack of religious credibility; in contrast, Ibn 'Abbas represents a superior knowledge that rests with the family of the Prophet.

Umayyad rulers and governors, including Mu'awiyya and al-Hajjaj, had attempted to establish the two calls to prayer, the *adhan* and *iqama*, as part of "official" practice for the Eid prayers. Though the rebel "anti-caliph" Ibn al-Zubayr took Ibn 'Abbas's advice against incorporating the two calls into Eid practice, he instituted them after falling out with Ibn 'Abbas.[56] In multiple narrations in the *Musnad*, Ibn 'Abbas firmly opposes the inclusion of calls to prayer in the Eid prayer. Some versions, all of which trace to a chain of Ibn Jurayj narrating from al-Hasan ibn Muslim, who in turn cites Tawus as his source, have Ibn 'Abbas name-dropping the first three caliphs, Abu Bakr, 'Umar, and 'Uthman, charging that Mu'awiyya had strayed from what they unanimously understood as correct practice. It's noteworthy here that Ibn 'Abbas neglects to include the fourth caliph, Mu'awiyya's opponent 'Ali, among the precedent-setting authorities.[57]

Questions over the correct practices of religious pilgrimage also became sites at which Ibn 'Abbas could flex 'Abbasid legitimacy over the Umayyads. When walking his ritual laps (*tawaf*) around the Ka'ba, Mu'awiyya touched every corner, for which Ibn 'Abbas scolded him. In Mujahid's version of this episode, Ibn 'Abbas told Mu'awiyya that the Prophet did not touch two of the corners, which Mu'awiyya could only answer with his personal feelings about the Ka'ba ("Nothing of the house is abandoned"). When Ibn 'Abbas corrected him with a verse of the Qur'an—"In the Messenger of God, you have a good example to follow" (33:21)—Mu'awiyya surrendered his argument.[58]

Mu'awiyya had also attempted to ban the joining of 'umra, the "lesser" pilgrimage (that is, a version of pilgrimage that only includes the Mecca-based rituals, rather than the complete hajj, which also includes rituals at sites in the surrounding area) to hajj. Again, Tawus (this time through a weak transmitter, Layth ibn Abi Sulaym) asserts that Muhammad had continued from his 'umra into hajj, adding that this practice was followed by Abu Bakr, 'Umar, and 'Uthman, and that Mu'awiyya was the first to reject it.[59] In a narration from Sa'id, 'Urwa ibn al-Zubayr argues that Abu Bakr and 'Umar prohibited the joining of 'umra and hajj, to which Ibn 'Abbas answers with apparent sarcasm, "I think they're going to be destroyed!"[60] According to Ibn Abi Mulayka, ʿUrwa accused Ibn ʿAbbas of misleading the community, charging that Abu Bakr and ʿUmar had forbidden the joining of ʿumra and hajj; Ibn ʿAbbas answered simply that Abu Bakr and ʿUmar had more knowledge of the Prophet than ʿUrwa.[61] In another Ibn Abi Mulayka account, Ibn ʿAbbas challenges ʿUrwa, "Ask your mother" (Asma, the daughter of Abu Bakr) about her father's pilgrimage praxis.[62]

Another tradition depicts Kurayb traveling from Syria to Medina at the start of the fasting month of Ramadan, which would have commenced with the sighting of the new moon. Upon his arrival in Medina, Kurayb told Ibn ʿAbbas that in Syria, Muʾawiyya had seen the new moon on Friday evening and then fasted; Ibn ʿAbbas answered that in Medina, they had seen the moon on Saturday evening and would count their days of fasting accordingly. When Kurayb asked if Muʾawiyya's sighting of the moon and commencement of the fast were not enough for Ibn ʿAbbas, Ibn ʿAbbas answered that they were not, and that it was the command of the Prophet.[63] This account is not self-evidently a polemic; it doesn't exactly discredit Muʾawiyya or expose him as in other hadiths; it simply establishes that the population in each locale adheres to its own moon sighting, rather than the caliph's sighting. But when read alongside a recurring theme in which Ibn ʿAbbas seems to enjoy putting Muʾawiyya in his place, this tradition can speak to more than the basic question of correct fasting practices: Ibn ʿAbbas lives in accordance with not the world city of Damascus and its high-powered elites but rather Medina, the simple city of the Prophet.

DID MUHAMMAD DRINK?

Two variants of a tradition in the *Musnad*, both traced to a pair of ʿAbbasid reporters (Husayn ibn ʿAbd Allah ibn ʿUbayd Allah ibn ʿAbbas and Ibn ʿAbbas's grandson Daʾwud), present Ibn ʿAbbas arguing against a challenger to defend the legitimacy of drinking *nabidh*, an alcoholic fruit beverage with an unclear relationship to the category of *khamr* (wine) and therefore a site of legal dispute.[64] In both variants of their account, Ibn ʿAbbas straightforwardly demonstrates that Muhammad consumed nabidh, and even favorably compares nabidh to milk and honey. But a third variant, traced to Basran traditionist Bakr ibn ʿAbd Allah, changes the question from one of legal permissibility to one of why Ibn ʿAbbas would give nabidh to drink when Mu'awiyya's family gives water and honey: "Are you stingy or poor?" Ibn 'Abbas then answers that he is not stingy or poor, but when the Prophet came with Usama ibn Zayd and asked for something to drink, they gave him nabidh, and Muhammad said that they had done well.[65] The shift between versions is interesting not only for one's injection of anti-Umayyad sentiment but also for the ways these traditions have Ibn 'Abbas defending nabidh on two different grounds: in Bakr's report, nabidh might appear low-class, but its legality is not the question.

Though many non-Muslims and Muslims alike would take it as a given that Islam universally and absolutely prohibits all intoxicating substances, the Islamic history of drinks and drugs is in fact rather complicated. Not only did new substances such as cannabis and coffee provoke legal uncertainty and debate when Muslims first encountered them, but even the question of drinking alcohol was surprisingly open for discussion. The problem was that while the Qur'an explicitly prohibited a beverage called khamr, the exact definitions and boundaries of that term were left for Muslims to figure out for themselves: Did khamr refer only to grape-based intoxicating drinks, or *all* intoxicants? Early in Islamic legal thought, the Hanafi school argued for a limiting of khamr to grape-based wine, though this school ultimately conformed to other schools that favored absolute bans on all intoxicants.[66]

Like so many controversies, different camps cited hadiths as evidence for their opinions, linking their arguments to Muhammad and authorities from the original Muslim community, such as Ibn 'Abbas. Did the Prophet drink nabidh? Did Ibn 'Abbas tell people that Muhammad drank nabidh? Within the Ibn 'Abbas transmissions that found their way into the *Musnad*, we find conflicting answers. As mentioned, some hadith reporters present Ibn 'Abbas as an advocate who would assert that drinking nabidh was part of the Prophet's personal habit. Along with Bakr ibn 'Abd Allah, 'Ikrima serves as a source for this position.[67] But 'Ikrima also tells us that according to Ibn 'Abbas, Muhammad prohibited a kind of nabidh made in green earthenware.[68] Abu-l-Hakam narrates that he asked Ibn 'Abbas about nabidh in earthenware jars, gourds, and green glazed pitchers, to which Ibn 'Abbas replied with the advice that if one wants to regard as forbidden what God and the Prophet regarded as forbidden, then regard nabidh as forbidden.[69] In a similar tradition from Kufan reporter Qays ibn Habtar, Ibn 'Abbas answered his question about various colors of earthenware with a statement that Muhammad had explicitly said, "Every intoxicant [*muskir*] is forbidden."[70]

Yusuf ibn Mihran, a poorly regarded transmitter, told ʿAli ibn Zayd (also considered a weak source) a story from Ibn ʿAbbas of Muhammad's arriving on his mount with Usama ibn Zayd and expressing approval when invited to drink from a water skin. ʿAli ibn Zayd in turn transmitted the story to Hammad ibn Salama, from whom two different scholars, ʿAffan ibn Muslim and Yunus, relate the story. Between these two later transmitters narrating roughly a century after Yusuf's death, the wording changes. In Yusuf's story as presented by ʿAffan, Ibn ʿAbbas is quoted as saying, "We gave him from this nabidh."[71] In Yunus's version, Ibn ʿAbbas explains only, "We gave him from this drink," but never names the beverage.[72] The difference could mean nothing more than someone remembering the gist of a story but getting the quote wrong, or perhaps Hammad (himself a somewhat controversial reporter) retelling the story without much regard for the exact words; or it could reflect a late edit, since the inclusion or erasure of nabidh could have meaningful consequences. Using the *isnad-cum-matn* approach advocated by Harald Motzki for tracking change between variants of a hadith, one could suggest that Yunus's version represents a sanitizing of content.

Surveying the pro-nabidh and anti-nabidh reports, we encounter the drink's container as a recurring theme. In narrations that present Ibn ʿAbbas as an eyewitness to Muhammad's drinking nabidh, Ibn ʿAbbas tends to explicitly state that the drink was made and/or offered to Muhammad in a leather skin. Meanwhile, narrations that declare nabidh to be forbidden (haram) usually appear in the context of someone asking Ibn ʿAbbas about particular kinds of pitchers and vessels. The distinction between leather skins and earthenware jars would impact the drink and thus produce different effects on the drinker. Likewise, since nabidh becomes intoxicating after several days, a pro-nabidh report gets very specific about how long Muhammad kept nabidh before disposing of it, making clear that he would not drink on a Wednesday night nabidh that had been made on Monday night.[73] Another establishes that when Muhammad consumed nabidh, he did not drink to fully quench his thirst, which would suggest that he maintained a safe distance from becoming intoxicated.[74] These subtle disclaimers often reflect ongoing legal debates as well as shifting views of Muhammad that motivated the circulation, editing, or even forgery of hadiths.

When I planned to embark on a deep exploration of a specific Companion's content in the *Musnad*, one of my more personally compelling reasons for choosing Ibn ʿAbbas was his prominence as a narrator of the Night Journey, Muhammad's miraculous flight to Jerusalem and ascension into the heavens. Ibn ʿAbbas was not the only Companion to whom ascension narratives were linked, but as Frederick S. Colby observes, Ibn ʿAbbas was frequently cited as the source for "highly embellished accounts" and "some of the most extensive and detailed of the Muslim ascension stories to have survived to the present."[75] Colby notes that long before modern scholarly skepticism, Muslim scholars rejected Ibn ʿAbbas ascension narratives as fabrications and forgeries with no legitimate transmission chains that could attach them to Ibn ʿAbbas.[76] This becomes a point at which we see divergence between Ibn ʿAbbas's legacy for the giants of hadith scholarship and other Islamic literary genres, such as Qurʾan commentary (tafsir). As Shahab Ahmed writes of hadith and Qurʾan tafsir, we're looking at "not only distinct literary genres but also overlapping yet ultimately distinct truth projects, with different goals, different practitioners, different materials, different methods, different forms, different values, and different meanings."[77] Ibn Hanbal was a jurist and hadith partisan, and had famously derided literary genres such as the Prophet's biography and Qurʾan commentary. In Ibn Hanbal's *Musnad*, the Night Journey doesn't read like a major theme of the Ibn ʿAbbas scholarly network. If we measure significance simply by counting reports, the Night Journey doesn't take up anywhere close to the space that we see Ibn ʿAbbas or his students and their later transmitters devoted to issues of correct pilgrimage praxis, ritual purity, the legality of nabidh in green earthenware jars, or sex laws. The *Musnad*'s Ibn ʿAbbas collection offers a handful of reports, mostly attributed to Mujahid ibn Jabr and Abu al-ʿAliya, and chiefly concerned with the physical appearance of Moses, Jesus, and Abraham. The reports differ slightly from each other, but tend to share a polemical purpose: of Moses, Jesus, and Muhammad, Muhammad bears the greatest physical resemblance to Abraham, seemingly privileging Muslims over Jews and Christians as Abraham's truest heirs.[78]

The relative lack of attention to the ascension might make sense, as Ibn ʿAbbas's core students were jurists, often speaking in official capacities as government-appointed judges and sought for their knowledge of legal matters; likewise, the later makers of our vast hadith compendiums, such as Ibn Hanbal, spent most of their energy on questions of how one properly *does* Islam. Though some hadiths present the Night Journey as the context in which Muslims were commanded to perform five daily prayers, the Night Journey itself does not itself answer an immediate question of correct Islamic practice. It's not likely, after all, that I'll ever need to know the right prayers to say when mounting and dismounting the Buraq, the winged steed that carried Muhammad between the vertically tiered heavens.

Asking questions about Muhammad's life, we'll get different answers depending on the scholarly archives we consult. This manifests again with the opposite of Muhammad's ascension through heavens: a story of Muhammad's temporary control by demonic forces. Versions of the famed "Satanic Verses" episode, in which Satan was able to momentarily deceive Muhammad and disguise concessions to polytheism as actual verses of the Qur'an, were widely circulated among early Qur'an commentators, as Shahab Ahmed has shown, though these accounts failed to find acceptance in canonical hadith texts. We don't see a version of the Satanic Verses incident in Ibn 'Abbas's *Musnad* reports, but outside the *Musnad* the story's circulation all but depends on hadiths from the Ibn 'Abbas network. Examining Shahab Ahmed's collection of early Satanic Verses accounts, we see that thirty-four of Ahmed's fifty reports are attributed to Ibn 'Abbas's students, both major (such as Mujahid, Sa'id, 'Ata, and Abu al-'Aliya) and minor (such as Isma'il al-Suddi al-Kabir, a Kufan proto-Shi'i who was said to have learned directly from Ibn 'Abbas but was nonetheless branded a liar by hadith scholars),[79] other figures in his extended network (as in his students' students, such as Dhahhak ibn Muzzahim), or Ibn 'Abbas himself.[80]

PROPHETIC SEXUALITIES

In his landmark work of scholarship and engaged theological reflection, *Homosexuality in Islam*, Scott Kugle rigorously investigates key sources of Islamic thought, such as the Qur'an, hadiths, and Muslim jurisprudence, to rethink the classical tradition and find new openings for inclusive and affirmational Islamic sexualities. In one of his chapters, Kugle turns to the hadith corpus to consider hadiths that treat same-sex intercourse as a punishable crime. Because the Qur'an and hadith corpus are very different sources — one being regarded as God's speech, perfectly preserved, while the other remains acknowledged by its own advocates as a body of fallible human scholarship—Kugle approaches these sources' capacities for homophobia in very different ways. In contrast to his chapter on the Qur'an's potential for homophobic meanings, in which Kugle critiques Muslim *interpretations* of the Qur'an but preserves the Qur'an itself as innocent, Kugle engages the hadith material with a critical skepticism that asks whether Muhammad really said the things that have been attributed to him. Kugle thus examines the chains of transmission, looking for patterns: Are certain ideas about Islamic sexuality linked to certain transmitters? Focusing on canonical hadiths that criminalize same-sex intercourse, Kugle finds his lens focusing on Ibn 'Abbas's former slave, 'Ikrima. Among thousands of hadith reporters in his generation, 'Ikrima became disproportionately responsible for the linking of violent homophobia to Muhammad's message. For Kugle, homophobic hadiths might tell us more about 'Ikrima than they do about Muhammad.

Ibn 'Abbas's material in the *Musnad* reads as exceptionally concerned with cursing and/or punishing sexual transgressions, but those reports almost always come through 'Ikrima. It's 'Ikrima who tells us that Ibn 'Abbas reported Muhammad's cursing bestiality and male-male anal penetration (*liwat*). It's 'Ikrima who narrates that Muhammad explicitly condemned men having sex with men and women having sex with women. It's 'Ikrima who reports a penalty of eighty lashes for adultery, and joins other transmitters in reporting a fine of one dinar to be paid by the man who has sex with his wife during her menstruation. And it's 'Ikrima who reports that Muhammad cursed people with transgender identities. Finally, it's also 'Ikrima who provides Ibn 'Abbas hadiths in which Muhammad issues commands to "kill the one who does it and the one he does it to"; depending on the version, the "it" in question is either bestiality, anal sex, or incest. Outside Ibn Hanbal's *Musnad*, Abu Dawud's collection includes an Ibn 'Abbas narration that prescribes the death penalty for unmarried men who are caught having anal sex with other men, but it does not come from 'Ikrima. The chain of reporters goes back to Ibn Khuthaym, who says he heard it from both Sa'id ibn Jubayr and Mujahid ibn Jabr.[81] This transmission is an obvious outlier, which Abu Dawud seems to recognize: he justifies its inclusion with a note regarding the weakness of similar narrations from 'Amr ibn Abi 'Amr, who appears in other hadith collections as a major narrator for 'Ikrima's violently homophobic reports. Some hadith critics would look skeptically at this "diving" chain of transmission, suggesting that it had been forged to compensate for the weakness of 'Amr's transmitting from 'Ikrima and create stronger evidence for the content.

Having reorganized Ibn 'Abbas's hadiths from the *Musnad* by topic, as an experiment I went through my section on sex, sex laws, and gender identity and crossed out every hadith that came from 'Ikrima. Just like that, the homophobia was gone from Ibn 'Abbas's archive. The transphobia was gone. Where Ibn 'Abbas had been made to represent Muhammad in ways that have harmed many people, he suddenly became silent, at least within the bounds of his public memory and this massive hadith collection.

Whether or not Muhammad or Ibn 'Abbas really said the words attributed to them, we have to ask how and why 'Ikrima came to be the chief source of these claims. Kugle engages in some speculation as to 'Ikrima's motivations, suggesting that his ties to the zealous Kharijiyya encouraged an obsession with policing morality. Kugle also mentions the possibility, noted by 'Ikrima's own contemporaries, that 'Ikrima exaggerated his knowledge of Ibn 'Abbas's teachings as a means of bolstering his own stature as an expert on the law.[82] This issue would not be unique in the hadith milieu.

The question of whether 'Ikrima accurately reported what he heard from Ibn 'Abbas leads me to another theme of hadith skepticism: the problem of knowledge flowing from a prolific teacher through single strands of transmission. As someone who teaches at a university in large lecture halls, I imagine a scenario in which my students—let's say there were 100 in this particular class—walk out of the room and tell their friends about my lecture's content. So we have 100 students, each providing an eyewitness account of what happened in the room. Out of these 100, a single student goes around and tells everyone they know that at some point during the lecture, I climbed onto the lectern, leaped into the air, and performed a flawlessly executed shooting star press in front of the class. The other 99 make no such claim, but this one student has widely circulated the story.

It's certainly possible that a teacher says or does something in class that only one student out of 100 remembers. But it's easy to question that recollection of events; and even if the student's report is accurate and I really did perform a shooting star press in front of everyone, one could question whether that shooting star press was the most important content. Again, 100 students narrated their firsthand memories of the lecture; only one mentioned a shooting star press; 99 either failed to see it, or saw it and found it unworthy of mention, compared to other details about the class. On top of that, let's say that someone who was not in the class really liked the story of my shooting star press and wanted everyone to believe it but grew concerned with the credibility of this singular narrator; so this person claimed that the story was corroborated by two better, more-trusted students. And to make matters even more complicated, let's say that this lecture took place several decades ago and no one who was physically in the room that day is alive to confirm or deny the statements attributed to them. If you want to know what they said about a lecture from generations earlier, you can interview their great-great-grandchildren's friends.

IBN 'ABBAS VERSUS IBN MAS'UD

Now that we've surveyed the 'Abd Allah ibn 'Abbas universe, let's put it in conversation with a whole other universe, reading Ibn 'Abbas alongside another 'Abd Allah: one of the earliest converts to Muhammad's move-ment, 'Abd Allah ibn Mas'ud (d. 652–54). Ibn 'Abbas and Ibn Mas'ud both became respected elder sages for their respective teaching circles and later interpretive tradition, representing authoritative traces of the original Muslim community, but their careers were somewhat separated by miles and years. These two 'Abd Allahs were based in different Iraqi garrison cities where they served as treasurer: Ibn 'Abbas went to Basra, where he ultimately became governor, and the caliph 'Umar sent Ibn Mas'ud as a resident scholar to Kufa; in their respective cities, their leg-acies and names became essential to the local knowledge traditions. Ibn Mas'ud was Ibn 'Abbas's senior by as much as two decades, which would mean that Ibn Mas'ud taught an older coterie of students—at least in theory. The most prominent source of Ibn Mas'ud narrations, Shaqiq ibn Salama (Abu Wa'il), was one of those *mu'ammarun* hadith transmitters who boasted supremely advanced age, reportedly claiming to have been a contemporary (though not precisely qualifying as a Companion) of the Prophet and living to be over 100 years old.[83] Another major Ibn Mas'ud transmitter, Zir ibn Hubaysh, was believed to be more than 120 years old at the time of his death.[84] At any rate, while the networks emanating from Ibn 'Abbas and Ibn Mas'ud contain numerous points of overlap and intersection, in the earliest layers of their transmission lineages these networks remain two distinct clusters. At the first layer, when we look at the transmitters acknowledged as major terminal nodes for Ibn ʿAbbas and Ibn Masʿud, we're seeing two different lists.

As both Ibn ʿAbbas and Ibn Masʿud became linked in different ways to scholarly traditions surrounding the Qurʾan, and an abundance of narrations offer their explanations of specific verses' meanings, their respective networks offer stories in which their credentials as Qurʾan scholars—and thus the authority of their students—become firmly established. In a number of varying accounts, Saʾid, ʿIkrima, and others narrate that Muhammad prayed for Ibn ʿAbbas to be endowed with gifts such as knowledge, wisdom, religion, al-kitab (the book, that is, the Qurʾan), and taʾwil (interpretation of the Qurʾan).[85] Abu Bishr narrates that when Ibn ʿAbbas was just a boy, ʿUmar deferred to his superior expertise on the Qurʾan's 105th sura.[86] Ibn Masʿud narrations likewise present him with endorsements from key figures: Muhammad asking Ibn Masʿud to recite the Qurʾan for him[87] and also proclaiming in front of Abu Bakr and ʿUmar that Ibn Masʿud's recitation was the best.[88] Ibn Masʿud additionally recalls the pairs of suras that Muhammad would recite in prayer.[89]

The construction of Ibn ʿAbbas as the greatest Qurʾan interpreter in early Islam (even reportedly hailed as such by Ibn Masʿud), as scholars have noted, reflects the later ʿAbbasid propaganda project, which infiltrated the world of hadith transmission.[90] Ibn Masʿud's assertions of his own expertise in the Qurʾan speak to his immediate political context. Like Ibn ʿAbbas, Ibn Masʿud experienced rising and falling positions with the regimes of his time, as is reflected in his body of reports. Ibn Masʿud's most famous controversy emerged when the caliph ʿUthman sought to establish an "official" state codex of the Qurʾan and called for the destruction of any alternative codices. Ibn Masʿud, who possessed his own copy of the Qurʾan and was regarded as an authoritative Qurʾan expert for his students in Kufa, refused to comply with the caliphal decree and continued to teach the Qurʾan as he knew it. Ibn Masʿud reportedly disagreed with ʿUthman's compilation of the Qurʾan on multiple points: he did not believe that the opening sura, al-Fatiha, was ever meant to be considered part of the Qurʾan proper, nor did he accept the final two suras, al-Falaq and an-Nas, as belonging to the revealed text. Given the antagonism surrounding Ibn Masʿud's positions on the Qurʾan, it shouldn't be surprising to see traces of this controversy in his narrations. In the Musnad, therefore, we find reports in which Ibn Masʿud boasts that he had learned seventy suras directly from the Prophet—sometimes with an added swipe at the scribe for 'Uthman's Qur'an project, Zayd ibn Thabit, whom he says had been just a child at the time.[91] Elsewhere in Ibn Mas'ud's corpus, he recalls having asked Muhammad about differences in recitation after Ibn Mas'ud and another Companion, both of whom had learned their recitation from the Prophet, recited in different ways; the Prophet, Ibn Mas'ud narrates, answers that each of them should recite as they had learned it, because differences caused preceding nations to be destroyed.[92]

Surveying these Companions' two bodies of reports, we find distinct themes, tropes, and answers to questions. At some points, the two Companions might disagree on an issue; and sometimes, an issue that appears critically urgent to one is neglected entirely by the other. With just a few examples below, we can see Ibn Mas'ud and Ibn 'Abbas emerge as unique voices, expressing not simply a Companion hive mind but rather their own subjectivities.

Future strife. Ibn Mas'ud died before 'Uthman's assassination, 'Ali's rise to the caliphate, A'isha's revolt, the Battle of the Camel, Mu'awiyya's rebellion, the dawn of the Umayyad dynasty, and the tragic battle of Karbala. Though hadith forgers would often insert commentary on current events in the mouths of people who had died decades earlier, Ibn Mas'ud's corpus in the *Musnad* doesn't seem to overtly violate his timeline's continuity. His reports exhibit a consistently positive treatment of Abu Bakr, but we don't see an obvious or undeniable partisanship for or against 'Ali. Nonetheless, Ibn Mas'ud does criticize ruling powers and present Muhammad giving warnings and dire predictions about the Muslims' future.

Like Ibn 'Abbas, who is depicted in hadith sources correcting, critiquing, and humiliating the Umayyads on questions of correct Islamic practice, Ibn Mas'ud can also speak truth to those in power. As we have seen, the most prominent example appears in Ibn Mas'ud's advocacy of differing Qur'an readings against 'Uthman's "official" Qur'an project. Ibn Mas'ud hadiths also present him as especially concerned with the unwarranted delaying of prayers, which reads as direct critique of Kufa governor (and 'Uthman's brother) al-Walid ibn 'Uqba, who left office in disgrace after being flogged for drunkenness.[93]

More than Ibn 'Abbas, Ibn Mas'ud seems exceedingly interested in dystopian futures, the decline of Islam, and various prophesied events that would signal the coming of the Hour. Ibn Mas'ud's narrations report not only that al-Walid had delayed the prayer but that future rulers would delay prayers.[94] More generally, future rulers will do what they had not been commanded to do,[95] and the Prophet himself will be told in the next world, "You don't know what your Companions did after you were gone."[96] Ibn Masʾud's hadith corpus envisions a future of rampant violence among Muslims and even offers a promise from Muhammad that the "millstone of Islam" would not last longer than seventy more years.[97] Ibn Masʾud is also cited as a source for the "three best genera-tions" hadith, in which Muhammad explains that the best *qarn* (gener-ation or nation) is his own, followed by the one after that, and followed in turn by the one after it.[98] This narrative of declining history fuels modern hadith-centered revivalism movements such as the Salafiyya, who authorize themselves as following the "pure" and "original" Islam of the Salaf, the first three Muslim generations.

Did Muhammad see jinns? Both Ibn ʿAbbas and Ibn Masʾud offer com-mentary on the "night of the jinns," an event vaguely referenced in the Qurʾan. The Qurʾan's seventy-second sura, popularly titled "The Jinn," begins with the declaration that a company of jinns listened to the Qurʾan and affirmed it as a divine revelation. A masjid, popularly known as *masjid al-jinn* ("mosque of the jinns"), was established in Na-khla (now within the expanded vicinity of Mecca) at the presumed site of the encounter and still stands today. But who were these jinns, and what was the context for their hearing the revelation? The Qurʾan does not name the jinns or give any kind of backstory as to how they were able to hear its recitation. Nor does it tell us how (or if) the Prophet in-teracted directly with the jinns. The Qurʾan's command, "Say, O Prophet, 'It has been revealed to me that a group of jinn listened to the Qurʾan'" (72:1) could suggest that Muhammad did not know about his jinn audi-ence until later, perhaps only learning of it when the verse came down, but this remains unclear. Hadith literature supplements the Qurʾan and fills some gaps, though as always, different hadith networks engaged this topic for different reasons, asked different questions, and relied on different Companions for their answers. So the information we have con-cerning the seventy-second sura and the jinns who listened to the Qurʾan will vary between two Companion archives such as those attributed to Ibn ʿAbbas and Ibn Masʾud.

An Ibn ʿAbbas transmission links the incident to devils who attempted to eavesdrop on divine communications in the heavens but were burned by shooting stars. Variant reports note that when they had previously spied on divine revelations, the devils would corrupt the revelations by adding nine or ten words to each one.[99] Recognizing that a major revelation must have been the reason for God to suddenly block their access to the news of heaven, the devils set forth on a journey to investigate. Between two mountains at Nakhla, their group intersected with Muhammad and his Companions as he led them in *fajr*, the pre-sunrise prayer. Hearing Muhammad's recitation of the Qur'an, they marveled at its truth and accepted it as a revelation. God then revealed verse 72:1 to Muhammad, telling him to publicly proclaim that the jinns had accepted the Qur'an (and perhaps informing him of it).[100] In another report, Ibn 'Abbas narrates that the jinns, astounded at the Companions' collective imitation of Muhammad's bodily movements, returned to their community and described them as a clinging mass around him. The Qur'an references this moment in the verse, "When the slave of God stood calling upon him alone, they became a clinging mass" (72:19). These Ibn 'Abbas transmissions contribute to an important part of Qur'an interpretation: the *asbab al-nuzul* or "occasions of revelation" literature, which seeks to enhance our understanding of Qur'an verses by providing the contexts in which they were revealed to Muhammad.

While narrating that a group of jinns observed Muhammad reciting the Qur'an in prayer, Ibn 'Abbas offers an important clarification: "The Messenger of God did not recite *to* the jinns and he did not see them." This statement, reported by Ibn 'Abbas's student Sa'id b. Jubayr, reads consistently with the rest of Ibn 'Abbas's archive, in which the jinns seem to come and go without interacting with Muhammad. Sa'id b. Jubayr does appear in tafsir literature as the source for a tale of jinns asking Muhammad a question that leads to the revelation of 72:18, but the story is unsourced rather than attributed to his teacher Ibn 'Abbas.[101] Moreover, the report of a jinn asking Muhammad a question does not itself betray Ibn 'Abbas's position that Muhammad did not see jinns or recite the Qur'an for them. Ibn 'Abbas's denial runs into friction with accounts from other Companions, such as Ibn Mas'ud, who tells us of an ominous "night of the jinns" in which Muhammad encountered a group of jinns and recited Qur'an verses to them. One report has Muhammad telling Ibn Mas'ud that he spent the previous night reciting the Qur'an for jinns who had accompanied him at al-Hajun (rather than Nakhla), the cemetery in Mecca where loved ones such as his mother Amina, uncle Abu Talib, wife Khadija, and others were buried.[102]

Traditions differ as to what Ibn Mas'ud himself witnessed or experienced that night. In one transmission, 'Alqama asks Ibn Mas'ud if anyone accompanied the Prophet on the night of the jinns, and Ibn Mas'ud answers that Muhammad was alone. Ibn Mas'ud adds that the Companions, fearing that Muhammad had been captured or even killed by the jinns, spent the "worst night that any people have ever spent," until Muhammad returned in the morning and told them what had happened. In other traditions, Ibn Mas'ud explicitly states that he was present, though it remains ambiguous as to whether he personally saw the jinns. Ibn Mas'ud's narrations become relevant to questions of practice, as Muhammad performs his ritual washing (*wudu*) with Ibn Mas'ud's nabidh, establishing the legitimacy of that practice, and tells Ibn Mas'ud not to use bones or dung in cleaning himself, since these are foods for the jinns.[103]

Did Muhammad see God? A point of contradiction among hadiths with major theological implications concerns the question of whether Muhammad personally saw God, and if he did, whether this vision was achieved with his physical eyes or in another sense. Companions reporting on the vision either affirmed that Muhammad saw God, denied the vision (often with the clarification that Muhammad saw Gabriel, not God), or allowed for some careful navigation between sides, such as clarifying that Muhammad saw God but not with his physical eyes, that the vision took place within the relative safety of a dream, or that Muhammad attested to only seeing a light and did not further explain the light's identity.

While A'isha appears in the hadith corpus as the most ardent opponent of the vision, charging that whoever claims such a thing about Muhammad is a liar, Ibn 'Abbas appears as one of the vision's major advocates. Examining the chains of transmission, Christopher Melchert has loosely linked support for Muhammad's seeing God to the city of Basra, and opposition to the vision in Kufa, though allowing for disagreement within each local network.[104]

Though the *Musnad* does not include the most intensely corporeal treatments of Muhammad's vision attributed to Ibn 'Abbas, in which Muhammad describes God's hair, clothing, furniture, and youthful appearance in vivid detail, Ibn 'Abbas does affirm that Muhammad saw God. Most of these affirmations (and all of the reports making it clear that the vision was with Muhammad's physical eyes) trace back to 'Ikrima.[105] Abu al-'Aliya also narrates that according to Ibn 'Abbas, Muhammad saw God on two occasions.[106] Abu Qilaba narrates a version in which Muhammad not only sees God but feels the touch of God's cold hand, though this version softens its theological impact with a disclaimer that the vision took place within a dream.[107]

Hadiths addressing the vision usually relate the incident not to Muhammad's heavenly ascension, as one might expect, but rather the *descent* of an unnamed being "intense in power" (*shadid al-qawwa*) to Muhammad, mentioned only vaguely in the Qur'an's fifty-third sura. In the *Musnad*, Ibn Mas'ud offers numerous reports on the fifty-third sura, and in all accounts, the shadid al-qawwa that Muhammad witnesses is not God but the angel Gabriel. Ibn Mas'ud thus appears more theologically compatible with A'isha than Ibn 'Abbas, which would correspond with the greater overlap between the Ibn Mas'ud and A'isha transmitter networks, though Ibn Mas'ud does not give the same scathing condemnations of the pro-vision camp that we see in A'isha's narrations.

Disagreement among Companions regarding Muhammad's vision of God provokes the question of what Islamic theology might have looked like for the first Muslims, particularly as they moved across the map in post-Muhammad years and became local centers of authority in newly conquered regions and garrison cities. In later generations, a sense of shared hadith canon would become an important—and according to some communities, the *only*—source for theological elaboration on the Qur'an, but what Islamic theologies were possible in a world before a canon? Instead of asking about the theology of the hadith corpus at large, we can disassemble the corpus and read Companion theologies alongside (or even against) each other.

Jews and Isra'iliyyat. Jews appear as frequent antagonists in both Companions' archives, as both Ibn 'Abbas and Ibn Mas'ud narrate variations of a "Jewish debate" motif in which Jews attempt to discredit Muhammad by asking him challenging questions, sometimes provoking the revelation of a new Qur'an verse, or in which Muhammad otherwise responds to something that Jews say to him.

The collected narrations of both Ibn 'Abbas and Ibn Mas'ud include materials that seem to reference Jewish and Christian scriptural sources as well as popular folklore. This shouldn't be surprising, since Muhammad lived in a world of biblical references, and one could expect that he'd say things about figures such as Moses in ways that elaborated on the bare references in the Qur'an. But Muslim scholars also feared that improperly sourced legends might smuggle their way into Islamic thought, in part as Jews (such as the important early writer Wahb ibn Munabbih) and Christians became Muslim and brought their prior knowledge and reference points into Muslim conversations.[108] ʿIkrima's material from Ibn ʿAbbas reads as a potential flow between Muslim and Jewish milieus. Examining sex laws in hadith literature, Scott Lucas suggests a reading of ʿIkrima's antibestiality reports alongside the Bible's prescribed punishment in Leviticus 20:15–16.[109] ʿIkrima also appears as the source for an Ibn ʿAbbas report in which Muhammad confirms a poet's description the four bearers of God's throne as a man, bull, eagle, and lion,[110] echoing the faces of the four throne-bearers in Ezekiel's visions (human, lion, ox, and eagle in 1:6; cherub, human, lion, and eagle in 10:14).

Different priorities. "What does Islam say about tattoos, plucked eyebrows, hair extensions, filed teeth, and bird omens?" does not appear to have been a question asked by Ibn ʿAbbas's students, as these topics don't show up in his *Musnad* corpus, but they read as serious concerns for Ibn Masʾud and/or his circle. In contrast, Ibn ʿAbbas transmitters have more to say about correct practices in the buying and selling of foodstuffs and the question of performing pilgrimage or other merit-earning deeds on behalf of elderly, disabled, or deceased family members who cannot perform the acts themselves. Breaking down the *Musnad* into its parts and allowing specific Companion-networks to speak for themselves, we don't really see a singular manual for "Islam" shared by every Companion's teaching circle. These circles often overlapped, but in many ways they remained distinct, resulting in diverse bodies of knowledge that reflected individual Companions' experiences and opinions, the specific contexts in which they lived and taught, the issues they faced, the unique sets of questions their students posed to them, and/or their power as "hadith brands" for those who would forge reports in their names. The consolidation of these local bodies into a larger one with the appearance of a universal system took generations. Whether or not the narrations attributed to a Companion "really" come from him or her—and in turn, whether or not a Companion's claims about Muhammad are assumed to accurately represent him—a Companion's body of reports can express the ways "Islam" in their time remained somewhat fluid: what you encountered as Islam in Basra or Medina might not have matched what you'd find in Kufa.

CONCLUSIONS

In academic conversations, "deconstruct" often sounds hostile; a mentor once told me that we engage in studies of hadith literature because we "either love it or we want to deconstruct it," with the unintended implication that we don't deconstruct what we love, or we don't love what we deconstruct. Maybe what I've done here can amount to a kind of loving deconstruction or, put more gently, a disassembly. I've placed a Ka'ba made from Lego bricks on the table. At first glance, it would look like a singular artifact. But then I started taking it apart, piece by piece, showing the bricks of different sizes and shapes, exploring their different powers of connection. The unity that they achieved in the Lego Ka'ba was not a "natural" or inevitable state but the result of a process. An external force had gathered the pieces and combined their powers of connection to make something new; external forces could also disassemble the new unity and find other ways the pieces could have connected to each other, producing alternative unities.

The forces that bring these pieces together to create new artifacts are first the Companions themselves and their teaching circles, which reflect diverse settings and distinct sets of teacher-student relationships but are not absolutely isolated from one another. From the very beginnings, we see points of connection. Over time, these teaching circles grew into networks that increasingly crisscrossed and grew entangled in one another. Long after the last of the Companions passed away, it became possible for hadith scholars to construct the "Companions" as a coherent category with fixed boundaries, and then to present the Companions as a collectively authoritative class of supreme knowers. And then a crystallizing network of hadith scholars, boasting a privileged connection to these supreme knowers through chains of transmission, was able to present itself as the only genuine representative of the Prophet. This network gathered its oral archives into massive collections of hadiths, some earning more canonical privilege than others, and arranged in different ways in accordance with the needs of their compilers. The *Musnad*'s style of organization, grouping hadiths by the Companion to whom they were attributed, reflects one way to put the Lego bricks together; the *musannaf* style, which arranged hadiths in accordance with their topics, reflects another. The musannaf style proved more useful for readers who regarded the Companions as a singular uncarved block rather than as individual subjectivities, and thus replaced the musnad format; all of the canonical Six Books are presented in musannaf style. The musnad-styled collections could have contributed to the evolving view of Companions as universally authoritative, but they were rendered obsolete by the establishment of that proto-Sunni position as later Sunni "orthodoxy." When you read a hadith collection organized by topic, the answer to a question becomes the Companions' answer. Reading these same traditions in the *Musnad*, we start to notice when one Companion has a lot to say on specific topics while remaining silent on others. The same Lego pieces, brought together by different forces with different priorities in mind, produce different unities.

Hadith networks in the early centuries of Islam became extraordinarily successful in creating a shared field on which different legal and theological schools could contest one another, which ironically served to unite them within a rubric that we'd call "Sunni Islam."[111] The full significance of that success cannot be overstated. Hadith scholars not only preserved the Sunna; they *created* it, that is, they advocated for a specific way of conceptualizing the Sunna and their preferred modes of accessing it, and they determined the kinds of concepts or behaviors that transgress it and take someone from *ahl al-sunna* ("people of the Sunna") to *ahl al-rayy* ("people of opinion") or *ahl al-bida'* ("people of innovation"). The Maliki school of jurisprudence favored an alternate model of thinking about the Sunna, defining the Sunna not through isolated hadith transmissions (though they were not opposed to hadiths, and their eponym, Malik ibn Anas, was a hadith scholar in his own right) but rather through the collective culture observed in the city of Medina. When arguments for the hadith-centered Sunna triumphed, the Maliki school adapted. But while the giants of classical hadith scholarship achieved immense norm-making power, the vast corpus that they produced still allowed for heterogeneities to persist among those who followed them. The corpus even includes Deleuzian "lines of flight" that can lead us out of the territory, such as the canonical hadith in which Muhammad attests to his appearances in believers' dreams. The question of whether Muhammad really said what's attributed to him in the hadith corpus only marks the starting point of adventures to be found in the texts.

CHAPTER FIVE

Jurists, Mystics, Philosophers

If you'd asked me this book's big question, "Who is Muhammad?" when I was a new Muslim teenager in the early-to-mid-1990s absorbing "intro to Islam" books and pamphlets through my local masjid and Islamic mail-order catalogs, I would have had an easy answer ready. With full confidence and not a moment's pause, I would have asserted that Muhammad was essentially a regular human being, who was conceived and born and lived his life and died like other human beings; that he did not claim supernatural powers or marvelous feats; that his only miracle was a divinely revealed book; and that when he died, his involvement in our worldly affairs came to an end: he cannot hear our prayers or mediate between us and God. He brought forth a clean and pure monotheism and advocated rational contemplation over blind faith. I also would have emphasized that because Muhammad is dead—really, *really* dead and gone—there is no usefulness whatsoever in trying to communicate with him or see him in our dreams. He did not want us to treat him as the Christians have treated Jesus. His grave is not a cosmically significant place; there is no special religious merit in visiting his mortal remains; and in fact, journeying to his grave as an act of love and veneration for him could even be dangerous to our status as monotheists. Muhammad's job was to deliver a message, and he did; we look to him as a template for how to live out that message, and we look to the Islamic society that he established in Medina as a precedent that modern nations should emulate in every sense. His prime value to us today is not as a supernatural power or magical force but as *content:* the text of the Qur'an and the record of his teachings and behavior, as preserved in Islamic scholarly tradition.

As far as I would have known at the time, the above summary of Muhammad would represent a universal Islamic norm; it was not the product of a particular time and place but simply Islam as Islam had always been. Anything else was a departure. This was how Muhammad presented himself to his Companions, and this remained his Companions' presentation to their own students. The Muslims around me presented Muhammad in more or less these terms. In my local context as a teen convert in upstate New York in the 1990s, learning about Islam from Muslims (both in literature and my flesh-and-blood community in Rochester) who wanted to emphasize Muhammad's monotheism, rationalism, opposition to superstition, and moral character, it represented the singular "Islamic" view of Muhammad.

Coming to Islam as an alienated Christian (representing much of the intended audience for the "intro to Islam" pamphlets), I was especially struck by the emphasis on Muhammad's humanity: if I had been dissatisfied with the narrative of God's having a son who was himself God but also somehow distinct from God, Muhammad's simplicity as a more or less regular human reached me through these pamphlets as the perfect antidote. As a young Muslim, I reached for a certain idea of Muhammad: the Muhammad who emerged from the textual sources and living communities most instantly accessible to me, and the Muhammad who appealed to my needs. Rejecting what I saw as the superstition and magic in my family's religious background, I looked for Islam to be the correction. I wanted the rational Muhammad, and people gave him to me. I had no idea how much editorial creativity went into our understanding of the Prophet, and it would have been deeply troubling to think about Islam undergoing historical change. In fact, when I read hadiths that depicted miracles such as water miraculously flowing out of Muhammad's hands, it was unsettling.

So we see the Muhammad that we see—the Muhammad that the world presents to us—and we run that Muhammad through our own internal filters to produce him again. We make Muhammad as a product of our own world and experience. Just as the philosopher Gilles Deleuze remarked that triangles would worship a triangular god, human beings understand Muhammad from where they stand. Jurists, for example, have sought Muhammad as a jurist and the supreme resource for their lawmaking project. This becomes true even of "secular" academics whose training is chiefly focused on Islamic law; ask them the flawed question, "What does Islam say about _____?" and they're likely to answer in terms of what classical jurists declared to be permissible or forbidden. That's the shape that Islam (and Muhammad) takes for them. Ask the same question to a scholar of Sufism, or an anthropologist, or someone who does Islamic art history, or a specialist in a specific sectarian, regional, or cultural context, and the answer to "What does Islam say?" could take a radically different form, produced from different archives, training, and priorities. So we all "make" Muhammad with the tools that we have.

In this chapter, I offer some glimpses of how this looks in Islamic interpretive traditions. Muslims across all spectrums might ask, "Who was Muhammad?" but have different reasons for needing an answer, as well as different sets of books and experts to guide them, and Muhammad takes diverse shapes in response to their needs. At the end of this discussion, I turn back to my own makings and remakings of Muhammad. Three decades removed from my teen conversion, now an academic who has climbed into the belly of critical theory and cannot find his way out, I find a new Muhammad confronting me with his own openings and limitations.

MUHAMMAD AS WARRIOR-PROPHET AND KING

Biographies tell us as much about their authors as their subjects. In the ways they approach a life and its evidence, biographers reveal their own personal priorities and values. When compiling and arranging the material to tell a person's life story, what topics and questions did the biographer consider most important? What was the engine that drove the biographer's research and writing? How did they get what they came to regard as "the facts" of that life? And in this case, what did Muhammad's biographers think was worth knowing about him, and what does this say about *them*? Situating the authors in their own historical moments, we have to ask about the world around them that made both their subjects and their work possible.

We cannot discuss the beginnings of Islamic historical writings, including the biography of Muhammad, without considering the interventions of early rulers. Even the practice of writing hadiths, which circulated chiefly as oral traditions, was controversial and opposed by some transmitters but became established through caliphal coercion. "We were unwilling to commit knowledge to writing," the foundational Umayyad-era scholar Ibn Shihab al-Zuhri recalled, "until these rulers forced us to do it."[1] The circulation of narratives that discourage or even forbid writing hadiths, Gregor Schoeler has argued, could reflect hadith scholars' resistance to the caliphate's attempt to appropriate their oral knowledge in book form.[2]

The early Umayyad caliphate has been treated in scholarship as a period in which rulers increasingly appropriated Muhammad for their own propaganda projects, leaving an impact on Islamic tradition. Fred Donner, for example, has argued that it was during this era, specifically the time of ʿAbd al-Malik (r. 685–705 CE), that an original "single shahadah," the testimony that there is no god but God, was replaced by a "double shahadah," testimony both to the oneness of God and the prophethood of Muhammad. Donner does not name a singular cause or motivation for the growing caliphal emphasis on Muhammad: it could have been a rhetorical co-opting from the Umayyads' "anticaliph" opponent, Ibn al-Zubayr (the first to issue coins bearing testimony to Muhammad as messenger of God),[3] and establish religious legitimacy for Umayyad rule. It could have been an effort to unite the community after factionalism and civil war; or, in the age of empires defining themselves by faith confessions—following centuries of the Christian Byzantine empire battling the Zoroastrian Sasanian empire—the Umayyads needed an imperial faith confession of their own. At any rate, the emphasis on Muhammad served to establish a clearer boundary between early Islam, which Donner terms the "Believers" movement, and Jews and Christians. According to Donner, ʿAbd al-Malik and his Umayyad successors "essentially defined 'Islam' as we know it today," establishing the Believers as a distinct religion more effectively separated from the other "Abrahamic" faiths.[4]

Through imperial patronage of scholars, Umayyad rulers actively contributed to early Islamic knowledge production, in a sense "making"

Muhammad as he would appear to later generations of Muslims. As Sean Anthony points out, this does not mean that the Umayyad ruling elites simply forged and fabricated a mass of biographical material about Muhammad as a top-down order to their court scholars.[5] The network of scholars collecting and transmitting hadiths was not at all a singular network with a shared connection to the Umayyad regime but rather a mass of networks with lots of intersection and overlap as well as distinct regional, tribal, and sectarian interests, and diverse relationships to the caliphate. Hadith scholarship existed independently of the government, and sometimes spoke in direct or implied opposition to it. For one example, while the Umayyad caliphate instigated the project of collecting hadiths in writing, we also see an abundance of hadiths that depict Muhammad condemning the practice of writing hadiths. Schoeler has argued that these "anti-writing" hadiths could be linked to anti-Umayyad feelings in Iraq and Medina, perhaps as an expression of hadith scholars' resistance to the Umayyad hadith project.[6] We also have to think not only about how hadith networks were impacted by the court propaganda machine but also about the reverse: scholars' connections shaped the imperial narrative. Ibn Shihab al-Zuhri, one of the most influential scholars in the Umayyad court, was a student of 'Urwa ibn al-Zubayr, the nephew of A'isha and grandson of the first "caliph," Abu Bakr. Among the multiple factors that led to A'isha's immeasurable significance in the development of the Sunni hadith corpus, we have to count the fact that her nephew, himself a foundational jurist in Medina, became a pioneer of Muslim historical writing.

Surveying the earliest biographies of Muhammad, a reader might be struck by the level of detail in descriptions of Muhammad's military expeditions: when and where particular campaigns took place, who participated, and how the spoils were distributed. Even the term for early biographical literature, *maghazi* ("campaigns" or "expeditions") highlights the aspect of Muhammad's life that most interested its producers. The early biographical sources on Muhammad cast him in the molds of both an epic war hero, immortalized for his bravery and sacrifice, and a biblical prophet who was favored by God against his enemies, often with miraculous intervention. Their information may or may not be "authentic," but it does tell us a lot about how early chroniclers of Muhammad's life wanted to think about him. Some of these details expressed specific agendas: amid tensions between Ansars and Mujahirs, the story of a particular campaign might depict one group more favorably than the other. The narrator of a raid could also tell the story in ways glorified his or her own clan, tribe, or family; storytellers often wanted to present their ancestors as "close to the action." Among accounts from the battle of Uhud, for one example, we encounter an odd incident in which a man named Malik ibn Sinan sucked the blood from a wound in Muhammad's cheek; Malik proudly affirms that he drank Muhammad's blood, and Muhammad proclaims that their blood has mixed and that "whoever touches his blood and my blood, the fire of hell will not wound him." The story traces back to Malik's grandson, Rubayh ibn ʿAbd ar-Rahman, who heard it from his father, prolific hadith narrator (and Malik's son) Abu Saʾid al-Khudri.[7] But we also see reporters rehabilitating their ancestors' images in historical memory. In the various stories of the Banu Qurayza, in which Saʾd ibn Muʾadh gives the judgment that the Qurayza's men should be killed, the version in which Saʾd displays the least agency and direct authority—acting not as an appointed judge who will personally decide the matter but only as a consultant to Muhammad—also comes from Saʾd's grandson, who could have sought distance between his grandfather and the verdict.[8]

Studying maghazi literature as it developed over time, Adrien de Jarmy observes that Muhammad grew from "only one character among many" in Islamic military historiography to become *the* central character, arguing, "The character of a Warrior-Prophet emerged only gradually."[9] De Jarmy attributes some of this development to the varied voices that produce Islamic historical memory: "rivalries among the great figures of the beginnings of Islam" could have contributed to a centering of Muhammad.[10] The development of maghazi sources also related to the imperial contexts in which they were produced: for the Umayyads, as memory of early conquests began to fade, maghazi literature preserved a sacred past, and also spoke to an empire experiencing multiple threats at its border. For the later ʿAbbasids, who shifted from an ambitious policy of conquest toward a more defensive strategy centered on the guarding of borders (and as territorial "borders" first appeared as a thinkable concept), the idea of jihad became relevant in ways it had not been before. With it came a new interest in understanding war through the sacred past, as well as a need to determine proper military conduct.[11] De Jarmy argues that as the Byzantines launched new offensives against the ʿAbbasids, and the ʿAbbasids also faced internal struggles amid pro-Umayyad revolts, Muslim traditionists circulated an increasing number of stories about Muhammad, producing a new image of Muhammad as Warrior-Prophet that spoke to the needs of that setting.[12]

Muhammad began his mission as a marginalized, persecuted street preacher, but by the time he passed away, he had become a kind of statesman: he made treaties, collected taxes, led an army, arbitrated disputes, passed legal judgments and handed down punishments, and presided over a growing territory. When he died, his prophetic office closed and the Qur'an's revelation concluded, but the consolidated tribes and towns now forming something like a "nation" or even a new "empire" still required leadership. In Muslim political histories, the notion of the caliphate or "khalifa," signifying meanings like "following," "substituting," and "succeeding"—came to signify an ideal ruler occupying Muhammad's position. The caliph was not a prophet (though we'll see that in premodern and early modern models of sacred kingship, rulers were often invested with a kind of mystical authority) but inherited Muhammad's duty of maintaining harmony, justice, and divine order in the world.

I say "in Muslim political histories" because the concept of khalifa did not exist during Muhammad's lifetime, or even those of his immediate successors—at least not in its modern recognizable meanings. The Qur'an makes reference to khalifa in its discussion of Adam's creation, when God declares an intention to "place a khalifa on the earth." But contrary to modern Qur'an translations that render the term in English as "vicegerent," it's not self-evident that God's designation of Adam signified anything like a political office or rulership. Sarra Tlili has argued that in the Qur'an, "khalifa" does not carry the overtly political meanings with which we have come to read it. Instead, the term's evolving political significance changed how Muslim scholars interpreted the Qur'an, leading Muslims to think of Adam (and the human species by extension) as a kind of divinely appointed governor over the earth.[13]

Just as the Qur'an does not articulate any concept of the caliphate as a political institution, it does not provide the details for any system of government whatsoever, nor does it prescribe Muhammad's specific role in government, apart from his leading the community as the Prophet. Nor does his treaty with the tribes of Medina, so often described as the "Medina Constitution," provide an actual constitution, if by "constitution" we mean the blueprint for a system of government and its processes for making laws. Neither the Qur'an nor the hadiths and biographical literature give any sense of a system by which power could be transferred to another leader in the event of Muhammad's illness or death. The community appears to have been caught completely unprepared for his absence, and even traditions that are interpreted to clearly indicate a successor (whether Abu Bakr or ʿAli) do not lay out a system by which that successor could prepare a government to last after his own demise. Among the four early leaders retroactively termed "rightly guided caliphs," we don't see a consistent process that we could term the model for a long-term "Islamic state." A group of Muslims elected Abu Bakr, who represented the best hope for reconciling rival factions within the community, each of which had their own ideas about how to proceed politically after Muhammad's death. Abu Bakr did not follow the precedent that led to his own election but instead named ʿUmar as his handpicked successor. On his deathbed after having been stabbed multiple times by his Persian slave, ʿUmar authorized a small council of six men to elect their next leader, resulting in the rise of ʿUthman, who would in turn rule for more than a decade before a mob of rebels stormed his house and killed him. Popular sentiment among the rebels and people of Medina gave support to ʿAli, who accepted the position that many believed had rightfully been his all along. Those who opposed ʿAli's regime, most famously Aʾisha, raised forces against him. Though ʿAli defeated Aʾisha's army, he still contended with the revolt by his Damascene governor, Muʾawiyya. Upon ʿAli's assassination, his son and successor Hasan abdicated any claim to power that he might have had; Muʾawiyya assumed what we now call the caliphate, and designated his own son Yazid as his successor. From the roughly thirty years from the death of Muhammad to Muʾawiyya's founding the Umayyad caliphate, we see men coming to power by a small election (Abu Bakr), handpicked designation (ʿUmar), a committee of six candidates choosing from among themselves (ʿUthman), election by mob rule in the aftermath of an assassination and occupation of Medina (ʿAli), victory in a civil war (Muʾawiyya), and hereditary succession (Yazid). While principles of leadership connected to moral virtue and religious knowledge could be traced to the Qurʾan and the Prophet,[14] efforts to formulate an "Islamic" government after Muhammad's death read as largely improvisational.

After less than a century in power, the Umayyad caliphate fell to the ʿAbbasid revolution, named for its leaders' descent from ʿAbbas, uncle of the Prophet. The ʿAbbasid cause of restoring political authority to the family of Muhammad may sound like an exclusively Shiʾi concern, but we have to remember that "Sunni" and "Shiʾi" were not yet fully formed distinctions, that people we might retroactively label as "Sunni" loved the family of the Prophet, and that various camps we might term "Shi'i" had not yet crystallized around a consistent theory of the Imamate as specifically bound to descendants of 'Ali and Fatima. At least in the beginning, the 'Abbasids enjoyed a wide coalition of support that would defy later Sunni-Shi'i binaries.

Mongol invasion in 1258 ended the 'Abbasid caliphate, and with it destroyed Muslim political culture. In the postcaliphate world, new models of kingship grew from Sufi shrines, lodges, and networks, leading to a context in which, as A. Azfar Moin explains, "the institution of kingship became locked in a mimetic embrace with the institution of sainthood . . . the greatest of Muslim sovereigns of the time began to enjoy the miraculous reputations of the greatest of saints."[15] Across the Timurid, Safavid, and Mughal empires, rulers linked themselves to the Prophet in charismatic and "mystical" ways. Though hadith literature condemns astrology, for example, a ruler could authorize himself with an astrological argument that identifies himself and Muhammad as both "Lords of Conjunction," their births linked to the auspicious conjunction of Jupiter and Saturn—thereby linking the king and the Prophet to each other in a grand unfolding of sacred history.[16] The Ottoman Empire would make its own claim on the caliphate, which it asserted more explicitly in an eighteenth-century treaty with Russia, since the title bolstered their claim to represent the interests of Muslims in Russian territory. As flimsy as the claim might have been, its symbolic weight proved immeasurable, particularly with the caliphate's formal dissolution in 1924.

THE JURISTS' MUHAMMAD

I'm going to make a bit of a dramatic statement here and then partially walk it back: there's no such thing as Islamic law.

Of course, Muslim societies have historically had laws, and yes, they presented these laws as Islamic: that is, in accordance with the commands of God and their implementation by Muhammad, and in turn the interpretation of Muhammad's actions by those closest in authority to him (whose identities will differ, depending on your sectarian orientation), and then the understanding of those acts and policies by a rising class of professional scholars, the 'ulama, who could theorize all of this into a working system. We would call this process *fiqh*, jurisprudence, rather than the more famous "shari'a," which literally translates to "way" or "road." If Muslims believe in a divine shari'a as God's prescriptions for human beings, fiqh represents the fallible human effort to understand those prescriptions. So sure, there's Islamic law.

But if by "Islamic law," you mean the image of Islamic law that we usually get in contemporary media—Muhammad arriving with a complete and eternally nonnegotiable legal system in hand—then no. Muslims did not have that, and so they had to make it; and in fact, they disagreed with each other about how to make it, resulting in a multiplicity of schools of fiqh. Across Islamic history, there were hundreds of these schools (*madhahib*), but in 1265 CE, the Ottoman Sultan Baybars gave imperial support to four Sunni schools (the Maliki, Shafi'i, Hanbali, and Hanafi), effectively determining the future of Sunni legal thought (most Shi'is adhere to a fifth madhab, the Ja'fari school). These five schools provide the functional sources of Islamic law.

The Qur'an issues *some* commands but does not itself really function as a legal code. Only a small portion of the Qur'an's verses address anything that we might call "law," and the Qur'an doesn't provide what a legal system needs more than actual laws: a method. The Qur'an gives rules and tells the believers to follow Muhammad, but it does not deliver jurisprudence. For the law to be a workable system and method of attaining truth, rather than simply a list of divinely ordered permissions and prohibitions, it must be postprophetic: it must come after divine revelation has ceased and fallible human jurists are left to make order of a messy world on their own. As Muslim scholars in the early generations sought answers to questions of practice that had not been addressed in Muhammad's lifetime, and Muslim rulers consulted with religious scholars to govern in accordance with God's wishes—which in turn opened up new questions—Muhammad's life, actions, and policies became increasingly important. It is in part through these efforts to *create* Islamic law that the concept of Muhammad's Sunna became so important.

Literally, "sunna" just means "custom" or "habit." The word never appears in the Qur'an in direct reference to Muhammad. Rather, the Qur'an speaks of sunna in reference to any past precedent. The Qur'an mentions the precedent (sunna) of past nations that God had destroyed for their disobedience (18:55), with warnings for Muhammad's contemporary opponents. The Qur'an also says that God had a custom (sunna) for dealing with them (8:38, 33:62), and the *sunnat Allah* does not change (48:23). While "sunna" in the earliest Muslim discourses had this general connotation—Umayyad rulers would boast that they followed the sunnas of the earlier "rightly-guided" caliphs[17]—hadith scholars somewhat quickly came to speak of *the* Sunna as exclusively the precedents set by Muhammad's actions, habits, verbal statements, likes, and dislikes. For those approaching the hadiths with a critical or skeptical eye, this discrepancy of meanings would raise red flags. For some scholars, the fact that words like "khalifa," "jama'a," and "sunna" mean different things in the hadith corpus than they do in the Qur'an demonstrates that these two bodies of text, which are obviously regarded as contemporary to each other, in fact speak from different historical settings.[18] The early origin of the Qur'an's text, in this view, comes at the expense of late hadiths.

Early Muslim jurists agreed that the Sunna was of utmost importance, but they defined and interpreted it in different ways. As I touched on in chapter 4, Malik ibn Anas (711–95 CE), foundational scholar for the Maliki school of jurisprudence, did not advocate the later position that hadiths, reported sayings and actions of Muhammad, served as the most authentic and authoritative source for determining the Sunna. Malik was by no means antihadith; he was a hadith scholar himself, and his *Muwatta* remains an important hadith collection. But in his famous quip, "The Qur'an was not revealed on the Euphrates,"[19] Malik challenged a rising Iraq-centered network of hadith scholars who constructed their grasp of the Sunna through isolated reports and the chains of transmission—individuals reporting from individuals in a line of (ideally) face-to-face encounters, ultimately tracing back to the Prophet—that vetted them. For Malik, there was a more efficient way of learning the Sunna than cataloging and comparing thousands of reports and their reporters: look to the norms of the Medina community as a collective precedent. After all, for Malik, who was born in Medina less than a century after Muhammad and his community of migrants arrived in the city, it was still possible to live among the great-great-grandchildren of the first Muslims who turned Yathrib into the *madinat al-nabi*, the "City of the Prophet." In Malik's view, hadiths were legitimate, but no hadith could overrule the power of an entire city with such a close relationship to Muhammad. Malik's position did not become the rule. Al-Shafi'i (767–820 CE), who had studied directly under Malik and later himself became the namesake for the Shafi'i school, made a convincing argument for the power of hadiths in determining the Sunna, and other schools adjusted to the new paradigm. According to al-Shafi'i, the hadith-determined Sunna was a divine revelation that worked alongside the Qur'an in the making of law; this idea would become foundational for Sunni jurisprudence.[20] As hadith scholars circled the wagons around their own professional field, arguing that their specific knowledge and expertise provided the basis for making and interpreting law, we would see the development of another cornerstone of Sunni thought: belief in Muhammad's Companions as entirely trustworthy reporters of his sayings and actions. Collectively authorizing the Companions in this way enhanced the truthmaking power of hadiths and protected the archive. Shi'i legal thought did not treat the Companions as universally authoritative, but it subscribed to the authority of statements traceable to the Imams. In both Sunni and Shi'i legal traditions, the Prophet's power to make law is mediated and supplemented by a privileged class of knowers.

As Sunni legal schools ground their authority with a claim to transmitted knowledge tracing back to the Prophet and his Companions, a believer trusting in the authority of this transmitted knowledge would engage in taqlid (imitation or following) of a particular school. But some modern Sunni revivalists charge that the tradition of "blindly" following a school is at best unnecessary, and at worst a flagrant deviation from the precedent of Muhammad and his Companions (since neither Muhammad nor the Companions formed "schools" of law). Discourses of the modern Salafiyya movement, emphasizing adherence to the ways of the Salaf (the first three generations of Muslims), would assert that rather than subscribe to a madhab, one can head straight to the sources, the Qur'an and the Sunna. In practice, these "Salafi" Muslims are generally compatible in both theology and practice with the Hanbali school; but their claim is that Muhammad's truthmaking precedent detonates the traditions of jurisprudence, cuts through all of the mediation, warpzones us through more than a dozen centuries, and places us back in direct conversation with the Prophet, his Companions, and their students.

THE PHILOSOPHERS' MUHAMMAD

Scholars of Western philosophy have sometimes struggled on the matter of "Islamic philosophy" as a thing that exists in the world. Some would rather categorize the work of Muslim Aristotelian philosopher Ibn Sina (Avicenna) as "Arabic philosophy" in part because they fail to catch his Islamic references or maintain an attitude that if Ibn Sina were really a committed Muslim with interest in Islamic frameworks, he wouldn't be a philosopher. More broadly, it's popular today to assume that the categories of "philosophy" and "religion" remain absolutely separate, defined by very obvious and nonnegotiable boundaries. We often treat philosophy as inherently secular and religion as inherently opposed to reason; by these terms, philosophy and religion can never come into contact with each other except in hostility and a zero-sum conflict that can only be won by one side. If one accommodates or mixes with the other, it immediately becomes less itself. In our contemporary world, this binary opposition of philosophy versus religion also tends to become racialized fuel for a "clash of civilizations" narrative, in which "the West," imagined as rational and scientific, is defined in contrast against an "East," imagined as mystical and religious.

As with so many binaries, however, a basic skim of history tears the whole opposition down. The philosophy-religion divide doesn't look the same in all times and places, and in many historical contexts, the division doesn't exist at all. This is true both for philosophy as it developed in European Christian settings and the tradition of Islamic philosophy, which remains not only *philosophy* but also *Islamic*. In the early centuries of Islam, Muslim thinkers grappled with the openings and challenges provoked by their readings of pre-Islamic literatures, including foundational Greek philosophers. Muslim engagements of philosophy sparked theological arguments and theories that would forever impact the course of Muslim history: at one point in the ninth century CE, the dominant Islamic caliphate was so committed to a specific reading of Islamic theology, informed by these philosophical engagements, that it imposed its ideas about rationalist interpretation as the official state religion. "By the early ninth century," Bruce Lawrence explains, "no reflection on Allah could avoid the major exponents of Aristotle in Arabic."[21] The Greek intellectual heritage entered into Islamic thought so early that we can't really imagine Islam without it. In turn, Carl Ernst writes that "it was only due to translations from Arabic into Latin that Aristotle was rediscovered in Paris and Oxford."[22] When we complain about the dangers of "mixture," the two things in question were probably already mixed long, *long* before we got there.

Muslim engagements of Greek, Indian, and Persian philosophical heritages emerged in large part through the 'Abbasid caliph al-Ma'mun (r. 786–833 CE), a Muslim philosopher-king whose patronage of translation projects enabled mass waves of literatures to enter into Islamic thought. Al-Ma'mun was also ruler of the above-mentioned regime that sought to establish a rationalist school of theology as state-sponsored, "orthodox" Islam. He was allegedly inspired to promote the translation movement by his dream of a man with "broad forehead, joined eyebrows, bloodshot eyes . . . sitting on his bed." The caliph asked the man to identify himself; the man answered, "I am Aristotle." Al-Ma'mun's account of his dream appears in multiple versions, but in these various retellings, we see Aristotle telling him that reason was fully harmonious with revelation and instructing him to commission the translation of Greek philosophical texts into Arabic. "Knowledge has no boundaries," the philosopher told the king. "To block out ideas is to block out the kingdom of God."[23] With some critical caution, we should note that al-Ma'mun's dream was probably not the cause of the 'Abbasid translation movement but either was caused by it or, more cynically, was a later narrative to privilege and authorize the caliph. Anyway, it would not be the last time that Aristotle showed up in a dream to guide Muslim thinkers. The martyred Sufi theosopher Suhrawardi (d. 1191 CE), whose Illuminationist system named Muhammad, Plato, and Hermes as the most advanced sages, received his own dream visit from Aristotle. In Suhrawardi's dream, Aristotle proclaimed Plato to be his superior, and also identified as the greatest philosophers the Sufi mystics Mansur al-Hallaj and Abu Yazid al-Bistami.[24] Between these dreams of the caliph and the mystic, separated by multiple centuries, we see the development of Aristotle as a fully Islamic figure, a source of *Islamic* knowledge to *Islamic* kings and sages. Muslim engagements of Aristotle and Plato turned them into resources for understanding Islam. Reflecting on their receptions in Islamic thought, Shahab Ahmed writes of their names in Arabic translation, respectively "Aristu" and "Aflatun," as almost corresponding to the creation of new literary characters: "Aristu does not, as a historical phenomenon, *mean* and *do* quite the same things as Aristotle; neither does Aflatun *mean* and *do* quite the same things as Plato."[25]

The contemporary prejudice that would imagine Aristotle not only as a foundational figure for "Western thought" but also as in fact the exclusive territory of a "Western civilization," defined by absolute incompatibility and eternally mutual antagonism with an "Islamic civilization," doesn't hold up against a casual survey of Aristotle's significance in Islam. Aristotle's translation into Arabic in the early centuries after Muhammad places him as a foundational thinker for Islamic theology and prophetology. In the case of theology, Muslim readers of Aristotle applied his thought to their ideas about God; in prophetology, they used Aristotle as a resource for thinking about Muhammad and explaining

Muhammad's status as the Prophet in terms that would make sense for them. Through Aristotle, as Frank Griffel writes, Muslim philosophers developed a "rationalist foundation for the belief that Muhammad was the most perfect of all humans."[26]

Building on Aristotle's conceptions of the soul and Ptolemaic models of the solar system, Muslim philosophers developed a theory of prophethood that presented Muhammad's supernatural experience as a natural phenomenon (and one that was at least theoretically accessible to other humans, with the "orthodox" disclaimer that Muhammad represented prophethood's conclusion). Besides developing a rationalist prophetology that could explain the revelation of knowledge from the unseen in ways that worked for them, these intellectuals also engaged the question of how they could understand Muhammad in relation to their own work: What separated prophets and philosophers?

The special experience of a prophet such as Muhammad or Moses, the philosophers argued, depended on a kind of power inherent to all human beings, though not in equal degrees. It depended on an "imaginative faculty" in the soul. It's through this faculty that we have dreams, which Muhammad had famously declared the one portion of prophethood that would remain accessible after him. Some humans are more developed in this faculty than others, just as humans differ from each other in the development of their rational faculty. With a supremely developed imaginative faculty, a prophet naturally accesses the emanations of knowledge from God that philosophers only access through their intellectual training. Prophetic religion, Griffel explains, was seen by these Muslim philosophers as "an imitation of philosophy, which also means there is no conflict between philosophy and religion"—and also that "the true prophet is also a philosopher," though this does not mean that the philosopher is a kind of prophet.[27]

The difference between prophets and philosophers ultimately rested with their intended audiences. Though a prophet produces (that is, receives) knowledge from the unseen that communicates the same universal truth as philosophers, prophets deliver their knowledge in a highly symbolic form that's more readily comprehensible by the masses. Muslim philosophers saw themselves as communicating a more advanced grasp of the truth than could be readily digested by regular people, who needed supports like anthropomorphic imagery, the Qur'an's descriptions of God as having human attributes and even body parts that seemingly corresponded to human anatomy. Muslim philosophers did not deny the Qur'an or even reject God's self-descriptions, but they believed that their elite intellectual training granted them access to a more advanced theology behind the Qur'an's words. Philosophy was not an opponent of Islam but rather "the version of the Muslim faith that is best for the intellectually gifted believer."[28] In contrast, Ibn Sina (Avicenna) would have seen Muhammad as a philosopher for people who can't do philosophy, but he nonetheless offered prayers and salutations upon "our master" Muhammad and his family, and understood his own thought as *Islamic* thought.[29]

THE MYSTICS' MUHAMMAD

There's a popular tendency to define Sufism as Islam's "mystical dimension" and take the "mystical" here to mean that Sufism prioritizes direct, unmediated experience of God. We can poke a lot of holes in this definition, starting with the ways this individualized and "mystical" definition speaks for a particular modern Sufism rather than the whole of Sufi tradition. When Sufism is transformed in modern "New Age" flows and reimagined as a personal, inner "spirituality," it's easy for us to forget that in many historical settings, Sufism has been deeply institutional and hierarchical, centered around pledges to charismatic masters and their lineages of authority. And while many Sufi luminaries of the past were marginalized and condemned as "heretics" and lawless misfits, others were social elites and enforcers of establishment "orthodoxy." The "New Age" version might present Sufism as an entirely personal, individualistic spirituality opposed to "organized religion" and completely removed from politics, but, historically, Sufism in many contexts has been defined by the power of Sufi lodges as political forces; Sufis have been kings, kingmakers, and revolutionaries. But in a book introducing Muhammad, my biggest complaint about the popular modern rendering of Sufism as "direct experience of God" is the way it often erases Muhammad from Sufi tradition.

In these contemporary rewritings of Sufism, one of the better-known Sufi concepts is *fana' fi-llah*, "annihilation in God," in which the spiritual seeker achieves a kind of "ego death" or dissolution of the self in God. As formulated by early Sufi thinker Junayd (d. 910 CE), the concept can be found in Muhammad's quotation of God as saying that as the seeker draws nearer to God, God becomes "his ear with which he hears, his eye with which he sees, his hand with which he grasps, and his foot with which he walks."[30] According to Junayd, it was impossible for a human being to adequately understand God's perfect unity while still bound to a "sense of self"; properly attaining knowledge of God's unity therefore required the self's disappearance.[31] But this station did not mean the attainment of new knowledge so much as a return to the "real." For example, in the Sufi order to which I had pledged, the Nimatullahi, I was taught that the Islamic testimony of faith, *la ilaha illa Allah* (There is no god but God) really meant that only God truly existed; to believe in my own existence and distinct selfhood was to commit a kind of idolatry. When we "forget" ourselves in God, from this point of view, we more accurately witness how the universe really works.

Fana' fi-llah now reflects the specific presentation of Sufism that circulates most widely in today's world. Lots of people, including many, many Muslims, would define Sufism in a way that centers these ideas: the point of Sufism is to become so conscious of God that you are no longer conscious of yourself. Less known is Sufism's deep tradition of *fana' fi-l-rasul*, "annihilation in the Messenger." In the thought of Ibn al-'Arabi (1156–1240 CE), Muhammad was a template of the *insan al-kamil*, "complete human," who served as the expression of God's attributes in perfect harmony and proportion. Muhammad's embodiment of God's names didn't make him an "incarnation" of God—such an idea would pose a major theological problem for a vast majority of Muslims (but not *all* of them, as we'll see)—but nonetheless meant that thinking about Muhammad or seeing him in dreams or even waking visions became a way of thinking about (and kind of "seeing") God. Ibn al-'Arabi taught that all worshipers of God were obstructed by their own subjectivity, essentially creating God within the limits of their own perception; he uses the example of how a mirror's shape determines what you see in it. But Muhammad himself, who embodied God's various names, offers a flawless mirror in which you can contemplate God (though of course, our perceptions of Muhammad are also limited by the quality of our "mirrors"). The more perfect one's perception of Muhammad, the more perfect one's knowledge of God. As Oludamini Ogunnaike explains in his treatment of the concept in the Tijani order, aspirants framed the self's annihilation in Muhammad in two ways: first, as a stage on the path toward achieving annihilation in God, and second, as a station that occurs *after* annihilation in God.[32]

Rather than conceptualize Muhammad as just a normal human who was born and died in normal human ways, some Sufi traditions favor the idea of a *nur muhammadiyya* or "Muhammadi Light" that preexisted the universe and even became the stuff from which God created everything else. This Muhammadi Light becomes the guidance that all prophets receive, meaning that Muhammad not only precedes prophets such as Jesus but also becomes their teacher in a sense. The concept of nur muhammadiyya varies in its articulations and is not uniquely Sufi (and it should also be remembered that Sufism does not exist as a "third party" outside of Sunni and Shi'i traditions; most Sufi orders are Sunni), but appears in hadith archives and can be found across Muslim traditions. It holds a special salience in Shi'i traditions, as the Muhammadi Light establishes the significance of the Imams' biological descent from the Prophet, as well as the closeness between Muhammad and ʿAli, who himself appears in some treatments as the first thing produced from the light.[33]

The direct experience of Muhammad, beyond its significance for the internal spiritual quest, could also transform one's position in the world. Nearly six centuries after Muhammad's death, he visited the Sufi master Ibn al-ʿArabi in Damascus. Muhammad brought a book, the *Fusus al-Hikam* (Bezels of Wisdom), and instructed Ibn al-ʿArabi to spread it throughout the world. The book is arranged into chapters, each relating a prophet to a key theme, and includes some reinterpretations of prophets' stories that Ibn al-ʿArabi's opponents would regard as evidence of his unforgivable heresies. The most famous example appears in the story of Noah, in which Ibn al-ʿArabi (or the Prophet, as he claimed) seems to depict God as siding with the polytheists against his own prophet! According to the story as retold in the *Fusus*, Noah's comprehension of monotheism was so limited by his belief in God's absolute transcendence that he failed to recognize God in the forms that his people worshiped.[34]

Besides the pursuit of Muhammad as a transcendent encounter, Sufis also achieve linkage to Muhammad through the earthly institution of the tariqas, Sufi orders. These orders demonstrate their connections to the Prophet through the *silsila*, a chain of lineage connecting an order's present master to Muhammad. The final node of connection to the Prophet is almost always ʿAli, whom Muhammad had called the gate to the city of knowledge; the relationship between Sufi master and initiated disciple draws on the template of the greatest master, Muhammad, and the greatest disciple, ʿAli. Sufi lineages mapped relations on the ground and were often politically engaged. As Sufi cultures became part of normative, public Muslim life, rulers could establish their own piety and Islamic credentials by funding the construction and maintenance of shrines for holy figures; the Ottoman construction of Ibn al-ʿArabi's masjid and mausoleum complex bears witness to the infusion of Sufism in the Ottoman Sunni regime. While sultans could appropriate the graves of Sufi saints for their own rhetorical purposes, living Sufi masters could also use their relationship to "baraka"—a term clumsily translated as "blessings" but in practice more like a holy energy or force—as a bargaining chip in negotiations with rulers.[35]

In their conceptions of Muhammad, Sufi traditions overlap with traditions of Islamic poetry, which themselves become routes to baraka and direct experience of the Prophet. In one example, Ogunnaike explains that twentieth-century Sufi master Shaykh Ahmadu Bamba (d. 1927 CE), founder of the Muridiyya order in Senegal, devoted two decades almost entirely to praising Muhammad in poetry.[36] Islam's rich poetry archive includes an abundance of poems praising Muhammad, either inspired by, or attempting to invite, Muhammad's appearance in dreams and visions. The most famous artifact in this genre is the *Qasidat al-Burda* ("Garment Ode") of al-Busiri (d. 1298 CE), an Egyptian Sufi in the Shadhiliyya order and contemporary of Ibn al-ʿArabi. After suffering a stroke, al-Busiri sought healing through Muhammad by composing poetry for him. In a vision, al-Busiri experienced Muhammad's direct presence: Muhammad wiped al-Busiri's face with his hand and placed his outer garment (*burda*) upon him. Al-Busiri's *Qasidat al-Burda* became a classic of poetic praise for Muhammad, recited throughout the world, translated into numerous languages, and an element of material culture, appearing in elaborate calligraphy on masjid walls. In Ottoman art and architecture, visual representations of the poem developed in stylistic correspondence to the *hilya* tradition of reproducing accounts of Muhammad's body from the hadith corpus in beautiful visual forms. Like hilya works, the *Qasidat al-Burda* was treated as a potent Islamic amulet; since the poem healed al-Busiri after his stroke, it was believed that the text's power could extend to those who read and recited the poem or carried it on their person.[37]

THE ASTROLOGERS' MUHAMMAD

No, Muhammad was not an astrologer, and while "never say never" is my general rule about big religious traditions overflowing with historical diversity, I don't know of any Muslim effort to portray him as one (though Muslim occult traditions have portrayed Idris, a prophet mentioned briefly in the Qur'an and usually identified as the biblical Enoch, as a teacher of astrology whose knowledge of the star was divinely revealed). But we could still have a conversation about the depictions of Muhammad in Islamic astrology.

Is there, or *can* there be, such a thing as "Islamic astrology?" Without getting into the question of who reads a religion "correctly," since I'm not writing from clerical authority here: yes, historically speaking, of course there's Islamic astrology, just as there's Christian astrology and Jewish astrology even if an abundance of Christian and Jewish authorities condemn astrologers. In the premodern world, Christian, Jewish, and Muslim astrologers argued with each other in defense of their religions, using their various calculations to contend that the stars proved them right. Astrology, after all, was a science, and the boundary between astrology and astronomy (or between the modern categories of science, religion, and magic)[38] wasn't always so clear in every time and place. If God made and controlled the stars, why wouldn't the stars contain signs of divine truth?

Many, many Christians would believe that Christianity "officially" condemns astrology as an occult practice, possibly even informed by demons, but they miss the presence of astrology in their most sacred narratives. My students from Christian backgrounds are often puzzled, for example, when I ask them to name the event in the New Testament in which Jesus is endorsed by Zoroastrian priestly astrologers. The notion of Jesus's truth being confirmed by both astrology and a separate religion beyond the Israelite or "Abrahamic" milieu seems completely unthinkable to them until we walk through the Gospel of Matthew's account of the Magi, popularly rendered as completely decontextualized "wise men," who come from the East to honor the birth of Jesus. How did the Magi know about him? They recognized that Jesus had arrived through their *science of reading the stars*. Christians who opposed astrology had some delicate navigation to do. Meanwhile, there were also early Christians who scheduled baptisms on astrologically auspicious days.[39]

Historically speaking, Islam also includes some tension on the point of astrology, namely the conflict between what some scholarly authorities present as "real" Islam and the ways other Muslim scholars—along with everyday Muslims in their regular lives—perceived astrology's relationship to their tradition. Astrology doesn't boast "orthodox" Islamic support today. You can visit any "e-fatwa" website in which an Internet cleric answers questions and makes proclamations about the nature of true Islam, and find an essentially universal condemnation of astrology, often expressed with the most severe charges possible: that to indulge in occult knowledge of the stars amounts to no less than *shirk*, basically making you an idol worshiper. They would cite as evidence a decent pile of hadith texts in which Muhammad issues these judgments on the science of interpreting stars. At the same time, hadith texts also depict Muhammad's arrival as recognized by an astrologer from another religious faith—in his case, the Christian emperor Heraclius.[40]

When the ʿAbbasid caliphate embarked on its momentous translation project, rendering heaps of Greek, Persian, and Indian volumes of philosophy and science into Arabic, translators intensified the flows of astrological knowledge in Muslim-majority societies. The hadith scholars who charged that the Prophet had declared all astrology to be illicit *sihr* (occultism or magic) did not have a monopoly on interpretation. Contrary to the objections of some Islamic authorities, many Muslims engaged astrology as not only a legitimate mode of knowledge but also as an Islamically affirmed one. The early Muslim astronomer and philosopher al-Kindi (d. 870) believed astrology to be a valid science, and moreover argued that it did not reflect a denial of God or worship of false idols. Just the opposite, al-Kindi held that astrology proved God's supreme unity and dominion over the universe. For al-Kindi, the notion that the movements of stars could have a relation to events on Earth demonstrated beyond doubt that a single creator and ruler was in charge.[41] The entire universe worked as one machine, designed and operated by one intelligence. Muslim intellectuals who upheld astrology's validity understood Islam through that lens. Muslim astrologers could see the truth of Islamic theologies and cosmologies in their work; they could also use their astrological archives to interpret Muhammad, as in early Muslim astrologer Abu Maʾshar (d. 886), who applied his knowledge of celestial bodies to interpret Muhammad's ascension through the seven spheres.[42] As mentioned in our discussion of Muslim sacred kingship, astrological readings, particularly grounded in belief that the alignment of Jupiter and Saturn corresponded to major world events and the appearances of transformative leaders, enabled Muslim rulers to present themselves as cosmologically linked to the Prophet. The age of mystical or sacred kingship has passed, however, and in today's world we don't see Jupiter-Saturn conjunction theory used in Muslim political projects, state rhetorics, or "proof of Islam" pamphlet literature. Whether or not astrology is acceptably "Islamic," of course, depends on the specific sources that a Muslim views as authentic and authoritative, along with the mediating figures—scholars, clerics, commentators, family members, informal mentors, and so on—that she or he trusts as reliable interpreters of those sources. So while I won't proclaim whether astrology can or cannot be "Islamic," I can at least say that in astrology's ups and downs throughout Islamic history, we see how Muslim intellectuals used the varied sciences and worldviews of their own historical moments to prove the greatness of Muhammad.

MUHAMMAD THE AVATAR?

For many readers, this will be the point at which we drive the car off the cliff. It's one thing to isolate and explore different aspects of Muhammad—breaking him down thematically as bringer of ritual praxis and law, mystical guide, idealized battlefield hero, philosopher-king, and so on—but it's something else to consider that multiple communities have imagined Muhammad as a representation of God. Of course, many would struggle to call such a phenomenon "Islamic"; my only answer is that if we're looking at Islam as a historical tradition, surrendering the question of whether a specific expression of Islam satisfies "orthodox" prerequisites, veneration of Muhammad as divine constitutes a historical, observable Islamic phenomenon.

Though my academic training inhibits me from indulging in an "all Muslims everywhere believe _____" kind of statement, this might be as close as we can get: it doesn't seem completely unreasonable to say that many, many, *many* Muslims would agree on the importance of monotheism as a central, nonnegotiable, and unchanging value of Islam. *There is no god but God.* As outsiders looking in, non-Muslims are also likely to take for granted that Islam commands absolute and "pure" monotheism, and no sincere Muslim would ever think of betraying or even complicating this apparently simple truth. In the heyday of colonial Orientalism, we saw a ton of Western scholars declaring Islam's fundamental core concept to be an uncompromising monotheism; some saw Islamic monotheism as kind of honorable in its alleged simplicity, while others treated it as a sign of intellectual backwardness, rigid fundamentalism, and even a kind of racial disability shared by Arabs and Jews, who were both seen by Aryanists as unable to think about God in more theologically abstract and sophisticated ways than as a sky-father sitting in a throne, throwing lightning bolts and issuing laws (mysticism and philosophy could only become Islamic, these Orientalists charged, when Islam became Persian—that is, "Aryan").[43]

Again, even as an academic who lives in constant fear of falling into essentialisms of one kind or another, it's hard to deny the importance of monotheism in Muslim traditions. Yes, as far as anything's "universal," we could call the belief in one god a universal priority for Muslims. But there's still a problem: How do we define monotheism? What are its key features and outer limits? Where's the line that, when crossed, takes you out of monotheism into something else? Even if Muslims agree on monotheism as a central value of Islam, they still disagree with each other over monotheism's terms and limits; and throughout history, Muslims have accused each other of violating monotheism's boundaries and becoming *mushrikun*, polytheists.

The Qur'an itself challenges people who self-identify as monotheists, most obviously Christians for the belief that God could father a son; but it has also been argued that the communities identified in the Qur'an as mushrikun, the practitioners of pre-Islamic "pagan" or jahiliyya religion, could have understood themselves as monotheists too. They worshiped the God of Abraham, after all, but like Christians, they apparently believed that God was a father, and worshiped a trinity of beings (al-Lat, al-Uzza, and Manat) as God's daughters (and/or angels). Rather than speak as a singular voice of monotheism to a world of polytheism, the Qur'an could be charging other monotheists with having "lapsed" in their commitment to God's unity.[44] In classical Muslim theological debates, questions over God's attributes, self-descriptions in the Qur'an, and relationship to the Qur'an itself (i.e., did God "create" the Qur'an or did the Qur'an, as *God's speech*, necessarily exist outside time?) led elite Muslim intellectuals to charge each other with violating God's transcendent unity. This is all to say that monotheism, like all of our concepts, amounts to a social construction. Human beings produce it in the course of their various arguments and truth-projects. Muslims might agree on a core value like "no god but God" but still struggle against each other to define what that means. In numerous contexts, there have been Muslim communities with ideas about God that the overwhelming majority of Muslims across history would reject as completely opposed to Islamic monotheism. And some of these ideas involve Muhammad.

Most Muslims would find it unthinkable, for example, to consider the idea of God's occupying a physical body or "incarnating" himself into a human being. In popular Islamic theological vocabulary, this concept would be called *hulul* and serves as grounds for disqualifying someone's claim to be Muslim. Many Muslims treat their opposition to hulul as a definitive feature of Islam in contrast to Christianity. When I was a teenager coming to Islam from a Christian background, this distinction appealed to me: Muhammad is not the "Muslim Christ," and we don't worship him. That's true most of the time, but it would not be accurate to call this the position of all Muslims across time and space. Some Muslims have, in fact, conceptualized Muhammad as divine. The early encounters between Muslim forces and the crumbling Persian Empire resulted in indigenous Iranian concepts becoming lenses through which people came to understand Muhammad. From these intersections flowed sectarian communities asserting that God had incarnated himself in Muhammad's body (as God also did with earlier prophets and/or members of Muhammad's family). While Muslim interpreters of the Qur'an disputed the meanings of Muhammad's encounter with the unnamed *shadid al-qawwa* (mighty in power) in the fifty-third sura, contesting whether Muhammad saw God or only the angel Gabriel, a movement known as the Mubayyida read the verses in question to reveal that God actually entered Muhammad's physical form.[45] A number of early Shi'i groups branded as *ghulat*, "exaggerators," identified 'Ali as God. The Mukhammisa held that God appeared in the forms of Muhammad (representing the divine essence) as well as his daughter Fatima, 'Ali, and their sons Hasan and Husayn.[46] Other groups believed that prior to Muhammad, God had occupied the bodies of earlier prophets, such as Noah and Moses, returning to his throne after each one died in turn. A group called the Minhaliyya believed that God could also incarnate himself in plants, animals, jinns, angels, or any other form he wanted; they reportedly argued that if some created beings (such as the angel Gabriel) could change their form, but God was unable to change his own form, God's creations possessed a power that he lacked.[47] In South Asian Islamic traditions, theological boundaries between Islam and Hinduism were not always so clearly defined; prior to the modern reification of these categories, the borders were more fluid and Muhammad's special ontology could be articulated in Hindu terms. As Ayesha Irani explains in her investigation of the *Nabivamsa*, the first epic on Muhammad in Bangla, the text presents

Muhammad as an *avatara* of Vishnu.[48] Irani adds that the *Nabivamsa's* treatment of Muhammad is not unprecedented in South Asian Islam, as a number of Muslim communities identified either Muhammad or ʿAli as Vishnu's tenth avatara.[49]

These traditions would sometimes come back onto my radar during my work with the Five Percenters. Most Five Percenters, believing that they were gods, did not consider themselves Muslims and would emphatically reject the label if asked; but even Five Percenters who self-identified as non-Muslims often claimed that their teachings were the very foundation of Islam. What they called "knowledge of self"—that is, recognition of one's self as Allah—represented the true message of Muhammad, which had been suppressed through the centuries but revealed itself at points along the way, most notoriously in the legend of Sufi martyr al-Hallaj's proclamation, "Ana al-Haqq" ("I am the Reality"), calling himself by a name of God. I've known multiple Five Percenters who drew from the thought of Ibn al-ʿArabi or even accepted initiation in Sufi orders, and some would refer to sayings of Muhammad in the most canonical hadith collections to articulate the *Islamic* character of Five Percenter theology.

If Muhammad, widely perceived as the paragon of nonnegotiable Abrahamic monotheism, could be reimagined by Muslims as an avatara of a Hindu god, have we landed at the conclusion that Muhammad is simply whatever people want him to be?

CONCLUSIONS, OR MUHAMMAD FOR POSTMODERNIST ACADEMICS

Muslims historically have asked, "Who is Muhammad?" and found their own answers, using their own knowledge and experience. If Muhammad is the template for how to live in this world as the most complete humans that we can be, we look to him as a resource for engaging the world as we know it. So kings want a Muhammad who represents the ideal ruler, mystics want Muhammad as the ideal mystic, philosophers want to rethink prophets as kinds of philosophers, and jurists want Muhammad as the supreme legislator. Muhammad's biographers in late antiquity envisioned him as the history-making "great man" whose special destiny was marked from cradle to grave with supernatural signs, miraculous survival, and epic victories on the battlefield. Muslims in the modern age of scientific rationality often seek a Muhammad who's not only compatible with modern science but in fact preceded or influenced its development in some way. Muslim converts coming from Christian or Jewish backgrounds will bring their prior knowledge and sources, such as the Bible, into their understanding of Muhammad, emphasizing his place in traditions of "Abrahamic" prophethood alongside figures such as Moses and Jesus. These different subjectivities can intersect, overlap, or complement one another (some kings are also mystics, after all, and some mystics are also philosophers); or they can even compete with one another. But it's simply how we as human beings work with the materials that we have, hoping to answer the unique problems of our respective times and places.

There is where I should make the perhaps surprising announcement, if it had not become clear already, that I am a human being with personal beliefs, values, and experiences, my understandings of which remain limited. When I compile sources and then subject them to my analysis for the purpose of presenting an artifact to you as "Muhammad," I am not performing these functions as a robot or as a brain in a jar, or as a mystical master receiving messages from beyond the clouds; I can only do the work of a human body fully embedded within this world. In addition to my identity as human, I am also a professional scholar. Sometimes these two identities feel mutually incompatible, but I keep going.

I entered this work because I believed that it was worth the years of graduate school and subsequent life of research, writing, and teaching. I became a professional scholar by entering a program of training at the hands of other professional scholars, who themselves cared about their work and believed that it could offer things of value to the world. None of us picked our academic specializations randomly out of a hat; my mentors and I were brought to each other by the things that we value. This means that even if I tried to perform a personally uninvested academic "objectivity," the fact would remain that I'm here because I care about something, and I was trained by humans who also care about things. I hope that students enroll in my courses because they care about things, and finally, my intended audience for this book consists of human beings who care about things; I hope that you wanted more from this book than a bare list of facts, names, and dates. So if I'm writing this book because I believe that it's a good thing for me to do, for whatever reason that might be, I am already manifesting an emotional investment, in fact a tangled mess of emotional investments, that makes this project happen.

One of my mentors told me, "Every project begins with a question." Calling a book *Who Is Muhammad?* at least implies that my question is obvious. But writing the book is not only a matter of giving you the answer (my version of the answer, anyway); it also forces me to return to my bookshelves and rethink my answer. I ask *myself*, "Who is Muhammad?," which of course means asking a thousand more questions. I ask the questions that I ask, and get the answers that I get, through the lens of my training in the academic study of religion, which means that my questions and answers would be different if I had been an art historian, or a military historian, or an archaeologist, or worked in psychoanalytic theory.

If it looks like I treat Muhammad as a fluid, shapeshifting thing, defined not by some absolute and nonnegotiable "real" Muhammad but always reinvented through the perspectives of human beings who imagine him, this is still not the "real" Muhammad, or at least not the only "real" Muhammad available. He's a Muhammad that reflects my own context, the world in which I inhabit and search for things like "truth" and "meaning" with the tools and concepts that I have.

As an academic working in the humanities, I think with and within something called "critical theory," the origins of which can be traced back to the Frankfurt School in 1920s Germany. Though I spent more time as a graduate student working directly with Islamic sources than reading foundational critical theorists such as Walter Benjamin, critical theory defined my field and the institutions in which I learned to read those Islamic sources. What does this mean for my Muhammad? You've seen it already. I'm generally skeptical of grand narratives, universalizing theories, and assumptions of timeless "natural" categories. Recognizing things like race and gender as malleable expressions of culture (rather than timeless, unchanging nature) that are socially constructed (and therefore inescapably shaped by issues of power and privilege), I turn to the category of "religion" and more specifically "Islam" with that same skepticism. This means that when I see someone claim, "Through the ages, religion has always _____" or "Islam says _____," I can't help but put up my guard. As a category, "religion" doesn't consistently mean the same things "through the ages"; as my mentor Carl Ernst would show his students, all we need to do to make this point is skim dictionary definitions of "religion" in recent centuries and track the ways they change. Likewise, "Islam" doesn't "say" things, and it certainly doesn't speak with the same voice through all Muslims who claim it, everywhere, across the centuries. I tell students that I don't study Islam as something outside or beyond human culture (a "glowing green ball" above the fray, as my mentor Juliane Hammer put it), since I have no access to such a thing, being contained within the limits of human culture and language myself. Instead of studying "Islam" as something with an intrinsic character that remains consistent forever, I only study *Muslims*, and what Muslims say, do, and think, which changes across different historical contexts.

Studying religion through human beings—who obviously differ from each other in their access to power and the capacity to speak for their tradition—we land at a sensitivity to religious "orthodoxy" as a product of these on-the-ground conditions. Like race or gender, religious orthodoxy is made by power. In religion class at my Catholic high school, I learned about the "true" Church's victories over early "heretical" sects; Sunni Muslim narratives would also recall the various "heretics" and "innovators" who tried (but failed) to take over "true" Islam. Even within Shiʾi tradition, defined in no small part by a self-consciousness of losing the struggle for power, one can find a sense of "true" or "orthodox" Shiʾism victorious over "false" or "heretical" variants. Somehow, the "correct" version of a religion always seems to survive and give its side of the story.

In my classroom, I tell students that I work with a *constructivist* framework, meaning that these religions are social constructions, rather than an *essentialist* one, in which each religion has a timeless, innate "core." Therefore, we'll be approaching religions with a *descriptive* lens, meaning that we engage them as observable phenomena in the world (i.e., "What do Muslims do?") rather than a *prescriptive* one (as in, "Which Muslims correctly understand the Qurʾan?"). I joke with them that academia has poisoned my soul forever, but in all seriousness, my academic training leaves a wound on my off-campus, personal experience of being Muslim. I remain mostly unable to approach the Qurʾan as a Muslim interested in what it "really" says and means, because I remain too sensitive to the issues of language, the problems of translation, the battles over interpretation, and all the baggage that we as readers bring to our texts. Whenever I come to a sense of what "real" Islam could look like for me, the speed bumps of my scholarship slow me down. Whether or not the Qurʾan actually speaks from a divine transcendence outside the world and worldly time, I can only access it *in* the world through my human language, concepts, and knowledge, all of which are of course limited. The idea of the Qur'an as God's eternal uncreated speech doesn't really help much in terms of what I can confidently do with it.

I remember a lecture that I gave on my book *Muhammad's Body*, which focuses its attention, as the title suggests, on ways Muslim sources (in this case, specifically Sunni hadith texts) depicted Muhammad's body in the early centuries of Islam. In the question-answer portion, someone asked about the discrepancy I observed in hadiths concerning Muhammad's physical appearance: some hadiths described his complexion as a mixture of "white" (which, in the skin color vocabularies of the historical setting, would have signified a light brown) and "red" (which would have been closer, in terms of skin color, to modern meanings of "white"), while others described his skin as neither extremely dark nor pale, but medium. My interlocutor in the audience had a very straightforward question: "Which was it?" I tried to explain that my interest was in the things these different hadiths told us about the people who circulated them. For whatever reason, hadiths describing Muhammad as a mixture of white and red were often linked to 'Ali, and narrations describing Muhammad as medium-complexioned or light brown were more typically attributed to Anas. At first glance, this could suggest a difference between how people remembered Muhammad's body in Medina as opposed to Basra nearly 900 miles away. The accounts of Muhammad's "medium" complexion accompany similar descriptions of his height and hair texture, imagining Muhammad's body as a balance between extremes. This resonated with Greek literature on physiognomy (which would have been circulating in Arabic fairly early in Islamic history), in which bodily moderation represented perfection; in fact, some hadiths describing Muhammad's appearance correspond closely to a Greek physiognomic text.[50] None of these hadiths are going to give us the equivalent of photographic evidence, but they offer insights into how early Muslims thought about bodies and how they would depict a perfect or idealized human form. I gave a very theoretical "academic study of religion" answer, but it was not enough for this person. To his eyes, my refusal to claim hard empirical "facts" about how Muhammad's body "really" looked only exposed a weakness in my work.

When introducing a religion to unfamiliar readers or students, I think that tracking multiplicity and historical change does something powerful, in part because we so often imagine religions as forever frozen in time or even violently resistant to change of any kind. For students who walk into the classroom with an idea of Islam as aggressively and absolutely consistent, capable of speaking with only one voice and one set of meanings wherever we find it, and instantly degrading into a compromised, "less Islamic" form whenever it encounters change, it's helpful to see just how many different ways Muslims have conceptualized Muhammad. But I want to do something more here than just throw my hands up and say that there's no "real" Muhammad, Muhammad is only what you make him in your own imagination, everything is fluid and malleable and subject to shocking transformations, and traditions are thus incoherent and unstable, forever in flux. That's all true, kind of. And calling attention to this historically undeniable messiness has been a big part of my work: as a scholar, I find it compelling for the ways it forces us to rethink our questions and the assumptions that drive them, and as a Muslim, I have found it personally empowering and enriching while I try to navigate Muhammad's significance in my own off-campus life. But Muhammad's *not* only what I want him to be, and he's not what I say he is. If I'm alone in my house and decide one day to make a new vision of Muhammad exactly as I desire him, pulling books from my shelves and choosing which sources and stories will contribute to my rethinking of the Prophet and which ones will be ignored and forgotten, I can do that. If I want to drink ayahuasca with a shaman and have a direct encounter with Muhammad that leaves me personally devastated (in good ways, healing ways) for years, I can do that; I *have* done that. But when I step out of my house, my Muhammad must negotiate with the available options.

After my first ayahuasca encounter with Muhammad, I slowly staggered into a Sunni masjid, washed for prayer as I had been taught two decades earlier, went to the prayer area, and performed a normative Sunni salat—again, consistent with the Hanafi school in which I had first learned Muslim prayer as a teenager. My personal dimethyltryptamine-powered reconstruction of Muhammad did not turn the masjid upside-down or destabilize Islam for anyone else in the room. Nor have we seen a swelling critical mass of ayahuasca-drinking Muslims emerge to provoke a new crisis in Islamic thought. With enough historical accidents, something like that could happen, but it would take an immeasurable shock to the system for a new hegemon of Islamic orthodoxy to emerge in which ayahuasca visions of Muhammad became an authoritative source for rewriting law. It's not technically *impossible*, since history gets weird sometimes, but I don't see it happening.

We can do our analysis based on the notion that "Muslims' ideas about Muhammad change over time, and we reinvent historic figures through the limited lenses of our own world," but my point would not be to deconstruct Muhammad beyond any hope of putting him back together, or imagine that Muslims have no way of making Muhammad coherently say, do, or mean things. Muhammad's meanings and values do change, the sources through which Muslims engage him change, and Muslims change too, meaning that we want different things from our Muhammad at different times. But rather than reduce Muhammad to "whatever Muslims want him to be," I would have to recognize that communities have ways of anchoring their meanings, and coherence comes as the product of a struggle.

I continue to access Muhammad more through academic literature than Friday sermons, which means that the image of a historically fluid, malleable Muhammad who means different things at different times to different people remains essentially the only Muhammad I have. This always-a-construct, always-fluid Muhammad isn't very helpful in solving problems of theology or practice: the "Muhammad's what you make him" shrug doesn't often provide satisfying evidence. But sometimes, I get a sense that with my Muslim academic friends, we share in this deconstructed Muhammad of seemingly infinite possibilities, as though such a Muhammad might nourish us and bring us into community with each other.

CHAPTER SIX

Modern Muhammads

What changes when religion enters the modern world? *Everything.* Everything has changed. The way we read our sacred books has changed. The way we imagine "sacred books" as a kind of thing that we expect all religions to have has changed. The books themselves have changed: the idea that any believer could be expected to possess a copy of the Qur'an or Bible, which she or he reads for content and that may even be translated into another language, is entirely modern. It couldn't have happened before mass printing, cheap paper, and standardized education. The way we think of ourselves as individuals relating to a religion, equipped with an intellect to make meaning in the religion for ourselves, has changed. And of course, as any decent intro to religious studies course tries to make clear, the definition of "religion" itself has changed. It's only a slight exaggeration to suggest that everything we imagine as "traditional" is perhaps 200 years old; and if it's more than 200 years old, it has been transformed immeasurably by historical processes of the past two centuries.

As much as modernity has impacted religion, traditions abound with seekers who pursue an escape tunnel through centuries of accumulated history to recover the lost "real," the pure origins buried under time. The idea that modernity's problems can be answered with a return to pure "tradition" and recovery of an original essence, however those things might be defined, leads in multiple directions. The desire for a time machine that can return us to a sacred past or lost "golden age" is itself neither conservative nor progressive but feeds all kinds of diagnoses about where exactly "modernity" went wrong and what we need to fix it. However your own values measure the spectrum of Muslim intellectuals, it's likely that the "best" and "worst" at your spectrum's far ends both rely on the idea that we need to reclaim the spirit at the origins but remain inescapably modern. ISIS might have looked "anti-modern" to many observers, but it remained modern at every step, from its inconsistent and radically destabilized approach to Islamic law to its uses of social media to its drawing from the strategies of drug cartels in its production of videos. At the other end, progressive Muslim thinkers who have articulated new visions of gender and sexual inclusivity do not always present their ideas as new but rather make their own claims to the truest meanings of the Qur'an and legacies of Muhammad. We all want to search the sacred past and find ourselves there.

"Who is Muhammad?," then, reads as a different question than "Who *was* Muhammad?," because modern Muslims, processing Muhammad's legacy while separated from him by more than fourteen centuries, will recode a modern Muhammad. Even if our sources are old, we can only perceive Muhammad through the lenses that the modern world has given us, and ask questions of him that are meaningful in our own feelings and experiences.

MUHAMMAD AND "FUNDAMENTALISM"

Are the changes brought by modernity always for the better? We often assume that when religions become more "modern," they must also become more "tolerant," progressive, and inclusive. However, all religions in the modern world are already modern because they're here now, and the violent bigotry that troubles modernity is itself modern, a product of the same forces that are supposed to produce new and "enlightened" forms of religion. Modern insistences on rationalist interpretation sometimes shut down resources that in another age would have helped to expand the meanings of a text. Modern obsessions with policing boundaries, particularly as expressed in modern nationalism, can also sever connections. The case could be made that Muslim-Hindu relations in South Asia, now driven by competing nationalisms, are more troubled than they had been in previous centuries; that the Sunni-Shiʾi divide, rather than some timeless and inevitable hostility, has been more exacerbated by antagonism between the modern nation-states of Saudi Arabia and Iran than it was in the era of the Ottoman Empire, which was a Sunni construct but maintained Shiʾi sites in the Arabian Peninsula and Iraq; and that minority "heterodox" communities such as the Ahmadiyya undergo more severe persecution under the modern state of Pakistan than they would have in an era more friendly to Sufism. And contrary to the notion that encounters with the West make everyone friendlier and more enlightened (since the "West" is so often conflated with idealized notions of the "modern"), we can argue that the impact of Western hegemony actually intensified homophobia in Muslim-majority societies, reconstructing sexuality in ways that erased preexisting resources and ironically *diminished* the possibilities for same-sex love in Muslim spaces.[1]

Before going any further, I need to get a bit punchy about the word "fundamentalism." In the first week of a semester, when I ask students what they hope to learn from our course, many will answer that they hope to have a better understanding of "Islamic fundamentalism." What I've learned is that whether or not I believe that "fundamentalism" is actually a meaningful term (and I don't), it gets people in the room. If only for the chance to do some deconstruction and antiracist work, I'm happy to have the "fundamentalism" conversation. The notion of "fundamentalism" speaks from a popular assumption, grounded in histories of Western Christianity and secularism, that the most intellectually rigid, antihermeneutic, uncompromising, intolerant, coercive, and ultimately violent version of a religion is in fact its most authentic and scripturally legitimate version. The truest reading of an ancient religion, in this view, is the one that puts it most at odds with the modern world. I've occasionally seen a soft expression of this view in Muslim communities, in which Muslims—particularly young Muslims who want to do the right thing but remain cautious, recognizing their lack of scholarly credentials—might take it as a natural given that when discussing issues of gender interaction as a community event, the most conservative answer to a question is probably the most genuine. Far, far removed from those contexts, we've also seen an ongoing flood of Islamophobic commentators who assume that groups such as al-Qaeda and ISIS represent the inescapable true essence of Islam, and that any Muslims who reject the Islamic grounds for these groups must be either dishonest or ignorant as to what Islam's canonical sources "really" say. The Islamophobic commentators tend to picture Islamic tradition as one timeless, unchanging, massive uncarved block with no internal diversity: it simply is what it is. In this sense, Islamophobes and the people that they describe as "fundamentalists" are strangely compatible in their views of how religions, scripture, and believers relate to one another; both sides read with a narrowness that betrays and defies history.

Since the label of "fundamentalism" comes from a North American Christian context (from Christians who self-identified as fundamentalists to boast of their faithfulness to the Bible), I'll leave it here and keep moving. When we talk about "fundamentalists" in Islamic contexts, we're often referring to a somewhat amorphous phenomenon known as the Salafiyya or Salafism, so let's start there. The term refers to the Salaf, the first three generations of Muslims. The basic idea of Salafism is that the most authoritative representatives of Muhammad are those Muslims who were chronologically closest to him, starting with the supremely authoritative generation of his Companions, then the Companions' students, and finally the students of the Companions' students. For a doctrinal point or practice to be considered genuinely Islamic, Salafi Muslims would argue, it must be grounded in the practices of the Salaf, who collectively embody the Sunna, the teachings and norms of the Prophet. In the Salafi view, the most profound challenge facing Muslims is the avoidance of *bida'*, "innovation," meaning any concept or practice that departs from the Salaf's example. We see this theme of Sunna versus bida' in all kinds of unresolved questions and debates in Muslim communities. Celebrating the Prophet's birthday, building elaborate shrines over the graves of holy people and performing ritual visitation (*ziyarat*) to them, joining Sufi orders, celebrating Christmas with non-Muslim friends and family, listening to music, going to mixed-gender parties, and engaging in group appeals to God after a congregational prayer are all points on which Muslims often disagree, and the disagreements hinge on the problem of bida'. At stake is the question of how one feels about the Sunna: what exactly the term means, where we go to find it, who best represents it, and how one either fulfills or violates it. Salafism also calls to a certain feeling about how to read the Qur'an; when we mine the Qur'an to uncover its esoteric meanings, trying to understand the Qur'an beyond the bare text of the words and Muhammad's explanations to his

Companions, we depart from the bounds of the real. If Muhammad's Companions represent the greatest generation of Muslims in history, the Salafi narrative holds, we don't need any interpretation of the Qur'an that they had not received from the Prophet or communicated to their own students. Islam as they understood it is better than whatever we might make for ourselves.

Looking to the example of the Salaf is not itself controversial, at least within Sunni traditions (Shi'i Muslims, drawing from a different understanding of early Islamic history, would not view all of the Salaf as collectively authoritative); both the valorization of the Salaf and condemnation of bida' find support in canonical Sunni hadith collections. But it shouldn't be a surprise that two believers in the same texts might hold opposing views of what those texts mean and how to best apply them.

Though an ironically *modern* phenomenon, Salafism traces back to important thinkers in classical Islamic traditions. These predecessors do not represent the organic "center" of original Islam but merely one option among many in the intellectually vibrant milieus in settings such as Iraq during the eighth through the tenth centuries CE. During this period, Muslims were approaching the Qur'an through numerous resources, including hermetic and "occult" traditions and Greek, Persian, and Indian philosophy. As we saw in chapter 5, Muslim thinkers formulated a prophetology in which Muhammad was reimagined as a kind of intuitive philosopher, and philosophers in turn could see their work as not exactly prophetic but at least capable of reaching prophets' intuitive insights through rigorous intellectual work. Elite Muslim theologians thus developed a hierarchy of understanding in which the masses depended on prophets to deliver revelation in a simple form that they could grasp, while the educated elites could look behind the words of revelation to engage those words in deeper ways. This meant that when God describes himself as having hands and sitting in a chair, seemingly defying God's absolute transcendence over all description and comparison to earthly things, the common believers should simply accept it without interpretation; but the intellectuals could probe such verses for metaphorical meanings, such as reading God's "hands" to signify his power.[2]

Amid diverse schools of thought flowering in early Islam, we find a network of hadith scholars that would gradually crystallize as a kind of sectarian group, popularly known as the *ahl al-hadith* or "Hadith Folk." Having devoted their lives to traveling and studying to become walking archives of prophetic traditions, the Hadith Folk naturally advocated the view that hadiths constituted the prime mode of accessing and learning the Sunna (as opposed to early scholar Malik ibn Anas's view, in which the collective public norm of Medina, not hadiths, offered the best way to learn Muhammad's Sunna), and that this hadith-based model of Sunna was the only legitimate resource for answering questions of belief and practice. With the elite theologians and philosophers, they shared the view that common believers could engage the Qur'an only on its surface level of meaning—an approach called *bi-la kayf*, "without asking how"— but they disagreed with the notion that higher levels of understanding awaited the intellectuals whose training in Greek philosophy earned them a privileged access behind the words. To this end, the hadith partisans read as somewhat egalitarian; while performing exclusions and upholding hierarchies of their own, they denounced the possibility of the Qur'an sharing private secrets with elite readers. The consequences were not only theological but also legal and political, because the hadith partisans held that all norm-making power rested in prophetic traditions, rather than independent reason. To this end, the ahl al-hadith disparaged their rivals as *ahl al-rayy*, "people of opinion."

From the rationalist readers of the Qur'an in eighth-century Basra emerged the Mu'tazila, who became especially important for Muslim history when embraced by the 'Abbasid caliph al-Ma'mun (r. 813–33 CE) and installed as the empire's official school of thought. Al-Ma'mun expected jurists and clerics to fall in line with Mu'tazili positions, most famously the notion that the Qur'an was created by Allah, rather than eternal and uncreated. When hadith partisans such as Ibn Hanbal refused to comply with the Mu'tazili platform, al-Ma'mun unleashed the Mihna, a series of persecutions, against them. Though the Mihna's historical significance might get overplayed (such as in the treatment of it as a Muslim "Spanish Inquisition"), it did have the effect of turning Ibn Hanbal and others into populist folk heroes for defending Muhammad's Sunna against an elitist imperial project. The caliphal Mu'tazilism experiment failed, and Ibn Hanbal's students became the core of a nascent Hanbali scholarly tradition. Today, Hanbali jurisprudence is recognized as one of the four surviving schools of Sunni law, and the Hanbali school enjoys special institutional privilege in the modern kingdom of Saudi Arabia. If we had to name a distant ancestor for modern Salafism, we could start with Ibn Hanbal.

Standing at roughly a middle point between Ibn Hanbal's world and our own, we encounter the highly important Hanbali jurist and theologian of Damascus, Ibn Taymiyya (1263–1328 CE), who died roughly five centuries after Ibn Hanbal and seven centuries before the time of this writing. Depending on whom you ask, he was either the greatest scholar of medieval Islam or the villain who ruined everything forever. In his own lifetime, Ibn Taymiyya was alternately revered for his piety or dismissed as a crackpot. He was even jailed. Anticipating popular modern tendencies to imagine that we're living in the worst of all times and the end must be near, Ibn Taymiyya—again, speaking nearly a thousand ago—lamented that Islam had been all but destroyed in his own setting, which was troubled by things like backgammon, Jews and Christians gaining influence in the government, heretical sectarian groups, Sufi charlatans duping gullible believers, and immodestly dressed women. He was deeply troubled by veneration of Muhammad that flagrantly defied Muhammad's own warnings to his followers, as witnessed in people revering Muhammad's alleged footprint or making pilgrimage to his tomb in Medina. But Ibn Taymiyya especially took offense at politically quietist scholars who offered no voice of resistance as Mongol invasions swept through Muslim lands, ravaged and plundered Muslim communities, and destroyed the caliphate. His advocacy of military jihad (and rejection of the notion that a "greater jihad" was to be found in internal spiritual struggle) does not merely express his interest in "pure" and "original" Islam but reflects the way a specific resource in the tradition—the chronicles of Muhammad's military conduct—could interact with the present world.

Several centuries later, Ibn Taymiyya's legacy became a useful resource for modern Muslim intellectuals who saw various aspects of his thought speaking to their own needs. Ibn Taymiyya's vicious polemics against brands of Sufism he deemed illegitimate resonated with a modern anti-Sufism. Ibn Taymiyya's particular scholasticism also appealed to Muslim intellectuals who saw in him a kind of systematic and rational approach to determining authentic Islam (I'll admit, there are times when investigating a hadith's transmission history feels almost mathematical). Finally, Ibn Taymiyya's courageous advocacy of jihad in the face of oppression would meet the needs of Muslims facing modern oppression in the form of European colonialism. While Ibn Taymiyya enjoyed a surging renaissance among Sunni revivalist networks in Egypt, Syria, and Iraq, the Arabian Peninsula experienced another revival movement, pejoratively named "Wahhabism" after its founder, ʿAbd Allah ibn ʿAbd al-Wahhab. "Wahhabism" would not be an acceptable term for so-called Wahhabi Muslims, since they would not identify their movement as something that developed in the eighteenth and nineteenth centuries or owed its origin to Ibn 'Abd al-Wahhab's own thought; Ibn 'Abd al-Wahhab, in their view, only called for a return to Islam as it was in its truest and original form. He opposed popular "folk" practices and what he regarded as heretical departures from the Salaf's authoritative customs and ventures into polytheism and idolatry, such as the veneration of graves. His followers destroyed the domed tombs over the graves of Muhammad's Companions in the cemetery of Jannat al-Baqi in Medina and even attempted to dismantle the dome over Muhammad's grave before they were stopped. Around the turn of the twentieth century, "Wahhabi" networks intersected with Sunni revivalist scenes in Damascus and Cairo, leading to modern Salafism as an amorphous but gradually concretizing vision for returning to original Islam.

In 1924, as the old world of sacred kingship and empire was fast giving way to modern nationalism, Mustafa Kemal Ataturk abolished the caliphate, finalizing the process of reconstructing post-Ottoman Turkey as a modern (and secular) nation-state. The loss of the caliphate, even if the Ottoman Empire's claim to it had only been symbolic by this time, provoked a crisis in Islamic political thought, but reformers and revivalists such as Rashid Rida looked to the rise of a Wahhabi kingdom in the new nation of Saudi Arabia as a trace of promise for Muslim futures. Across the twentieth century, many notable Muslim authors and intellectuals sought a recoding of Muhammad as the ideal statesman, author of a "Constitution of Medina," who established a universal template for Muslim societies to follow—even though the modern concepts of a nation-state and constitution would have been unrecognizable to him.

Since its founding in the 1920s, the modern kingdom of Saudi Arabia has become a new center of Islamic gravity in ways the Arabian Peninsula had almost never been; not since the caliphate's capital moved from Medina to Damascus and later Baghdad had the Hijaz region been so politically crucial. The Saudi government has exported its Wahhabi platform throughout the world, provoking recalibrations of "correct" Islamic thought and practice seemingly everywhere. Popular religious practice, architecture, art, music, political movements, legal thought, Sunni-Shi'i relations, Sufism, and conversations on Islam and gender have all been touched by global Wahhabi revivalism. But as I witnessed when I hiked the Mountain of Light outside Mecca, joining other pilgrims as we ignored the government's advisory signs warning that visitation to the mountain was not a legitimate Islamic practice, Wahhabism's success was never absolute. Lovers of Muhammad still made their way up the mountain.

AN ALTERNATE REVIVAL: MUHAMMAD, JUSTICE, AND REFORM

In 2005, I worked security at what gender-progressive Muslims would remember as a definitive and foundational moment for rethinking the tradition and its possibilities: a public gender-integrated prayer in which the believers assembled as a congregation behind a woman imam. In classical Islamic jurisprudence, the idea that women could perform as imams and lead men in prayer was (almost) universally regarded as unthinkable; the event drew heated objections and condemnations from throughout the world and has contributed to a heaping of abuse on the event's imam, amina wadud, in the decades since.

Advocates for woman-led prayer often make arguments from within the tradition and canonical sources, asserting the case of Umm Waraqa, a woman whom Muhammad had authorized to lead her house in prayer. Muhammad himself thereby becomes the agent of reform, which is no longer "reform" at all but a revival of what Islam had originally been; at least on this point, progressive Muslims advocating for gender equality in ritual prayer can return to the same canonical texts and frameworks as conservatives or so-called fundamentalists. Opponents of woman-led prayer counter either on the grounds of the hadith's transmission or the way it had been received in the classical tradition. But just as often as we see the Umm Waraqa hadith cited in arguments that use traditional methods to create new concepts and practices, we also see a departure from those structures in favor of a Qur'an-centered (or Qur'an-only) argument. It's perhaps fitting that the 2005 prayer's imam was a scholar of the Qur'an, rather than hadith, as the Qur'an remains unquestionably favored above hadith sources in progressive Muslim circles. Progressive Muslim thinkers, treating the Qur'an as a revelation from outside the world, generally uphold the text as a message of justice and equality; problems within the Qur'an's text rise from the accumulated traditions of subjective human interpreters rather than the revealed words them-selves. In contrast, the hadith corpus is entirely a project of subjective humans, who may or may not have reliably preserved Muhammad's actual words. As I discussed in chapter 4, Muslims such as scholar Scott

Kugle might challenge homophobic readings of the Qur'an by rethinking the interpretation of specific verses but challenge homophobic readings of hadiths by rethinking the hadiths themselves, questioning their authenticity. As Kugle argues, the fact that 'Ikrima, freed slave of Muhammad's cousin Ibn 'Abbas, becomes such a disproportionately prolific source of homophobic hadith reports could tell us more about 'Ikrima's own prejudices or issues than it does about what Muhammad or even Ibn 'Abbas actually said and did.[3] The point here is not necessarily to throw away the entirety of the hadith corpus (though I have seen many progressive Muslims call for that approach, and sometimes even ironically cite "antihadith" hadiths as their evidence) but to at least recognize the human subjectivity that accompanies every hadith report, as well as those of the great hadith scholars and their methods for vetting narrations.

In progressive Muslim circles, questions over Muhammad's legacy often center the tensions that persist between facts of his life (insofar as the reported facts are "facts"), the vision of Muhammad as our model for justice, and our own conceptions of what "justice" means. The big questions tend to focus on his marriages and wars. Did Muhammad marry A'isha when she was only a child? Canonical hadith sources depict A'isha narrating that she was six years old when the marriage was contracted, and nine when she began to live with Muhammad as his wife. A vigorous hadith investigation can offer one way out of that problem; a recent dissertation (unpublished at the time of this writing) by J. J. Little argues that the child marriage hadiths were fabricated by Hisham ibn 'Urwa ibn al-Zubayr, A'isha's great-nephew, in order to preserve claims of A'isha's virginity against Shi'i polemics.[4] But as Kecia Ali has explained, A'isha's own narrations of her age appear in Sunni Muslims' most canonically privileged sources; for Sunni Muslims, rejecting those narrations would essentially mean leaving the entire canon up for grabs and conceding that we have no reliable information for understanding Muhammad's life.[5] Likewise, sources on the genocide of the Banu Qurayza allow us to consider variance between different narrations and question Muhammad's precise involvement, but an argument that it simply never happened would depend on an attitude toward hadiths that threatens to erase Muhammad as a knowable personality.

Some Muslims in today's world would be okay with that, taking comfort in the relative simplicity of the Qur'an over the vast, unmanageable, and perhaps treacherous terrain of the hadith corpus. But at the same time, when Islamophobic voices cite specific verses to imagine that the Qur'an commands endless war against all non-Muslims, our ability to better understand those verses often depends on context: the more we can relate the verses to a specific time and place, considering why and when a particular verse came down, the more tools we have for countering a naive, decontextualized hot take on what the verse says to an uninformed commentator. Sometimes our evidence for details of Muhammad's life will be the problem, and sometimes it will be the solution.

Classical hadith scholarship, of course, doesn't require faith that all hadiths are authentic; the whole project of developing methodologies for vetting hadiths was a response to the reality that hadith scholarship abounded with forgers, fabricators, and otherwise unreliable sources. Bukhari was moved to produce his canonical work after seeing Muhammad covered by flies in a dream; interpreting the flies to be false hadiths, Bukhari sought to serve Muhammad by purifying the hadith corpus. Bukhari's collection boasts supreme canonical privilege, but today, modern Salafi hadith critics such as Nasr ad-Din al-Albani would even challenge specific reports in Bukhari's prestigious *Sahih*. One could conceivably reject a hadith from Bukhari without throwing out the entire canon; but the struggle faces an additional obstruction in the fact that modern hadith studies tend to privilege A'isha's narrations to her nephew 'Urwa as the most strongly evidenced (in a "secular" critical framework).

With all of the critical problems concerning our sources on Muhammad's "real" life aside, if we allow that a man who lived nearly fifteen centuries ago probably said and did things that make sense in his own time and place but not our own, a sensitivity to historical context can help reconcile Muhammad's biography with progressive Muslim platforms. Modern Muslim thinkers have produced some tools for this approach. Sudanese intellectual Mahmoud Muhammad Taha, for example, distinguished between the Meccan and Medinan periods of Muhammad's life, arguing that his call to God in the Meccan period represented a universal message, while his entry into politics at Medina meant that he became more defined by the limits of a local context. South Asian scholar Fazlur Rahman argued for a theory of "double movement" in which we identify the progressive and ethical dimensions in the Qur'an and read thematically for these larger messages over the letter of a specific verse. The challenge that troubles "historical context" arguments lies in Muhammad's transcendence as the mercy to all worlds and our own power as readers of his life. As the readers, we are ultimately the ones who determine his meanings, which risks imposing our own presentist judgments, which we imagine to be universal, on his life. Because "Progressive Islam" constitutes a diverse field of communities, thinkers, and priorities, there is no singular "progressive" attitude toward Muhammad or the hadith corpus. Some progressive Muslims find their answer in rejecting the view that Muhammad remains central to Islam, while others find in Muhammad a resource and foundation for their progressive ethics and values.

MUHAMMAD AND SCIENCE

In my interactions with Muslim Students Association booths on various campuses over the years, I have engaged in more than one impromptu lecture about a particular "intro to Islam" pamphlet often found on their tables. The pamphlet argues that we can instantly recognize the truth of Islam by looking to verses of the Qur'an that exhibit a knowledge of scientific phenomena, ranging from geology to embryology, that would not have been possible in Muhammad's own lifetime. Due to this bewildering compatibility between a seventh-century text and modern science, the argument goes, the Qur'an could not have been produced by a human author. I'd go off about the problems with the pamphlet and how it's a terrible look for Muslims, and then share an anecdote from my teen years.

As a new convert to Islam, I viewed religion as a battlefield in which one faith had to be right, all the others had to be wrong, and the religion with superior facts, evidence, and rational argument would win. My model for the convert's intellectual path was Malcolm X, who embraced Islam and devoted himself to obsessive reading from whatever resources the prison library offered, searching for the evidence that could illuminate the truth of Islam as he understood it. With Malcolm as my template of the autodidact convert, I consumed whatever books I could find to arm myself with the best facts and arguments possible. It was crucial that when talking religion with friends and family, I could establish that Islam was the most rational and scientifically oriented choice. If they took it for granted that religion and science existed in perpetual conflict and mutual antagonism and could never reconcile, it was only due to their anchoring in Western Christian history: repeating the pamphlet tropes, I was sure that no such conflict could ever exist in Islam.

One afternoon, I called one of my beloved masjid uncles with excitement over the latest proof that I had found: apparently, someone had discovered a "mathematical code" running throughout the Qur'an that evidenced its divine origin beyond all doubt. The masjid uncle knew more about this "mathematical code"—and the controversial figure behind it—than me. He did not shut down the possibility of the Qur'an containing a mathematical miracle but simply answered, "Brother, there is an integrity to Islam that makes it stand on its own. Once you really have it, you don't have to prove it."

We were later in Pakistan together. I had left the United States at seventeen to spend a chunk of my senior year of high school at Faisal Mosque in Islamabad, Pakistan, where I would spend all day hearing lectures at the adjacent Daw'ah Academy and visiting the library. He had come to teach for the Daw'ah Academy program that I was attending. In Islamabad, I again shared my readings with him: this time, I had been getting into scholars who argued that numerous Qur'an verses display a knowledge of scientific phenomena that would not have been possible for a human being in seventh-century Arabia. There were no microscopes in Muhammad's time; how could the Qur'an speak on the fetus in ways that anticipated modern science by more than a thousand years? I was stunned by the evidence and couldn't wait to return to the United States and share it with my mother, whom I feared was meant for the hellfire if she did not convert. In the face of these clear proofs, how could anyone deny the Qur'an?

Strangely, he was not impressed.

"Brother," he said, "Why did the Sahabas believe in the Qur'an?" The Sahabas were the Companions of the Prophet, the first generation of the Salaf. "Did the Sahabas believe in the Qur'an because it gave them advanced knowledge about the development of the fetus in the womb?" The "scientific proofs of Islam" argument, in his eyes, missed far more profound evidence for Islam, namely the changes that our love for the Prophet initiated in our hearts. A better proof for the truth of Islam would be found in the kinds of human beings that Islam produced. Rather than argue for the Qur'an's supernaturally advanced ideas about geology, look to the way the Prophet treated people who heaped garbage on his head as he prayed. Islam would show itself through the people who best imitate the Prophet's example.

The "Qur'an and science" project isn't very scientific, since science relates not to the answer that you get but your method and the ability to reliably test your answer. "Does my religious scripture agree with science?" is not an answerable question, since our personal judgment of whether a verse sounds enough like science to hold up is not measurable, and the answer cannot be tested. If the book reads to our subjective eyes as compatible with science, then praise God, the book has proven itself. If we perceive the book to be in conflict with science, we can answer that the verse reflects some deeper mystical meaning that we haven't yet comprehended; or we can suggest that the verse meets its original readers where they are (i.e., the seventh-century Hijaz) and must be read with that context in mind, just like an adult might answer a child's question in a way that's not precisely correct but still appropriate for the child; finally, we can just insist that science is wrong and will eventually catch up. Moreover, the pamphlets claiming that the Qur'an provides knowledge of topics such as embryology that would not have been possible in the seventh century CE don't seem to know the actual state of knowledge in the world at that time. Rather than necessarily reflect insight from the unseen, the Qur'an's embryology reads in line with ancient Greek medical science.[6]

The effort to establish Islam's compatibility with science doesn't go away; claims found in pamphlets that flooded the world in past decades continue to circulate online. These pamphlets are not unique to Muslims; Christian networks, after all, have produced entire museums and mountains of textbooks to boast "scientific" proof of the Bible's literal inerrancy. On the point of evolution, Muslim versions of the "intelligent design" argument repeat claims and logics found in Christian antievolution media. Contrary to the "reason versus faith" opposition, these literatures attempt to state their cases with hard facts and empirical science; they employ scientific proofs precisely because they believe, on some level, in the ability of science to arrive at the truth. In a sense, the supposed opponents of secularism are essentially secularizing their scriptures, asking secular science to endorse their faith convictions. This kind of work extends beyond the "Abrahamic" religious milieu; it was also evident in early twentieth-century Japan, where Shinto intellectuals argued for Japan's indigenous gods as the true sources of modern science,[7] as well as colonial India, where Hindu and Buddhist intellectuals presented modern scientific findings as having been present all along in their respective archives.[8]

The emphasis on science and rationality informs ways we look at Muhammad's Night Journey through the heavens, during which he ascended through a vertically tiered cosmos, conversing with angels and prophets along the way. Muhammad's ascension often fails to appear in modern treatments as a major event of his life; it's certainly not one of the most debated and reassessed aspects of his biography, in comparison to his marriages or military policies—that is, things that "really" happened in his "real life." Muhammad's ascension isn't a point of high-stakes controversy. But when Muslims do talk about the heavenly journey, we can catch a glimpse that our imaginary has changed. We might forget that Muhammad's ascent corresponds to the *physical* structure of the universe as it was understood in his time: to enter the transcendent realm of angels and prophets and ultimately God, you go *up*, and then you go further *up*, and still further *up*, and if God wants to draw near to the believers, he comes *down*. The term for the Qur'an's revelations, *nazul*, signifies descent. Knowledge emanates downward through the tiers of heavens, each associated with a specific planet ("planet" here also including the sun and moon), into our sublunar realm. As our knowledge changes, different resources in the tradition become favored; A'isha, after all, argued that her husband's ascension had been entirely visionary and that his body never left the house that night.

In our scientific, rational, and somewhat antimystical rereading of Muhammad's life, Sufism doesn't disappear, but in many contexts it is purged and recoded. In North American Muslim contexts, I've sometimes encountered Sufism as something like a secular technology of human development, flowing from the intersections of Muslim traditions and contemporary wellness practices. Muslim scholars have also worked to produce a sanitized and more "orthodox" construction of Sufism, in which the point of Sufi tradition is to spiritualize our practices—and definitively *not* to become mystical masters who receive entire texts from the Prophet in visionary encounters or invite any new concepts and practices that depart from the "normative" tradition.[9] Sufism as a technology of Muslim selfhood, producing a sober Islamic consciousness through our bodily discipline, becomes the acceptable version; Sufism as a source of new information from the unseen is erased.

MUHAMMAD AND ART

In classrooms and community events, I have sometimes provided as a visual aid a large poster depicting Muhammad as a smiling young man. The poster clearly identifies its subject, providing the caption in Arabic,

Muhammad Rasul Allah (Muhammad, Messenger of God). When I slowly unroll the poster, I know what it's about to do. More than once, the poster has provoked surprise and confusion. On one occasion, a Muslim asked me to put it away on the grounds that it's against Islam and hurtful to Muslims. He couldn't register that the poster was made by *Muslims*, for *Muslims*, as *Islamic* art intended to touch *Muslim* hearts and produce *Islamic* feelings, and that it had circulated as such not in a fringe corner or marginal community but a nation of more than 80 million people, and had been embraced by one of the most important Islamic clerics of the twentieth century as his favorite image of the Prophet.

For my conversation partner on that day, and for many Muslims, it remained completely off the map to consider a visual image of Muhammad as a legitimately *Islamic* image. Given the degree of anti-Shi'ism and anti-Iranian prejudice that can run throughout Sunni communities, it did not help the poster's legitimacy to connect it to Shi'ism, Iran, or the Ayatollah Khomeini. For many non-Muslims as well, it felt like an incontrovertible fact of nature that Muslims everywhere objected to the depiction of living things in visual art, and that they absolutely and universally opposed the visual depiction of Muhammad with a special intensity that would make them freak out and burn down cities if they saw one.

This assumption comes from somewhere. I wouldn't overstate my case and suggest that it's entirely an invention of modernity with no basis in historical tradition, but I would say that modern forces have gone a long way in erasing past archives and narrowing the field of possibilities. So today it's a very popular given that Islamic art includes no history of depicting Muhammad, at least none that would include a full depiction of his face. But this simply isn't historical, and it's certainly not to be found in the Qur'an. Nor do the traces left by premodern Muslims, whether in texts or archaeological evidence, give us reason to imagine that wherever Muslims went, they made it a priority to cleanse the terrain of all images. Rather, it's often the case that they not only preserved images but made their own, including images of Muhammad, including his face.

Back to the Qur'an; people who expect the Qur'an to operate as the "Muslim Bible" and provide Muslims with all of their answers might be struck by the Qur'an's lack of a judgment on art. No verse of the Qur'an self-evidently speaks on whether it's appropriate for artists to depict living things in general or Muhammad in particular. At best, one could read the Qur'an's discussions of Abraham and idols as expressing a negative attitude toward statues, though this attitude appears entirely in connection with images that are treated as gods. The Qur'an reminds its audience that neither the images nor their human makers were actual creators themselves (21:58, 37:93); a reader of the Qur'an could therefore draw the conclusion that artists risk a slight against God's creativity when they assert themselves as creator. But the Qur'an also reminds men that they are not the creators of the semen that they ejaculate (56:59), without this being taken as an antisemen polemic. The Qur'an seems to suggest a connection between visual art and polytheism, in which people who worship multiple beings make images, and people who worship the God of Abraham do not; but readers looking for a clearly stated "Qur'anic judgment on art" will not find it.

As with many topics, points of ambiguity or silence in the Qur'an are supplemented by more decisive content in the hadith corpus. The most obvious evidence from the Prophet's life is found in his conquest of Mecca, which culminated in his purging the precincts of the Ka'ba (and apparently the roof and interior of the Ka'ba itself) of its numerous idols. We're not sure if the "idols" were actually statues, since the artifacts destroyed in this purging are more prominently described with a word signifying "altars," suggesting that they were more likely the stone slabs on which animals were slaughtered in devotion to deities. Further complicating the consequences of Muhammad's reported purge, we find reports in which he did not destroy an image of Jesus and Mary that he found in the Ka'ba, though other reports state that it was an image of Abraham, and that Muhammad *did* order the image erased. But even the Abraham version allows more than one interpretation, since Abraham was reportedly depicted holding divination arrows, and Muhammad's objection to the image could have more to do with the representation of Abraham engaged in a practice of polytheists and diviners.

Numerous hadiths in the most canonical collections depict Muhammad condemning images and the artists who make them, even charging that in the hellfire, the artists would be punished by their own art. Again, the problem lies in the imitation of God's creative power, as the artists will be asked to breathe life into their works as God had breathed into Adam. The angel Gabriel once explained that he had missed a scheduled meeting with Muhammad because angels would not enter homes that contained images. Muhammad then learned that there were images on a pillow or curtain owned by A'isha (in an alternate version, however, the angel is deterred by a dog that 'Ali's sons had brought inside, and explains that angels do not enter houses containing dogs).

There could be more to these aniconic hadiths than simply a straightforward reporting of what Muhammad said. Hadiths condemning the depiction of living things in visual art may or may not reflect Muhammad's actual position. But whether grounded in his "real" words or not, it's possible that Muhammad's opposition to the makers of images could have circulated in post-Muhammad contexts for reasons that spoke to those specific contexts.

Among early Umayyad caliphs, attitudes toward art did not match those found in later hadith collections. In fact, the first Islamic coins, relying on Sasanian mints, included a human portrait. Though the image originally depicted Chosroes, one might ask whether the image was interpreted differently when appearing on coins in the Islamic era, adjacent to the Arabic phrase "bism Allah" (in the Name of God). Moreover, the other side of the coin featured an image of a Zoroastrian fire temple and its attendants![10] 'Abd al-Malik (r. 685–705), fifth Umayyad caliph, initiated a reform in which images were removed from coins and replaced by Islamically oriented text. His move seems to mark movement in a new direction that would be accelerated by the ninth Umayyad caliph, Yazid II (r. 720–24), who briefly attempted to ban all depictions of living things and ordered their destruction. The poorly enforced executive order did not last long before it was withdrawn.[11]

The idea that Islam absolutely opposed all depictions of living things was not in force as an established "orthodoxy" during the early Umayyad caliphs. So what changed? How did opposition to images take on the veneer of a universally accepted tradition? Scholarship has speculated that the key could be Muslim-Christian relations in the Umayyad period, which generally saw a firmer sense of boundaries drawn between Muslims and other monotheists. Those boundaries were not always there with the same intensity. Muhammad, after all, had seen himself as another prophet in the line of Moses and Jesus, and the Qur'an particularly displays a friendliness to Christians, even when disagreeing with them. Muhammad did not self-present as the founder of a "new" and separate religion, but we see a trend in this direction among the early Umayyads.[12] Taking a harder stance on visual art could have become a means by which the Muslim-Christian distinction was more firmly established. This wouldn't have to mean that hadith scholars invented pro-aniconic hadiths out of nowhere but could at least suggest that such hadiths were favored and accentuated for the way they spoke to the needs of the moment.

The hadiths could have targeted Christians, but they could also reflect conflicts between the hadith scholars and the Umayyad ruling elites. The Umayyad era was characterized in part by an ongoing oppression and exploitation of Muslims in Iraq (an increasingly vital center for the hadith transmission network) by the government centered in Damascus. Hadith scholars were even known to participate in military uprisings against the Umayyad regime. On other topics, these hadith scholars also circulated traditions as critiques of Umayyad extravagance; hadiths condemning men who wear silk and gold, for example, could have served hadith scholars speaking truth to Umayyad power. Hadiths that seemingly object to the writing of hadiths could also have expressed hadith scholars' opposition to Umayyad projects of compiling, writing, and circulating "official" government hadith collections.[13] If Umayyad scholars were decorating coins and palaces with visual art, anti-Umayyad hadith masters could have expressed their resistance to the empire through hadiths of Muhammad condemning the makers of images.[14]

It should always be remembered that these hadith transmitters never held a monopoly in terms of how Muslims were supposed to engage ideas about Muhammad. Despite the hadith network's vehement aniconism, Muslim artists produced Muhammad images for Muslim consumption, with the best-known examples being painted miniatures. It's often assumed that the makers of such images consistently avoided depicting Muhammad's face, with the rationale often being a concern to refrain from making Muhammad an "idol." However, this is inaccurate on both counts. Islamic art traditions do include numerous images of Muhammad depicted with his face fully shown. Moreover, it has been argued that when Muslim artists avoided showing Muhammad's face, it was not to keep him anchored in his mere humanity but the opposite: Christiane Gruber asserts that paintings of Muhammad began to veil his face around the sixteenth century CE, as Iranian Safavid artists endeavored to emphasize Muhammad's transcendence, turning him into a "veiled, luminous, and secret mystery."[15]

In the modern world, Islamic art in Iran again underwent a transformation. The twentieth century saw a proliferation of Muhammad images, such as the famous poster of young Muhammad preferred by the Ayatollah Khomeini, though Muhammad (and the Shi'i Imams descended from him) were also often depicted without their faces shown. After the 2005 "Danish cartoon" controversy, in which the newspaper *Jyllands-Posten* published inflammatory cartoons of Muhammad and sparked international outrage, the Iranian government moved toward discouraging Muhammad images. The rise and fall of a Muhammad poster does not prove Islam's timeless opposition to art or even Muhammad images but rather illustrates the malleability that characterizes our ideas of Muhammad across history.[16] Today, a more popular go-to reference for the "Muhammad in Islamic art" question would be the hilya, a genre of calligraphic devotion to the Prophet that developed in the early modern Ottoman Empire and reached a somewhat standard form in the seventh century. Drawn from practices in which textual descriptions of Muhammad are believed to hold protective and curative properties, functioning as potent talismans, the hilya tradition incorporates ornately written hadiths that describe Muhammad's physical appearance (the word "hilya" literally means "decoration" or "ornament"). Though not a "picture" that seeks to graphically depict Muhammad, the hilya works like a sacred icon. Even in this more abstracted form, hilya pieces evoke the Prophet's transcendent beauty, linking his aesthetic perfection to his status as God's greatest creation and mercy to the worlds and the venerated texts of the hadith corpus.

MUHAMMAD AND WESTERN ESOTERICISM

In 1888, the French Spiritualist journal *Le Spiritisme* published an interview with the spirit of Muhammad, after the Prophet had been summoned in a séance. Muhammad proceeds to tell the interviewer or summoner that he had knowingly taught a false doctrine but with good intentions: he only wanted to guide his idolatrous people toward belief in one God, rather than the stone gods that they worshiped. Muhammad first confesses, "I fought Christianity," but then corrects himself: "No, I fought the doctrine that took that name." Muhammad pleads that if he could have read the Gospel, he would have become its propagator, and that it shames him when Muslims mention his name adjacent to the name of God; but he also deflects some blame to those "great culprits" who modified Christianity for their own selfish purposes. When asked about his present afterlife condition, Muhammad explains that he's in the process of purifying his soul but has not completed that process. When asked whether Spiritualism could influence Islam today,

Muhammad first defers to God's will but also recognizes Spiritualism as superior to all religions.[17]

Including a confession of Islam's fraudulence, condemnation of Christian churches for having corrupted Jesus's true teachings, and praise for Spiritualism, the "interviewer" finds Muhammad's ghost confirming his/her own prejudices. Of course, as anti-Spiritualist critics noted, "Muhammad" speaks for the views of the person who summoned his ghost.[18] But with that much clear, I'm also interested in the alternate histories that a Spiritualist encounter with Muhammad could have produced. The "interview" with Muhammad did not make a meaningful impact in Spiritualist networks or broader Western esoteric and occult scenes, and certainly did not leave a mark on Muslim readerships. But what might have changed if another Spiritualist reinvention of Muhammad had been more successful? The Buddha, after all, had been the subject of radical reinventions by Western esotericists. Most notably through the nineteenth-century work of the Theosophical Society and legions of Theosophy-adjacent thinkers through the early decades of the twentieth century, the Buddha became something new. For better or worse (and I'm not going to get prescriptive here about where "true Buddhism" exists), Western imaginaries of Buddhism produced a "New Age" Buddha, often divorced from the lived realities of Buddhist communities and traditions, who speaks for new and distinct expressions of Buddhism. The forces that shaped the milieu of concepts, materials, and practices known collectively as "New Age" did not embrace Muhammad with anything close to its appropriations of the Buddha. We can speculate as to why one was more popular than the other. I suggest that it at least partly relates to race: during the era of peak Aryanism, white Buddhists frequently imagined the Buddha as their cousin on a shared Indo-European family tree, while Muhammad was imagined as the most excessive case of non-Aryan—that is, Semitic—religion. As I've heard it said, "New Age" discourses often claim to draw from all of the world's great spiritual traditions, but you rarely see this vision of global spirituality include anything from Africa (except for Egypt) or Islam (except for Sufism, more specifically a curated presentation of Sufism all but purged of explicit references to Islam). While we see plenty of evidence for New Age spirituality within contemporary Muslim thought-networks, it's harder to find a place for Islam in New Age.

Nonetheless, Muhammad does show up in the work of some Western esotericists. The most famous example is the prominent early convert

Muhammad Alexander Russell Webb (1846–1916), who was a member of the Theosophical Society when he found Islam. Rather than choose Islam over Theosophy, Webb saw the two as mutually compatible, even "almost identical."[19] Webb regarded Islam as a perfect expression of Theosophical concepts. His views were not shared by many in his Theosophical circles, who favored "Aryan" Buddhism and Hinduism and at times disdained "Semitic" monotheisms.[20]

Writers in Western esotericism of the nineteenth and early twentieth centuries, informed by readings in Sufism and Freemasonry, sometimes imagined Muhammad as the founder of hidden lodges, holding that his truest teachings were not reflected in "mainstream" Islamic tradition. Godfrey Higgins, believed to have been an important author for Nation of Islam founder W. D. Fard, writes in his *Anacalypsis* (1836) of the "secret doctrine of Mohamed," which he terms "Sopheism," describing it as a four-stage progression through which Muslims grow from mere obedience to God's ritual commands to attaining a knowledge equal to that of angels and then surpassing the angels to reach union with God.[21] According to Higgins, Muhammad's "original esoteric religion" was suppressed in public but existed among his "cabinet" of twelve imams, who maintained a hierarchy of knowledge and understanding in which they were entitled to higher levels of religion than the crude orthodoxy of everyday believers.[22] Later in the nineteenth century, Theosophical literature made claims of a secret Islam, known only to ʿAli, who taught students at his Medina school on topics such as reincarnation and "the divinity in man."[23] ʿAli's school was later destroyed by Umayyad invasion, leaving the knowledge with no institutional support. Completely unacceptable to public orthodoxy, the esoteric teachings that Muhammad imparted to ʿAli were either destroyed without a trace or managed to survive underground, through secret transmissions from ʿAli's students to younger generations.[24]

These esoteric and occult imaginaries of Muhammad's life didn't exactly "win" or create a new Islamic orthodoxy anywhere, but they did contribute to a pool of resources that would nourish the most significant American Muslim movement, the Nation of Islam. Founded in 1930s Detroit by Fard Muhammad, a Muslim of mostly likely Afghan heritage, the Nation attracted scores of thousands of African Americans to Muslim conversion, including most famously its national minister, Malcolm X, Malcolm's student Louis Farrakhan, and heavyweight boxing champion Muhammad Ali. Many of the Nation's concepts, such as its deification of Fard as Allah and recognition of Fard's student, Elijah Muhammad, as the Messenger of Allah, have been widely denounced as heretical, but the Nation's contribution to American Muslim histories and the Black freedom struggle cannot be denied. Fard's deification and the concept of godhood as human self-perfection, along with other Nation concepts, such as its belief in a hidden council of wise scientists who administered the world and claim that Freemasonry secretly acknowledged the truth of Islam, speak from a milieu of esoteric and metaphysical discourses in the early decades of the twentieth century. Malcolm X left the Nation in early 1964, reconverted as a Sunni Muslim, and was assassinated in 1965; Muhammad Ali remained in the Nation but followed Elijah Muhammad's son, Wallace D. Muhammad (later Warith Deen Mohammed), who launched a series of reforms after Elijah's death in 1975 that would reinvent the Nation as an "orthodox" Muslim community. Though most Nation members from the Elijah Muhammad years and their descendants are recognizable as "orthodox" Muslims today (aside from Farrakhan's Nation revival group and a number of small Nation communities), the Nation tradition's story cannot be told without recognition of these entangled genealogies in which "heresy" made "orthodoxy" possible. In many contexts, whether South Asia or Central Asia or China or Iran or what Fard called the "wilderness" of North America, Muslim consciousness first developed organically in conversation with local concepts and traditions, producing new expressions of Islam that Muslims in other contexts would have considered beyond the pale (such as Muhammad's being the tenth avatar of Vishnu), only later entering negotiation with globalizing orthodoxies.

CONCLUSIONS

One morning in graduate school, I brought my open laptop down the hall to surprise a mentor with an exciting new toy: IslamWeb's online hadith database, which offered seemingly the entire Sunni hadith corpus in a searchable and well-organized archive, and even provided extensive biographical details and critical assessments of every reporter in each hadith's chain of transmission. As we scrolled down the various hadith collections and clicked on the names of transmitters, my mentor casually noted, "A thousand years ago, that was all in their heads," speaking to the traditions of memorization that characterized classical hadith scholarship. Bukhari didn't need a searchable online database. The remark left me wondering how the technologies that supported my research resulted in the kind of project I wrote, spiraling me into reflection on the inescapable modernity of even our most "traditional" attempts at hadith scholarship.

Many would measure a religion's truth as dependent on its consistency. If the religion is truly what its advocates claim for it, especially if that claim relates to knowledge received from beyond the world and time, it can't change its answers to the big questions. I would not deny that Islamic traditions exhibit consistencies; but the ways Muslims understand those consistencies, and the values that they place on them, absolutely change. Muhammad has been transformed by modern phenomena of colonialism, nationalism, and racism; modern technology and, with it, changes in literacy, education, and the access to texts provided first by modern mass printing and later by broadcast media and the Internet; the ascent of scientific rationality as a mode of truth with which religious discourses must engage, whether seeking reconciliation or resistance; the impact of modern rethinking of gender, which challenges the ways we read the life of a man in the seventh century CE and threatens some believers with an upending of the entire foundation on which the tradition rests; and the combined regimes of capitalism and secularism, which reshape the religious seeker into a shopper staring down an aisle offering seemingly infinite choices. The question is not whether Muhammad has changed but rather how we could measure the impact of modernity on our own readings of his life and legacy.

CHAPTER SEVEN

Future Muhammads

So you're proposing that Muhammad is whatever people say he is?

Kind of, yes. But I hope that my own dissatisfaction with that answer is already clear. The answer that I can give is not an answer that consistently gives me peace. It does not clean up the mess I've made.

If Muhammad is whatever people say he is, we must recognize that these diverse Muhammads are often irreconcilable with each other, that they differ in their relationships to power and privilege, and that some Muhammads are therefore more enforceable and advantaged than others. Thinking about Muhammad as an ongoing historical construction, characterized by a bewildering diversity, does not land us at a happy and harmonious theoretical deconstruction in which everyone recognizes the limits of their own subjectivities and surrenders their claims to the absolute. Muhammad remains a passionately contested territory. These irreconcilable visions of him engage in conflict and struggle for the right to "make" Muhammad with authority. Sure, every individual can imagine Muhammad however they want, but these private imaginaries negotiate with larger public constructions of the Prophet. In the modern world, that can mean everything from the coercive power of states (as in

Pakistan's government including an "orthodox" prophetology in its constitution, legally codifying the persecution of Ahmadiyya Muslims) to the bigotry of Islamophobic media (which often focuses on the person and image of Muhammad, as seen in a proliferation of anti-Muhammad cartoons).

Over the course of nearly fifteen centuries, the life of Muhammad has been told, retold, questioned, contested, and reinterpreted more times, in more ways, than I can track here. Those rewritings continue in our own increasingly polarized settings, both in the contests between Muslim and non-Muslim voices and within Muslim communities. In the case of the former, non-Muslims (not all of them writing antagonistically against Islam) have produced a body of content regarding Muhammad's life, teachings, and significance. Whatever their intentions, they have participated in the ongoing construction of Muhammad, both through Muslims reading them and Muslim authors responding to them in subsequent works. As Kecia Ali has observed in her study of modern biographical treatments of Muhammad, a kind of ironic collaboration takes place in non-Muslim and Muslim authors of Muhammad's life: when anti-Muslim polemicists and Muslim apologists aim to refute each other, they end up choosing the same topics (such as Muhammad's marriages or military conflicts) as their points of focus. Muslim writers (and sympathetic non-Muslim writers), facing a common portrayal of Muhammad as a lust-driven warlord, answer negative depictions of Muhammad by dwelling on those same questions. In the perpetual back-and-forth between visions of Muhammad, therefore, Muhammad's modern opponents and defenders collaborate toward a shared outline in which marriages and wars define his character and value. As anti-Muslim writers looked to Muhammad's practice of plural marriage and especially the age of A'isha to brand him a sex fiend and pedophile, Muslim biographies of Muhammad would emphasize his monogamous marriage with Khadija, casting their relationship in terms of modern "soulmates," and stress that his later plural marriages were primarily for the purpose of building political coalitions. Answering the charge of pedophilia in Muhammad's marriage to A'isha, modern Muslim biographers favor traditional sources that depict Khadija as forty years old, fifteen years Muhammad's senior at the time of their marriage—though traditional sources also make a more probable claim (given the number of children that they had together) that they were both in their twenties, Khadija a few years older.[1]

The Aʾisha question often undergoes the "historical context" treatment, namely that we have to place ourselves in the seventh century CE and examine its specific constructions of marriage and adulthood, before projecting our judgments and diagnoses upon Muhammad's sex life. That approach can be useful, but it in turn forces the new question of our own subjectivity when it comes to determining which aspects of Muhammad's life constitute the timeless, transcendent Sunna and which ones can be reduced to "a different time." Different Muslims will locate that line of distinction at different places. This brings us to the ways Muslims contest other Muslims on the proper sources, methods, and values through which we can best understand Muhammad.

Some Muslims search the hadith corpus and find evidence for Muhammad as antiracist and feminist, a prophet who can speak from the seventh century CE to those working in our present to achieve greater equity and justice in our communities and the world at large. There are also Muslims today who, using the same sources, produce a "red-pill" and "antiwoke" Muhammad who serves the same function for which "alt-right" white supremacist men promote ancient Greek and Latin texts: in their respective archives of "classical Islam" and "classical Western civilization," Muslims and white supremacists alike search for citable ancient authorities who can defend "tradition" against what they perceive as modern feminist oppression.[2] A special flash point of conflict between progressive and red-pill visions of Muhammad persists on the question of what constitutes *Islamic* sexuality. Progressive Muslims, using the various tools at their disposal, whether Qurʾan interpretation or hadith studies or classical Islamic jurisprudence, work to open new spaces within the tradition that prioritize consent as an essential value of Islamic sexual ethics. For red-pill Muslims, it's simply a given that while mutual consent has become a key value in "modern" societies as the singular factor that makes a sexual act legitimate, consent does not exactly hold that place in classical Islamic tradition. They're comfortable with the idea that in Islam, certain kinds of consensual sex are viewed as detestable in God's eyes, while certain kinds of nonconsensual sex remain blessed.

The problem is not reducible to a "Muhammad problem" or unique to Muslims. Within American Muslim communities, these debates take place against the larger US backdrop of debates and "culture wars" over rape culture, "cancel culture," critical race theory, and transgender and nonbinary identities. It's not hard to find loud online voices expressing the grievances of heterosexual cisgender men, Muslim and non-Muslim alike, who believe that the world is now oppressing heterosexual cisgender men; some voices in Muslim "manosphere" conversations would completely align with the Right were it not for the Right's investments in white nationalism, xenophobia, and Islamophobia. The racialized nature of Islamophobia closes the possibilities for many American Muslims to fully participate in the Right; but I have also seen (non-Black) Muslims hesitant to engage in pursuits of racial justice in part because they feared the theoretical frameworks informing Black Lives Matter and other freedom struggles to be gateways into critical theories of gender and sexuality.

At almost every step of Donna Zuckerberg's analysis of antifeminists weaponizing the Greek and Roman classics of "Western civilization" against the modern world, I couldn't help but extend her insights to contemporary Muslim debates over Muhammad and the hadith corpus. Zuckerberg remarks, "Although their analyses of ancient sources rarely display much understanding of context and nuance, Red Pill writers nevertheless are adept at manipulating ancient sources to make them speak meaningfully to contemporary concerns."[3] The description will ring a bell for those of us familiar with US Muslim communities' public intellectuals and online personalities. Likewise, online progressive Muslim groups often face intrusions by reactionary trolls who demand engagement of their simplistic "what the books clearly say" arguments and manipulations of sacred sources and scholarly tradition.

Zuckerberg observes more hopefully that the same classical Greek and Roman texts are also in the hands of a "long and rich history of brilliant progressive and feminist thinkers" who have used the ancients in their own work on patriarchal oppression.[4] This goes for Muslim communities as well, as evidenced by a deep and growing corpus of progressive Muslim literature. Though Muslim feminist scholarship has tended to treat Qur'an interpretation, rather than the hadith corpus, as the key site at which battles for gender justice must take place, a field of feminist hadith studies has also started to develop. Progressive hadith scholarship can take many forms. Scholars scrutinize specific hadiths for the integrity of their transmission, as seen in Scott Kugle's critical examination of homophobic hadith traditions; they reconsider the process by which hadiths became positioned as a sacred source virtually on par with the Qur'an, as in the work of Aisha Y. Musa;[5] they investigate the entire process of hadith production, as seen in Asma Sayeed's study of women's varying inclusion and exclusion as hadith transmitters;[6] they expose the inescapable modernity in our engagements of the material, as shown in Kecia Ali's *Lives of Muhammad*; they engage critical questions of how hadiths participate in the construction of gender, as in the work of Ash Geissinger;[7] and they read the hadiths through a confessional lens of Islamic feminist epistemology, exploring new possibilities for hadiths that have been historically read as misogynistic, as in the work of Sa'diyya Shaikh.[8] A new corpus is taking shape.

Whose Muhammad will win? After centuries of dispute, and the fields of contest always moving and changing, it is not my guess that a future Muhammad of perfect unity and coherence awaits. Muslims will continue to engage each other, as well as non-Muslims, in argument over Muhammad's true nature and significance, and those debates will lay out the terms on which future Muhammad are constructed. In the meantime, I find some comfort in the famous tradition of "hair and skin." Muhammad reportedly told his Companions that if they heard a hadith attributed to him that their hearts could recognize and that gave them peace in their hair and skin, they could know that it was really from him. Muhammad assured them that if they feel it near to themselves, "I am the nearest of you to it." But if they heard a hadith that was unrecognizable to their hearts and a source of discomfort that they felt in their hair and skin, it could not speak for Muhammad. If we feel distant from the hadith, Muhammad tells us, "I am the most distant of you from it."[9] Of course, that will not fulfill the needs of every project, whether in academic or community settings. If you want to know who the historical Muhammad really was, you might not accept the evidence provided in my hair and skin; or, for that matter, the Muhammad who showed up in my dreams or the Muhammad who appeared in my ayahuasca vision, comforted and healed in 'Ali's arms as sunbeams snuck through a thick forest ceiling to warm them. The Muhammad of my ayahuasca vision is my private Muhammad; when I participate in Muslim community spaces, I share in multiple public Muhammads. But while there will not be a universal consensus on the Prophet to settle every argument, the hadith of hair and skin gives me hope for my Muhammad, the mercy to my world.

Notes

CHAPTER 1

1. X and Haley, *The Autobiography of Malcolm X*.

CHAPTER 2

1. Hart, *The 100*.
2. Bukharin, "Mecca on the Caravan Routes in Pre-Islamic Antiquity."
3. Evans, *The Emperor Justinian and the Byzantine Empire*, xxx.
4. Evans, *The Emperor Justinian and the Byzantine Empire*, xxviii.
5. Evans, *The Emperor Justinian and the Byzantine Empire*, xxix.
6. Ehrman, *The Triumph of Christianity*, 51–51.
7. Healey, *The Religion of the Nabataeans*, 6.
8. Healey, *The Religion of the Nabataeans*, 112–16.
9. Healey, *The Religion of the Nabataeans*, 114–16.
10. Healey, *The Religion of the Nabataeans*, 108.
11. Healey, *The Religion of the Nabataeans*, 37.
12. Ibn al-Kalbi, *The Book of Idols*, 23; Ibn Hisham, *The Life of Muhammad*, 37.
13. Healey, *The Religion of the Nabataeans*, 37.
14. Daryaee, *Sasanian Persia*, 71.
15. Daryaee, *Sasanian Persia*, 77.
16. Daryaee, *Sasanian Persia*, 26–27.
17. Daryaee, *Sasanian Persia*, 78.
18. Donner, *Muhammad and the Believers*, 20–21.
19. Payne, *A State of Mixture*, 10.
20. Payne, *A State of Mixture*, 13.
21. Payne, *A State of Mixture*, 177–78.
22. Payne, *A State of Mixture*, 179.
23. Daryaee, *Sasanian Persia*, 78.
24. Cole, "'It Was Made to Appear to Them So.'"
25. Mokhtarian, *Rabbis, Sorcerers, Kings, and Priests*, 104.
26. Dandamayev and Gyselen, "2Fiscal System i. Achaemenid ii. Sasanian."
27. Payne, *A State of Mixture*, 53–55.
28. Fisher and Wood, "Writing the History of the 'Persian Arabs.'"
29. Fisher, "The Political Development of the Ghassan between Rome and Iran."
30. Bosworth, "Lakhmids."
31. Toral-Niehoff, "Late Antique Iran and the Arabs."
32. Kister, "Al-Hira," 145.
33. Toral-Niehoff, "The 'Ibad of al-Hira."

34. Bosworth, "Hira."

35. Evans, *The Emperor Justinian and the Byzantine Empire*, 66–67, 102.

36. Bosworth, "Hira."

37. Toral-Niehoff, "The 'Ibad of al-Hira."

38. Demichelis, "Arab Christian Confederations and Muhammad's Believers."

39. Demichelis, "Arab Christian Confederations and Muhammad's Believers."

40. Lecker "Were the Ghassanids and the Byzantines behind Muhammad's Hijra?"

41. Haas, "Mountain Constantines."

42. Robin, "The Judaism of the Ancient Kingdom of Himyar in Arabia."

43. Robin, "The Judaism of the Ancient Kingdom of Himyar in Arabia."

44. Robin, "The Judaism of the Ancient Kingdom of Himyar in Arabia."

45. Bowersock, *The Throne of Adulis*, 80.

46. Robin, "The Judaism of the Ancient Kingdom of Himyar in Arabia."

47. Bowersock, *The Throne of Adulis*, 94.

48. Bowersock, *The Throne of Adulis*, 97.

49. Ibn Hisham, *The Life of Muhammad*, 16–20.

50. Bowersock, *The Throne of Adulis*, 90.

51. Bowersock, *The Throne of Adulis*, 112–15.

52. Ibn Hisham, *The Life of Muhammad*, 27.

53. Bowersock, *The Throne of Adulis*, 111.

54. Bukharin, "Mecca on the Caravan Routes in Pre-Islamic Antiquity."

55. Finster, "Arabia in Late Antiquity."

56. Hoyland, *Arabia and the Arabs*, 157.

57. Hoyland, *Arabia and the Arabs*, 158.

58. Hoyland, *Arabia and the Arabs*, 161.

59. Finster, "Arabia in Late Antiquity."

60. Finster, "Arabia in Late Antiquity."

61. Jallad, *The Religion and Rituals of the Nomads of Pre-Islamic Arabia*, 85.

62. Mazuz, *The Religious and Spiritual Life of the Jews in Medina*, 6.

63. Crone, "The Religion of the Qur'anic Pagans."

64. Mazuz, *The Religious and Spiritual Life of the Jews in Medina*, 6.

65. Bowersock, *The Throne of Adulis*, 83–84.

66. Jallad, "The Pre-Islamic Basmala."

67. Jallad and Sidky, "A Paleo-Arabic Inscription on a Route North of Ta'if," 211.

68. Jallad, *The Religion and Rituals of the Nomads of Pre-Islamic Arabia*, 7–8.

69. Jallad, *The Religion and Rituals of the Nomads of Pre-Islamic Arabia*, 7.

70. Hawting, *The Idea of Idolatry and the Emergence of Islam*.

71. Crone, "The Religion of the Qur'anic Pagans."

72. Crone, "The Religion of the Qur'anic Pagans."

73. Crone, "The Religion of the Qur'anic Pagans," 171.

74. Crone, "The Religion of the Qur'anic Pagans," 171–77.

75. Crone, "The Religion of the Qur'anic Pagans," 177.

76. Bukhari, *Sahih al-Bukhari*; Muslim ibn Hajjaj, *Sahih al-Muslim*.

77. Bukhari, *Sahih al-Bukhari*.

78. Tirmidhi, *Jami' al-Tirmidhi*.

79. Nasa'i, *Sunan al-Nasa'i.*

80. Ibn Hanbal, *Musnad al-Imam Ahmad ibn Hanbal,* no. 1302.

CHAPTER 3

1. Schoeler, *The Biography of Muhammad.*

2. Schoeler, *The Biography of Muhammad,* 119.

3. Vorisco, "Metaphors and Sacred History."

4. Ibn Hisham, *The Life of Muhammad,* 63.

5. Ibn Hisham, *The Life of Muhammad,* 69.

6. Ibn Hisham, *The Life of Muhammad,* 68–72.

7. Ibn Hisham, *The Life of Muhammad,* 70.

8. Hawting, *The Idea of Idolatry and the Emergence of Islam.*

9. Kister, "'A Bag of Meat.'"

10. For some examples, see 4:8–10; 76:8; 89:17–19; 93:9; and 107:2.

11. Knight, *Muhammad's Body,* 53–56.

12. Ibn Hisham, *The Life of Muhammad,* 82–83.

13. For a discussion of this phenomenon, see Kermani, *God Is Beautiful,* 303–11.

14. Ibn Hisham, *The Life of Muhammad,* 106–7.

15. Ibn Hisham, *The Life of Muhammad,* 106–7.

16. Ibn Hisham, *The Life of Muhammad,* 179.

17. Ibn Hisham, *The Life of Muhammad,* 180.

18. Ibn Hisham, *The Life of Muhammad,* 180.

19. Ibn Hisham, *The Life of Muhammad,* 145.

20. Ibn Hisham, *The Life of Muhammad.*

21. Ibn Hisham, *The Life of Muhammad,* 151.

22. Ibn Hisham, *The Life of Muhammad,* 152.

23. Ibn Hisham, *The Life of Muhammad,* 152.

24. Husayn, "Treatises on the Salvation of Abu Talib."

25. Modified translation from Colby, *Narrating Muhammad's Night Journey,* 14.

26. Ibn Hisham, *The Life of Muhammad,* 183.

27. Ibn Hisham, *The Life of Muhammad,* 183.

28. Colby, *Narrating Muhammad's Night Journey,* 15.

29. Ernst, *Following Muhammad,* 88.

30. Ibn Hisham, *The Life of Muhammad,* 186.

31. Melchert, "The Early Controversy over whether the Prophet Saw God."

32. Ibn Hisham, *The Life of Muhammad,* 165–66.

33. Ahmed, *Before Orthodoxy.*

34. Knight, *Muhammad,* 109–11.

35. Lecker, "Constitution of Medina."

36. Cole, "'It Was Made to Appear to Them So.'"

37. Lecker, "The Bewitching of the Prophet Muhammad by the Jews."

38. Haider, "Contesting Intoxication."

39. Waqidi, *The Life of Muhammad,* 87–88.

40. Waqidi, *The Life of Muhammad,* 87–88.

41. Ibn Hisham, *The Life of Muhammad*, 437.

42. Anthony, *The Expeditions*, 298n140.

43. Alajmi, "The Examination of Isnad Validity in Early Islamic History Sources."

44. Kister, "The Massacre of the Banu Qurayza."

45. Schoeler, *The Biography of Muhammad*, 119.

46. Gorke and Schoeler, "Reconstructing the Earliest Sira Texts."

47. Neuwirth, *The Qur'an in Late Antiquity*, 317.

48. Lecker, "The Hudaybiyya Treaty and the Expedition against Khaybar."

49. Cole, "Muhammad and Justinian."

50. Saleh, "The Arabian Context of Muhammad's Life."

51. Cole, "Muhammad and Justinian," 190.

52. Cole, "Muhammad and Justinian," 193.

53. Cole, "Muhammad and Justinian."

54. Kohlberg, "Shi'i Views of the Death of the Prophet Muhammad."

55. Knight, *Muhammad's Body*, 141.

56. Knight, *Muhammad's Body*, 139.

57. Knight, *Muhammad's Body*, 140.

58. Knight, *Muhammad's Body*, 142–43.

59. Knight, *Muhammad's Body*, 142–43.

60. Knight, *Muhammad's Body*, 153.

61. Donner, *Muhammad and the Believers*, 99, 211.

62. Gunther, "Modern Literary Theory Applied to Classical Arabic Texts." See also Gunther, "Fictional Narration and Imagination within an Authoritative Framework."

CHAPTER 4

1. Gorke, "Al-'Abbas b. 'Abd al-Muttalib."

2. Ibn Hanbal, *Musnad*, nos. 2283, 2601, 3125, 3357–543.

3. Gorke, "Al-'Abbas b. 'Abd al-Muttalib."

4. Gorke, "Al-'Abbas b. 'Abd al-Muttalib."

5. Gorke, "Al-'Abbas b. 'Abd al-Muttalib."

6. Knight, *Muhammad's Body*, 113.

7. Dahmani, *Sayyid al-Tabi'in*, 12–13.

8. Mizzi, *Tuhfat al-Ashraf bi Marifat al-Atraf*, 130–896.

9. Dhahabi, *Siyar A'lam al-Nubala'*, 5:378–93.

10. Berg, "Lexicological Hadith and the 'School' of Ibn 'Abbas," 67–88, 84.

11. Harvey, "Slavery, Indenture, and Freedom."

12. Dahmani, *Sayyid al-Tabi'in*, 9.

13. Bosworth, "Raja' ibn Haywa al-Kindi and the Umayyad Caliphs."

14. Ibn Hanbal, *Musnad al-Imam Ahmad ibn Hanbal*, no. 2256.

15. Harvey, "Slavery, Indenture, and Freedom."

16. Harvey, "Slavery, Indenture, and Freedom."

17. Harvey, "Slavery, Indenture, and Freedom."

18. Harvey, "Slavery, Indenture, and Freedom."

19. Dhahabi, *Siyar A'lam al-Nubala'*, 5:378–93.

20. Dhahabi, *Siyar A'lam al-Nubala'*, 5:266–70.

21. Dhahabi, *Siyar A'lam al-Nubala'*, 5:423–29.

22. Dhahabi, *Siyar A'lam al-Nubala'*, 5:267–70.

23. Dhahabi, *Siyar A'lam al-Nubala'*, 5:423–29.

24. Dhahabi, *Siyar A'lam al-Nubala'*, 5:186–98.

25. Dhahabi, *Siyar A'lam al-Nubala'*, vol. 5.

26. Dhahabi, *Siyar A'lam al-Nubala'*, 5:396.

27. Dhahabi, *Siyar A'lam al-Nubala'*, 5:424.

28. Dhahabi, *Siyar A'lam al-Nubala'*, 5:384, 385.

29. Kugle, *Homosexuality in Islam*, 105–6.

30. Dhahabi, *Siyar A'lam al-Nubala'*, 5:186–98.

31. Dhahabi, *Siyar A'lam al-Nubala'*, 5:285.

32. Dhahabi, *Siyar A'lam al-Nubala'*, 5:284–85.

33. Ahmed, *Before Orthodoxy*, 146–58.

34. Donner, "Maymun b. Mihran."

35. Juynboll, *Encyclopedia of Canonical Hadith*, 60–61.

36. Juynboll, "Some Isnad-Analytical Methods."

37. Motzki, "'Amr b. Dinar."

38. Ibn Hanbal, *Musnad al-Imam Ahmad ibn Hanbal*, no. 6441.

39. Ibn Hanbal, *Musnad al-Imam Ahmad ibn Hanbal*, no. 6416.

40. Motzki, *Reconstruction of a Source of Ibn Ishaq's Life of the Prophet and Early Qur'an Exegesis*, 4.

41. Lucas, *Constructive Critics, Hadith Literature, and the Articulation of Sunni Islam*, 338.

42. Ibn Hanbal, *Musnad al-Imam Ahmad ibn Hanbal*, nos. 1871, 2551, 2552.

43. Ibn Hanbal, *Musnad al-Imam Ahmad ibn Hanbal*, nos. 2112, 2434.

44. Ibn Hanbal, *Musnad al-Imam Ahmad ibn Hanbal*, nos. 2165, 2553.

45. Ibn Hanbal, *Musnad al-Imam Ahmad ibn Hanbal*, nos. 3062, 3063, 3542.

46. Ibn Hanbal, *Musnad al-Imam Ahmad ibn Hanbal*, nos. 1905, 2496, 3262.

47. Ibn Hanbal, *Musnad al-Imam Ahmad ibn Hanbal*, nos. 2432, 3385.

48. Ibn Hanbal, *Musnad al-Imam Ahmad ibn Hanbal*, no. 2026.

49. Ibn Hanbal, *Musnad al-Imam Ahmad ibn Hanbal*, nos. 2055, 3355, 3189, 3356.

50. Husayn, "Treatises on the Salvation of Abu Talib."

51. Ibn Hanbal, *Musnad al-Imam Ahmad ibn Hanbal*, nos. 2636, 2690.

52. Ibn Hanbal, *Musnad al-Imam Ahmad ibn Hanbal*, nos. 2374, 2999.

53. Ibn Hanbal, *Musnad al-Imam Ahmad ibn Hanbal*, nos. 2875, 3310.

54. Ibn Hanbal, *Musnad al-Imam Ahmad ibn Hanbal*, no. 2734.

55. Ibn Hanbal, *Musnad al-Imam Ahmad ibn Hanbal*, no. 2661.

56. Abd-Allah Wymann-Landgraf, *Malik and Medina*, 408.

57. Ibn Hanbal, *Musnad al-Imam Ahmad ibn Hanbal*, nos. 2173, 3227.

58. Ibn Hanbal, *Musnad al-Imam Ahmad ibn Hanbal*, nos. 1877, 2210, 3074, 3532, 3533.

59. Ibn Hanbal, *Musnad al-Imam Ahmad ibn Hanbal*, nos. 2664, 2865, 2866, 2879.

60. Ibn Hanbal, *Musnad al-Imam Ahmad ibn Hanbal*, no. 3121.

61. Ibn Hanbal, *Musnad al-Imam Ahmad ibn Hanbal*, no. 2277.

62. Ibn Hanbal, *Musnad al-Imam Ahmad ibn Hanbal*, nos. 2977, 3351.

63. Ibn Hanbal, *Musnad al-Imam Ahmad ibn Hanbal*, no. 2790.

64. Haider, "Contesting Intoxication."

65. Ibn Hanbal, *Musnad al-Imam Ahmad ibn Hanbal*, nos. 2946, 3114, 3528.

66. Haider, "Contesting Intoxication."

67. Ibn Hanbal, *Musnad al-Imam Ahmad ibn Hanbal*, nos. 2606, 3495.

68. Ibn Hanbal, *Musnad al-Imam Ahmad ibn Hanbal*, no. 2831.

69. Ibn Hanbal, *Musnad al-Imam Ahmad ibn Hanbal*, no. 3157.

70. Ibn Hanbal, *Musnad al-Imam Ahmad ibn Hanbal*, nos. 2476 (long), 2625, 3274.

71. Ibn Hanbal, *Musnad al-Imam Ahmad ibn Hanbal*, no. 2655.

72. Ibn Hanbal, *Musnad al-Imam Ahmad ibn Hanbal*, no. 2207.

73. Ibn Hanbal, *Musnad al-Imam Ahmad ibn Hanbal*, no. 2143.

74. Ibn Hanbal, *Musnad al-Imam Ahmad ibn Hanbal*, no. 2946.

75. Colby, *Narrating Muhammad's Night Journey*, 2–3.

76. Colby, *Narrating Muhammad's Night Journey*, 3.

77. Ahmed, *Before Orthodoxy*, 20.

78. Ibn Hanbal, *Musnad al-Imam Ahmad ibn Hanbal*, nos. 2197, 2198, 2347, 3179, 3180, 2324, 2501, 2502, 2697.

79. Ahmed, *Before Orthodoxy*, 159.

80. Ahmed, *Before Orthodoxy*.

81. Kugle, *Homosexuality in Islam*, 102.

82. Kugle, *Homosexuality in Islam*, 107–8.

83. Dhahabi, *Siyar A'lam al-Nubala'*, vol. 5.

84. Dhahabi, *Siyar A'lam al-Nubala'*, 5:91–93.

85. Ibn Hanbal, *Musnad al-Imam Ahmad ibn Hanbal*, nos. 1840, 2397, 2422, 2881, 3023, 3033, 3102, 3379, 3061.

86. Ibn Hanbal, *Musnad al-Imam Ahmad ibn Hanbal*, no. 3127.

87. Ibn Hanbal, *Musnad al-Imam Ahmad ibn Hanbal*, nos. 3550, 3551.

88. Ibn Hanbal, *Musnad al-Imam Ahmad ibn Hanbal*, nos. 4255, 4340, 4341.

89. Ibn Hanbal, *Musnad al-Imam Ahmad ibn Hanbal*, nos. 4350, 4410.

90. Berg, *The Development of Exegesis in Early Islam*, 214.

91. Ibn Hanbal, *Musnad al-Imam Ahmad ibn Hanbal*, nos. 3599, 3697, 4372, 4412, 4330, 4217.

92. Ibn Hanbal, *Musnad al-Imam Ahmad ibn Hanbal*, nos. 4322, 4364.

93. Ibn Hanbal, *Musnad al-Imam Ahmad ibn Hanbal*, no. 4298.

94. Ibn Hanbal, *Musnad al-Imam Ahmad ibn Hanbal*, nos. 4386, 4347.

95. Ibn Hanbal, *Musnad al-Imam Ahmad ibn Hanbal*, nos. 4363, 4402.

96. Ibn Hanbal, *Musnad al-Imam Ahmad ibn Hanbal*, nos. 3639, 4351, 4332, 4180.

97. Ibn Hanbal, *Musnad al-Imam Ahmad ibn Hanbal*, no. 4315.

98. Ibn Hanbal, *Musnad al-Imam Ahmad ibn Hanbal*, no. 3594.

99. Ibn Hanbal, *Musnad al-Imam Ahmad ibn Hanbal*, no. 2978.

100. Ibn Hanbal, *Musnad al-Imam Ahmad ibn Hanbal*, no. 2271.

101. Dahmani, *Sayyid al-Tabi'in*, 85.

102. Ibn Hanbal, *Musnad al-Imam Ahmad ibn Hanbal*, no. 3954.

103. Ibn Hanbal, *Musnad al-Imam Ahmad ibn Hanbal*, nos. 3781, 3810, 4296, 4301, 4353, 4375.

104. Melchert, "The Early Controversy over whether the Prophet Saw God."

105. Ibn Hanbal, *Musnad al-Imam Ahmad ibn Hanbal*, nos. 1916, 3500, 3546, 2580, 2634.

106. Ibn Hanbal, *Musnad al-Imam Ahmad ibn Hanbal*, no. 1956.

107. Ibn Hanbal, *Musnad al-Imam Ahmad ibn Hanbal*, no. 3484.

108. Wasserstrom, *Between Muslim and Jew*, 171–75.

109. Lucas, "'Perhaps You Only Kissed Her?'"

110. Ibn Hanbal, *Musnad al-Imam Ahmad ibn Hanbal*, no. 2314.

111. Lucas, *Constructive Critics, Hadith Literature, and the Articulation of Sunni Islam*; Brown, *The Canonization of al-Bukhari and Muslim*.

CHAPTER 5

1. Anthony, *Muhammad and the Empires of Faith*, 138.

2. Schoeler, "Oral Torah and Hadith."

3. Donner, *Muhammad and the Believers*, 205–13.

4. Donner, *Muhammad and the Believers*, 205–13, 211.

5. Anthony, *Muhammad and the Empires of Faith*, 176.

6. Schoeler, "Oral Torah and Hadith."

7. Knight, *Muhammad's Body*, 87–88.

8. Alajmi, "The Examination of Isnad Validity in Early Islamic History Sources."

9. de Jarmy, "Dating the Emergence of the Warrior-Prophet in Maghazi Literature," 95.

10. de Jarmy, "Dating the Emergence of the Warrior-Prophet in Maghazi Literature," 95.

11. de Jarmy, "Dating the Emergence of the Warrior-Prophet in Maghazi Literature."

12. de Jarmy, "Dating the Emergence of the Warrior-Prophet in Maghazi Literature."

13. Tlili, *Animals in the Qur'an*, 116–23.

14. Afsaruddin, "Where Earth and Heaven Meet."

15. Moin, *The Millennial Sovereign*, 5.

16. Moin, *The Millennial Sovereign*, 23–55, 88–92.

17. Crone and Hinds, *God's Caliph*, 43–57.

18. Donner, *Narratives of Islamic Origins*, 40–51.

19. Dutton, *The Origins of Islamic Law*, 43–45.

20. Lowry, "The Prophet as Lawgiver and Legal Authority."

21. Lawrence, *Who Is Allah?*, 60.

22. Ernst, *Following Muhammad*, 6.

23. Wagner and Briggs, *The Penultimate Curiosity*, 133.

24. von Stuckrad, *Locations of Knowledge in Medieval and Early Modern Europe*, 87.

25. Ahmed, *What Is Islam?*, 437.

26. Griffel, "Muslim Philosophers' Rationalist Explanation of Muhammad's Prophecy."

27. Griffel, "Muslim Philosophers' Rationalist Explanation of Muhammad's Prophecy."

28. Hall, "Intellect, Soul and Body in Ibn Sina."

29. Ahmed, *What Is Islam?*, 13.

30. Karamustafa, *Sufism*, 16.

31. Karamustafa, *Sufism*, 16.

32. Ogunnaike, "Annihilation in the Messenger Revisited."

33. Rubin, "Pre-existence and Light."

34. Ibn al-'Arabi, *The Bezels of Wisdom*, 71–73.

35. Safi, "Bargaining with Baraka."

36. Ogunnaike, *Poetry in Praise of Prophetic Perfection*, 7.

37. Gruber, *The Praiseworthy One*, 276, 287–88.

38. Styers, *Making Magic*.

39. Denzey, "A New Star on the Horizon."

40. Knight, *Magic in Islam*, 81.

41. Knight, *Magic in Islam*, 91.

42. Caiozzo, "The Horoscope of Iskandar Sultan as a Cosmological Vision in the Islamic World."

43. Almond, *History of Islam in German Thought*, 37.

44. Hawting, *The Idea of Idolatry and the Emergence of Islam*.

45. Crone, *The Nativist Prophets of Early Islamic Iran*, 221.

46. Crone, *The Nativist Prophets of Early Islamic Iran*, 212.

47. Crone, *The Nativist Prophets of Early Islamic Iran*, 224–25.

48. Irani, *The Muhammad Avatara*, 155.

49. Irani, *The Muhammad Avatara*, 351.

50. Knight, *Muhammad's Body*, 35–40.

CHAPTER 6

1. Rouayheb, *Before Homosexuality in the Arab-Islamic World*.

2. Lawrence, *Who Is Allah?*, 64nn10, 11.

3. Kugle, *Homosexuality in Islam*, 102.

4. Little, "Why I Studied the Aisha Hadith for My PhD."

5. Ali, *Sexual Ethics and Islam*, 137.

6. Kueny, *Conceiving Identities*, 32.

7. Josephson, *The Invention of Religion in Japan*, 109–17.

8. McMahen, *The Making of Buddhist Modernism*, 96–97.

9. Jackson, *Sufism for Non-Sufis?*

10. Donner, *Muhammad and the Believers*, 111.

11. Sahner, "The First Iconoclasm in Islam."

12. Donner, *Muhammad and the Believers*, 194–224.

13. Schoeler, "Oral Torah and Hadith."

14. Natif, "'Painters Will Be Punished.'"

15. Gruber, *The Praiseworthy One*, 20.

16. Gruber, "Images of the Prophet in and out of Modernity."

17. "An Interview with Mahomet!"

18. "An Interview with Mahomet!"

19. Bowen, *A History of Conversion to Islam in the United States*, 110.

20. Abd-Allah, *A Muslim in Victorian America*.

21. Higgins, *Anacalypsis*, 728.

22. Higgins, *Anacalypsis*, 727.

23. Morris, "Golden Threads in the Tapestry of History," 349.

24. Morris, "Golden Threads in the Tapestry of History," 353.

CHAPTER 7

1. Ali, *The Lives of Muhammad*, 119.

2. Zuckerberg, *Not All Dead White Men*, 11.

3. Zuckerberg, *Not All Dead White Men*, 185.

4. Zuckerberg, *Not All Dead White Men*, 185–86.

5. Musa, *Hadith as Scripture*.

6. Sayeed, *Women and the Transmission of Religious Knowledge in Islam*.

7. Geissinger, "'Are Men the Majority in Paradise, or Women?'"; Geissinger, "'Umm al-Darda' Sat in Tashahhud Like a Man'"; Geissinger, "Mary in the Qu'ran"; Geissinger, "The Portrayal of Hajj as a Context for Women's Exegesis."

8. Shaikh, "Knowledge, Women, and Gender in the Hadith."

9. Ibn Hanbal, *Musnad al-Imam Ahmad ibn Hanbal*, no. 15725; Brown, "The Rules of Matn Criticism."

Bibliography

Abd-Allah, Umar F. *A Muslim in Victorian America: The Life of Alexander Russell Webb.* Oxford: Oxford University Press, 2006.

Abd-Allah Wymann-Landgraf, Umar F. *Malik and Medina: Islamic Legal Reasoning in the Formative Period.* Leiden, the Netherlands: Brill, 2013.

Afsaruddin, Asma. "Where Earth and Heaven Meet: Remembering Muhammad as Head of State." In *The Cambridge Companion to Muhammad,* edited by Jonathan E. Brockopp, 180–98. Cambridge: Cambridge University Press, 2010.

Ahmed, Shahab. *Before Orthodoxy: The Satanic Verses in Early Islam.* Cambridge, MA: Harvard University Press, 2017.

———. *What Is Islam? The Importance of Being Islamic.* Princeton, NJ: Princeton University Press, 2015.

Alajmi, Abdulhadi. "The Examination of Isnad Validity in Early Islamic History Sources: 'Sa'd ibn Mu'adh's Judgment of Banu Qurayza' as a Case Study." *Anaquel de Estudios Árabes* 21 (2010): 7–34.

Ali, Kecia. *The Lives of Muhammad.* Cambridge, MA: Harvard University Press, 2014.

———. *Sexual Ethics and Islam: Feminist Reflections on Qur'an, Hadith, and Jurisprudence.* Oxford, UK: Oneworld, 2006.

Almond, Ian. *History of Islam in German Thought.* New York: Routledge, 2009.

Anthony, Sean W. *The Expeditions: An Early Biography of Muhammad.* New York: New York University Press, 2014.

———. *Muhammad and the Empires of Faith.* Oakland: University of California Press, 2020.

Berg, Herbert. *The Development of Exegesis in Early Islam: The Authenticity of Muslim Literature from the Formative Period.* New York: Routledge, 2000.

———. "Lexicological Hadith and the 'School' of Ibn 'Abbas." In *The Meaning of the Word: Lexicology and Qur'anic Exegesis,* edited by S. R. Burge, 67–88. Oxford: Oxford University Press, 2015.

Bosworth, C. E. "Hira." In *Encyclopaedia Iranica.* https://www.iranicaonline.org /articles/hira. Last updated March 22, 2012.

———. "Lakhmids." In *Encyclopaedia Iranica.* https://www.iranicaonline.org /articles/lakhmids. Last updated December 20, 2012.

———. "Raja' ibn Haywa al-Kindi and the Umayyad Caliphs." In *The Articulation of Early Islamic State Structures,* edited by Fred Donner, 89–134. New York: Routledge, 2016.

Bowen, Patrick D. *A History of Conversion to Islam in the United States.* Vol. 1. Leiden, the Netherlands: Brill, 2017.

Bowersock, G. W. *The Throne of Adulis: Red Sea Wars on the Eve of Islam.* Oxford: Oxford University Press, 2013.

Brown, Jonathan A. C. *The Canonization of al-Bukhārī and Muslim: The Formation and Function of the Sunnī Ḥadīth Canon.* Leiden, the Netherlands: Brill, 2007.

———. "The Rules of Matn Criticism: There Are No Rules." *Islamic Law and Society* 19 (2012): 356–96.

Bukhari, Muhammad ibn Isma'il. *Sahih al-Bukhari: Kitab al-tafsir.* Sunnah.com. Accessed March 2022.

Bukharin, Mikhail. "Mecca on the Caravan Routes in Pre-Islamic Antiquity." In *The Qur'an in Context,* edited by Angelika Neuwirth, Nicolai Sinai, and Michael Marx, 115–34. Leiden, the Netherlands: Brill, 2009.

Caiozzo, Anna. "The Horoscope of Iskandar Sultan as a Cosmological Vision in the Islamic World." In *Horoscopes and Public Spheres: Essays on the History of Astrology,* edited by Günther Oestmann, H. Darrel Rutkin, and Kocku von Stuckrad, 115–44. Berlin: De Grutyer, 2012.

Colby, Frederick S. *Narrating Muhammad's Night Journey: Tracing the Development of the Ibn 'Abbas Ascension Discourse.* Albany: State University of New York Press, 2008.

Cole, Juan. "'It Was Made to Appear to Them So': The Crucifixion, Jews and Sasanian War Propaganda in the Qur'an." *Religion* 51, no. 3 (2021): 404–22.

———. "Muhammad and Justinian: Roman Legal Traditions and the Qur'an." *Journal of Near Eastern Studies* 79, no. 2 (2020): 183–96.

Crone, Patricia. *The Nativist Prophets of Early Islamic Iran: Rural Revolt and Local Zoroastrianism.* Cambridge: Cambridge University Press, 2012.

———. "The Religion of the Qur'anic Pagans: God and the Lesser Deities." *Arabica* 57, no. 2/3 (2010): 151–200.

Crone, Patricia, and Martin Hinds. *God's Caliph: Religious Authority in the First Centuries of Islam.* Cambridge: Cambridge University Press, 1986.

Dahmani, Taraki ibn al-Hasan al-. *Sayyid al-Tabi'in: Sa'id ibn Jubayr.* Oman: Amwaj, 2012.

Dandamayev, Mohammad A., and Rika Gyselen. "Fiscal System i. Achaemenid ii. Sasanian." *Encyclopedia Iranica* 9, no. 6 (2012): 639–46.

Daryaee, Touraj. *Sasanian Persia: The Rise and Fall of an Empire.* New York: I. B. Tauris, 2014.

de Jarmy, Adrien. "Dating the Emergence of the Warrior-Prophet in Maghazi Literature." In *The Presence of the Prophet in Early Modern and Contemporary Islam.* Vol. 1, edited by Denis Gril, Stefan Reichmuth, and Dilek Sarmis, 79–99. Leiden, the Netherlands: Brill, 2022.

Demichelis, Marco. "Arab Christian Confederations and Muhammad's Believers: On the Origins of Jihad." *Religions* 12, no. 710 (2021).

Denzey, Nicola. "A New Star on the Horizon: Astral Christianities and Stellar Debates in Early Christian Discourse." In *Prayer, Magic and the Stars in the Ancient and Late Antique World,* edited by Scott Nogoel, Joel Walker, and Brannon Wheeler, 207–21. University Park: Pennsylvania State University Press, 2003.

Dhahabi, Shams ad-Din al-. *Siyar A'lam al-Nubala'.* Cairo: Dar El-Hadith, 2006.

Donner, Fred. "Maymun b. Mihran." *Encyclopaedia of Islam.* 2nd ed., edited by P. Bearman, T. Bianquis, C. E. Bosworth, E. van Donzel, and W. P. Heinrichs.

https://referenceworks.brillonline.com/entries/encyclopaedia-of-islam-2
/maymun-b-mihran-SIM_5074?s.num=652&s.start=640. Accessed January 4,
2023.

———. *Muhammad and the Believers: At the Origins of Islam*. Cambridge, MA:
Belknap Press of Harvard University Press, 2010.

———. *Narratives of Islamic Origins: The Beginnings of Islamic Historical Writing*.
Princeton, NJ: Darwin, 1998.

Dutton, Yasin. *The Origins of Islamic Law: The Qur'an, the Muwatta' and Madinan
Amal*. New York: Routledge, 2013.

Ehrman, Bart D. *The Triumph of Christianity: How a Forbidden Religion Swept the
World*. New York: Simon & Schuster, 2018.

Ernst, Carl. *Following Muhammad*. Chapel Hill: University of North Carolina Press,
2003.

Evans, James Allan. *The Emperor Justinian and the Byzantine Empire*. Westport, CT:
Greenwood, 2005.

Finster, Barbara. "Arabia in Late Antiquity: An Outline of the Cultural Situation
in the Peninsula at the Time of Muhammad." In *The Qur'an in Context*, edited
by Angelika Neuwirth, Nicolai Sinai, and Michael Marx, 61–114. Leiden, the
Netherlands: Brill, 2009.

Fisher, Greg. "The Political Development of the Ghassan between Rome and Iran."
Journal of Late Antiquity 1, no. 2 (Fall 2008): 311–34.

Fisher, Greg, and Philip Wood. "Writing the History of the 'Persian Arabs': The
Pre-Islamic Perspective on the 'Nasrids' of al-Hirah." *Iranian Studies* 49, no. 2
(2016): 247–90.

Geissinger, A. "'Are Men the Majority in Paradise, or Women?' Constructing Gender
and Communal Boundaries in Muslim b. al-Hajjaj's (d. 261/875) Kitab al-Janna."
In *Roads to Paradise: Eschatology and Concepts of the Hereafter in Islam*, edited by
Sebastian Guenther and Todd Lawson, 309–40. Leiden, the Netherlands: Brill,
2016.

———. "Mary in the Qur'an: Rereading Subversive Births." In *Sacred Tropes: Tanakh,
New Testament, and Qur'an as Literature and Culture*. Biblical Interpretation Series
98, edited by Roberta Sterman Sabbath, 379–92. Leiden, the Netherlands: Brill,
2009.

———. "The Portrayal of Hajj as a Context for Women's Exegesis: Textual Evidence
in al-Bukhari's (d. 870 C.E.) *Sahih*." In *Insights into Classical Arabic Literature and
Islam*, edited by Sebastian Guenther, 153–79. Leiden, the Netherlands: Brill,
2005.

———. "'Umm al-Darda' Sat in Tashahhud Like a Man': Towards the Historical
Contextualization of a Portrayal of Female Religious Authority." *Muslim World*
103, no. 3 (July 2013): 305–19.

Gorke, Andreas. "Al-'Abbas b. 'Abd al-Muttalib." *Encyclopedia of Islam* 3.
https://referenceworks.brillonline.com/entries/encyclopaedia-of-islam-3/al
-abbas-b-abd-al-muttalib-COM_22582?s.num=19. Accessed January 4, 2023.

Gorke, Andreas, and Gregor Schoeler. "Reconstructing the Earliest Sira Texts: The
Higra in the Corpus of 'Urwa b. al-Zubayr." *Der Islam* 82 (2005): 209–20.

Griffel, Frank. "Muslim Philosophers' Rationalist Explanation of Muhammad's Prophecy." In *The Cambridge Companion to Muhammad*, edited by Jonathan E. Brockopp, 158–79. Cambridge: Cambridge University Press, 2010.

Gruber, Christiane. "Images of the Prophet in and out of Modernity: The Curious Case of a 2008 Mural in Tehran." In *Visual Culture in the Modern Middle East: Rhetoric of the Image*, edited by Christiane Gruber and Sune Haugbolle, 3–31. Bloomington: Indiana University Press, 2013.

———. *The Praiseworthy One: The Prophet Muhammad in Islamic Texts and Images*. Bloomington: Indiana University Press, 2019.

Gunther, Sebastian. "Fictional Narration and Imagination within an Authoritative Framework: Towards a New Understanding of Hadith." In *Story-Telling in the Framework of Non-fictional Arab Literature*, edited by Stefan Leder, 433–71. Weisbaden, Germany: Harrassowitz, 2000.

———. "Modern Literary Theory Applied to Classical Arabic Texts: Hadith Revisited." In *Understanding Near Eastern Literatures*, edited by Verena Klemm and Beatrice Grundler, 171–76. Weisbaden, Germany: Harrassowitz, 2000.

Haas, Christopher. "Mountain Constantines: The Christianization of Askum and Iberia." *Journal of Late Antiquity* 1, no. 1. (Spring 2008): 101–26.

Haider, Najam. "Contesting Intoxication: Early Juristic Debates over the Lawfulness of Alcoholic Beverages." *Islamic Law and Society* 20, no. 1/2 (2013): 48–89.

Hall, Robert. "Intellect, Soul and Body in Ibn Sina: Systematic Synthesis and Development of the Aristotelian, Neo-Platonic and Galenic Theories." In *Interpreting Avicenna: Science and Philosophy in Medieval Islam*, edited by Jon McGinnis, 62–86. Leiden, the Netherlands: Brill, 2004.

Hart, Michael. *The 100: A Ranking of the Most Influential Persons in History*. New York: Citadel Press, 1992.

Harvey, Ramon. "Slavery, Indenture, and Freedom: Exegesis of the 'Mukataba Verse' (Q. 24:33) in Early Islam." *Journal of Qurʾanic Studies* 21, no. 2 (2019): 68–107.

Hawting, G. R. *The Idea of Idolatry and the Emergence of Islam: From Polemic to History*. Cambridge: Cambridge University Press, 1999.

Healey, John F. *The Religion of the Nabataeans: A Conspectus*. Leiden, the Netherlands: Brill, 2001.

Higgins, Godfrey. *Anacalypsis: An Attempt to Draw Aside the Veil of the Saitic Isis; or An Inquiry into the Origin of Languages, Nations and Religions*. New York: Macy-Masius, 1927.

Hoyland, Robert G. *Arabia and the Arabs: From the Bronze Age to the Coming of Islam*. New York: Routledge, 2001.

Husayn, Nebil. "Treatises on the Salvation of Abu Talib." *Shii Studies Review* 1 (2017): 3–41.

Ibn al-ʿArabi, *The Bezels of Wisdom*. Translated by R. W. J. Austin. Ramsey, NJ: Paulist, 1980.

Ibn al-Kalbi, Hisham. *The Book of Idols*. Translated by Nabith Amin Faris. Princeton, NJ: Princeton Legacy Library, 1952.

Ibn Hanbal, Ahmad. *Musnad al-Imam Ahmad Ibn Hanbal*. Beirut: ʿAlam al-Kutub, 1998.

Ibn Hisham, 'Abd al-Malik. *The Life of Muhammad.* Translated by A. Guillaume. Oxford: Oxford University Press, 2012.

"An Interview with Mahomet." *Light: A Journal of Psychical, Occult, and Mystical Research* 8 no. 408 (1888): 531.

Irani, Ayesha A. *The Muhammad Avatara: Salvation History, Translation, and the Making of Bengali Islam.* Oxford: Oxford University Press, 2021.

Jackson, Sherman. *Sufism for Non-Sufis? Ibn 'Ata' Allah al-Sakandari's Taj al-'Arus.* Oxford: Oxford University Press, 2012.

Jallad, Ahmad al-. "The Pre-Islamic Basmala: Reflections on Its First Epigraphic Attestation and Its Original Significance" (draft). Academia.edu. Accessed March 2022.

———. *The Religion and Rituals of the Nomads of Pre-Islamic Arabia: A Reconstruction Based on the Inscriptions.* Leiden, the Netherlands: Brill, 2022.

Jallad, Ahmad al-, and Hythem Sidkey. "A Paleo-Arabic Inscription on a Route North of Ta'if." *Arabian Archaeology and Epigraphy* 33, no. 1 (2021): 202–15.

Josephson, Joseph Ananda. *The Invention of Religion in Japan.* Chicago: University of Chicago Press, 2012.

Juynboll, G. H. A. *Encyclopedia of Canonical Hadith.* Leiden, the Netherlands: Brill, 2007.

———. "Some Isnad-Analytical Methods Illustrated on the Basis of Several Women-Demeaning Sayings from Hadith Literature." *Al-Qantara* 10 (1989): 343–83.

Karamustafa, Ahmet T. *Sufism: The Formative Period.* Berkeley: University of California Press, 2007.

Kermani, Navid. *God is Beautiful: The Aesthetic Experience of the Qur'an.* Translated by Tony Crawford. Oxford: Wiley Blackwell, 2015.

Kister, M. J. "Al-Hira: Some Notes on Its Relations with Arabia." *Arabica* 15, no. 2 (June 1968): 143–69.

———. "'A Bag of Meat': A Study of an Early 'Hadith.'" *Bulletin of the School of Oriental and African Studies, University of London* 22, no. 2 (1970): 267–75.

———. "The Massacre of the Banu Qurayza: A Re-examination of a Tradition." *Jerusalem Studies in Arabic and Islam* 8 (1986): 61–96.

Knight, Michael Muhammad. *Magic in Islam.* New York: TarcherPerigee/Penguin Random House, 2016.

———. *Muhammad: Forty Introductions.* Berkeley, CA: Soft Skull, 2019.

———. *Muhammad's Body: Baraka Networks and the Prophetic Assemblage.* Chapel Hill: University of North Carolina Press, 2020.

Kohlberg, Etan. "Shi'i Views of the Death of the Prophet Muhammad." In *Medieval Arabic Thought: Essays in Honour of Fritz Zimmermann*, 77–86. London: Warburg Institute, 2012.

Kueny, Kathryn. *Conceiving Identities: Maternity in Medieval Muslim Discourse and Practice.* Albany: SUNY Press, 2013.

Kugle, Scott. *Homosexuality in Islam.* Oxford: Oxford University Press, 2010.

Lawrence, Bruce. *Who Is Allah?* Chapel Hill: University of North Carolina Press, 2015.

Lecker, Michael. "The Bewitching of the Prophet Muhammad by the Jews: A Note à propos ʿAbd al-Malik b. Habib's *Mukhtasar fi ʿl-tibb.*" *Al-Qantara* 13 (1992): 561–69.

———. "Constitution of Medina." *Encyclopedia of Islam* 3, edited by Kate Fleet, Gudrun Krämer, Denis Matringe, John Nawas, and Everett Rowson. https://referenceworks.brillonline.com/entries/encyclopaedia-of-islam-3 /constitution-of-medina-COM_24415?s.num=0&s.rows=20&s.f.s2_parent=s.f .book.encyclopaedia-of-islam-3&s.q=Constitution+of+Medina. Accessed January 4, 2023.

———. "The Hudaybiyya Treaty and the Expedition against Khaybar." *Jerusalem Studies in Arabic and Islam* 5 (1984): 1–9.

———. "Were the Ghassanids and the Byzantines behind Muhammad's Hijra?" In *Les Jafnides: Des rois arabes au service de Byzance*, edited by Denis Genequand and Christian Julien Robin, 277–94. Paris: De Boccard, 2014.

Little, Joshua. "Why I Studied the Aisha Hadith for My PhD: Some Reflections on Religious Interpretation, Sunni Orthodoxy, and Islamophobia." Islamic Origins: Essays on History, Religion, and Politics. https://islamicorigins.com/why-i -studied-the-aisha-hadith/. Accessed March 15, 2023.

Lowry, Joseph E. "The Prophet as Lawgiver and Legal Authority." In *The Cambridge Companion to Muhammad*, edited by Jonathan E. Brockopp, 83–102. Cambridge: Cambridge University Press, 2010.

Lucas, Scott C. *Constructive Critics, Hadith Literature, and the Articulation of Sunni Islam: The Legacy of the Generation of Ibn Saʿd, Ibn Maʾin, and Ibn Hanbal.* Leiden, the Netherlands: Brill, 2004.

———. "ʿPerhaps You Only Kissed Her?ʾ A Contrapuntal Reading of Illicit Sex in the Sunni Hadith Literature." *Journal of Religious Ethics* 39, no. 3 (September 2011): 399–415.

Mazuz, Haggai. *The Religious and Spiritual Life of the Jews in Medina.* Leiden, the Netherlands: Brill, 2014.

McMahen, David L. *The Making of Buddhist Modernism.* Oxford: Oxford University Press, 2008.

Melchert, Christopher. "The Early Controversy over whether the Prophet Saw God." *Arabica* 62, no. 4 (2015): 459–76.

Mizzi, Yusuf al-. *Tuhfat al-Ashraf bi Marifat al-Atraf.* Vol. 11. Edited by Bashur Maruf. Tunis: Dar al-Gharb al-Islami, 2019.

Moin, A. Azfar. *The Millennial Sovereign: Sacred Kingship and Sainthood in Islam.* New York: Columbia University Press, 2012.

Mokhtarian, Jason Sion. *Rabbis, Sorcerers, Kings, and Priests: The Culture of the Talmud in Ancient Iran.* Berkeley: University of California Press, 2021.

Morris, Kenneth. "Golden Threads in the Tapestry of History, Part III, Chapter V—The Lion of God." *Theosophical Path* 11, no. 4 (October 1916): 346–53.

Motzki, Harald. "ʿAmr b. Dinar." *Encyclopaedia of Islam* 3, edited by Kate Fleet, Gudrun Krämer, Denis Matringe, John Nawas, and Everett Rowson (2009). https://referenceworks.brillonline.com/entries/encyclopaedia-of-islam-3

/amr-b-dinar-COM_22955?s.num=0&s.f.s2_parent=s.f.book.encyclopaedia-of
-islam-3&s.q=%CA%BEAmr+b.+Dinar. Accessed January 4, 2023.

———. *Reconstruction of a Source of Ibn Ishaq's Life of the Prophet and Early Qurʾan Exegesis: A Study of Early Ibn ʿAbbas Traditions*. Piscataway, NJ: Gorgias, 2017.

Musa, Aisha Y. *Hadith as Scripture: Discussions on the Authority of Prophetic Traditions in Islam*. New York: Palgrave and Macmillan, 2008.

Muslim ibn Hajjaj. *Sahih al-Muslim: Kitab al-Maghazi wa al-Siyar*. Sunnah.com. Accessed March 2022.

Nasaʾi, Ahmad ibn Shuʾayb al-. *Sunan al-Nasaʾi, Kitab tahrim al-dam*. Sunnah.com. Accessed March 2022.

Natif, M. "'Painters Will Be Punished': The Politics of Figural Representation amongst the Umayyads." In *The Image Debate: Figural Representation in Islam and across the World*, edited by Christiane Gruber, 32–45. London: Gingko, 2019.

Neuwirth, Angelika. *The Qurʾan in Late Antiquity*. Translated by Samuel Wilder. Oxford: Oxford University Press, 2019.

Ogunnaike, Oludamini. "Annihilation in the Messenger Revisited: Clarifications on a Contemporary Sufi Practice and Its Precedents." *Journal of Islamic and Muslim Studies* 1, no. 2 (November 2016): 13–34.

———. *Poetry in Praise of Prophetic Perfection: A Study of West African Arabic Madīḥ Poetry and Its Precedents*. Cambridge, UK: Islamic Texts Society, 2020.

Payne, Richard E. *A State of Mixture: Christians, Zoroastrians, and Iranian Political Culture in Late Antiquity*. Berkeley: University of California Press, 2015.

Robin, Christian Julien. "The Judaism of the Ancient Kingdom of Himyar in Arabia." In *Diversity and Rabbinization: Jewish Texts and Societies between 400 and 1,000 CE*, edited by Gavin McDowell, Ron Naiweld, and Daniel Stokl Ben Ezra. Cambridge: University of Cambridge and Open Book, 2021. https://www.openbookpublishers.com/books/10.11647/obp.0219. Accessed January 4, 2023.

Rouayheb, Khaled el-. *Before Homosexuality in the Arab-Islamic World*. Chicago: Chicago University Press, 2005.

Rubin, Uri. "Pre-existence and Light: Aspects of the Concept of Nur Muhammad." *Israel Oriental Studies* 5 (1975): 62–119.

Safi, Omid. "Bargaining with Baraka: Persian Sufism, 'Mysticism,' and Pre-modern Politics." *Muslim World* 90, no. 3/4 (2000): 259–88.

Sahner, C. "The First Iconoclasm in Islam: A New History of the Edict of Yazid II (AH 104/AD 723)." *Der Islam* 94, no. 1 (2017): 5–56.

Saleh, Walid A. "The Arabian Context of Muhammad's Life." In *The Cambridge Companion to Muhammad*, edited by Jonathan E. Brockopp, 21–38. Cambridge: Cambridge University Press, 2010.

Sayeed, Asma. *Women and the Transmission of Religious Knowledge in Islam*. Cambridge: Cambridge University Press, 2013.

Schoeler, Gregor. *The Biography of Muhammad: Nature and Authenticity*. New York: Routledge, 2010.

———. "Oral Torah and Hadith: Transmission, Prohibition of Writing, Redaction." In *Hadith: Origins and Developments*, edited by Harald Motzki, 111–41. Burlington, VT: Ashgate/Valorium, 2004.

Shaikh, Saʾdiyya. "Knowledge, Women, and Gender in the Hadith: A Feminist Interpretation." In *The Hadith*, edited by Mustafa Shah, 4:252–61. Critical Concepts in Islamic Studies. London: Routledge, 2010.

Styers, Randall. *Making Magic: Religion, Magic and Science in the Modern World.* New York: Oxford University Press, 2004.

Tirmidhi, Muhammad ibn Isa. *Jamiʾ al-Tirmidhi, Kitab al-tafsir*. Sunnah.com. Accessed March 2022.

Tlili, Sarra. *Animals in the Qurʾan*. Cambridge: Cambridge University Press, 2012.

Toral-Niehoff, Isabel. "The ʿIbad of al-Hira: An Arab Christian Community in Late Antique Iraq." In *The Qurʾan in Context*, edited by Angelika Neuwirth, Nicolai Sinai, and Michael Marx, 323–47. Leiden, the Netherlands: Brill, 2009.

———. "Late Antique Iran and the Arabs: The Case of al-Hira." *Journal of Persianate Studies* 6 (2013): 115–26.

von Stuckrad, Kocku. *Locations of Knowledge in Medieval and Early Modern Europe.* Leiden, the Netherlands: Brill, 2010.

Vorisco, Daniel Martin. "Metaphors and Sacred History: The Genealogy of Muhammad and the Arab 'Tribe.'" *Anthropological Quarterly* 68, no. 3 (July 1995): 139–56.

Wagner, Roger, and Andrew Briggs. *The Penultimate Curiosity*. Oxford: Oxford University Press, 2016.

Waqidi, Muhammad ibn ʿUmar al-. *The Life of Muhammad: Al-Waqidi's Kitab al-Maghazi*. Translated by Rizwi Faizer. New York: Routledge, 2013.

Wasserstrom, Steven M. *Between Muslim and Jew: The Problem of Symbiosis under Early Islam*. Princeton, NJ: Princeton Legacy Library, 1995.

X, Malcolm, and Alex Haley. *The Autobiography of Malcolm X*. New York: Ballantine, 1965 [1989].

Zuckerberg, Donna. *Not All Dead White Men: Classics and Misogyny in the Digital Age.* Cambridge, MA: Harvard University Press, 2018.

Index

Ka'ba, 11, 19, 23, 33, 34, 37–40, 45, 46, 52, 54, 58, 66, 81, 88, 104, 153

Karbala, 8, 85, 98

Khadija (bint Khuwaylid), 19, 47, 49, 50, 65, 85, 100, 162

al-Khandaq, 62; Battle of Khandaq, 62–63

Kufa, 15, 77, 79, 81, 82, 86, 90, 93, 96, 97, 98, 101, 103

Lakhmids, 26–29

Mecca, 3, 6, 18, 19, 23, 27, 28, 30, 33, 35–40, 42, 46, 49, 51–54, 57–62, 64–67, 69, 76, 79, 83–85, 88, 99, 100, 144, 147, 153

Medina, 6, 15, 18, 30, 31, 35, 39, 45, 53, 58–62, 65, 66, 69, 82, 84, 89, 103, 105, 107, 110, 112, 113, 116, 134, 142, 144, 147, 158

Nabataeans, 23, 37

Qur'an interpretation (tafsir), 76, 80, 92, 100

Quraysh, 19, 23, 45, 46, 64, 82

Sahabas, 74, 149. *See* Companions

Salaf/Salafism, 4, 5, 9, 99, 117, 140–42, 144, 147, 149

Sasanian Empire, 13, 14, 20, 24–28, 33, 39, 109, 154

Shi'ism, 4, 6, 8, 9, 15, 44, 53, 66, 69–71, 80, 82, 85, 86, 93, 114, 115, 117, 123, 129, 133, 139, 141, 144, 146, 152, 155

shrines, 6, 19, 34, 38, 52, 114, 124, 140

Sufism, 6, 7, 9, 15, 108, 114, 119, 121–24, 130, 139, 140, 143, 144, 151, 157, 158

Sunna, 105, 115–17, 140, 142, 163

Sunnism, 3, 4, 6, 8, 15, 44, 53–55, 66, 69, 70, 73, 74, 80, 81, 85, 105, 110, 113–17, 123, 124, 133–35, 139, 141–44, 146, 152, 159

Syria, 19, 22, 23, 26–28, 33, 34, 47, 49, 61, 62, 79, 89, 143

tafsir. *See* Qur'an interpretation

Umayyads, 15, 76, 79, 81, 82, 85–88, 90, 98, 110–13, 115, 154, 155, 158, 170, 177, 183

Vishnu, 16, 130, 159

wadud, amina, 145

Wahhabism, 143–45

X, Malcolm, 3, 36, 148, 158, 159, 167

Yemen, 7, 14, 18, 19, 25, 27, 30, 31, 33, 78, 83

Ziyarat, 140

Zoroastrianism, 20, 24, 25–27, 67, 109, 125, 154